*Moray McLaren*

# Bonnie Prince Charlie

A PANTHER BOOK

**GRANADA**
London Toronto Sydney New York

Published by Granada Publishing Limited in 1974
Reprinted 1980

ISBN 0 586 03879 5

First published in Great Britain by
Rupert Hart-Davis Ltd 1972
Copyright © Moray McLaren 1972

Granada Publishing Limited
Frogmore, St Albans, Herts AL2 2NF
and
3 Upper James Street, London W1R 4BP
866 United Nations Plaza, New York, NY 10017, USA
117 York Street, Sydney, NSW 2000, Australia
100 Skyway Avenue, Rexdale, Ontario, M9W 3A6, Canada
PO Box 84165, Greenside, 2034 Johannesburg, South Africa
61 Beach Road, Auckland, New Zealand

Made and printed in Great Britain by
Richard Clay (The Chaucer Press) Ltd
Bungay, Suffolk
Set in Linotype Baskerville

Granada ®
Granada Publishing ®

When Charles Stuart sailed from the Western islands of Scotland for France after the smashing defeat of Culloden, the Bonnie Prince Charlie of legend, poetry and fact sailed out of the history books; the long period of frustration, humiliation and drunkenness that followed have been almost entirely obliterated in the popular mind, but Moray McLaren has here given a full and lively account of these years in exile.

This new biography of Charles Stuart is a highly individual portrait of the best-loved of all the Royal Stuarts by a great Scottish patriot.

'Tremendously colourful and well-illustrated biography ... told with simplicity and clarity as well as with a magnificent light touch. It is sad that Moray McLaren has not lived to witness the success of what may come to be known as his finest work'
THE SCOTSMAN

'Moray McLaren has done more than any other Jacobite historian to put Bonnie Prince Charlie's later record straight into proper perspective. Our Stuart hero's *mores* were those of his *tempora*. For he was a hero in the classical tradition'
*Sir Iain Moncreiffe* BOOKS AND BOOKMEN

# Contents

## List of Illustrations

# Introduction

> Let private persons, who repine at their little mis-
> fortunes, read the history of this prince and his
> ancestors.
>
> François-Marie Arouet de Voltaire

Ever since the accession of James I as King of Scotland
in 1406, the story of the Royal House of Stuart had
been one of extraordinary misfortune. This was the
legacy bequeathed to the new-born Charles Edward
Louis Philip Sylvester Casimir Maria on 31 December
1720.

The birth was duly reported by the Rome newspaper *Gracas*, which also recorded the names of the il-
lustrious who had been present at the event in the
Palace of the Santissimi Apostoli. Among them were
the Bishop of Albano, Fabrizio Paulucci, Prime Minister, Secretary of State and Great Penitentiary to His
Holiness the Pope. There was also the Cardinal of St
Peter's, Howard, brother of the Duke of Norfolk, the
premier baron of England. In congratulation for the
happy event, the Pope sent an Agnus to the babe's
father, James, acknowledged King of Great Britain at
the courts of Rome, Madrid and Paris. Unknown to
the players, the last act in the Stuart tragedy had begun. An émigré son had been born to an émigré king,
but the new prince was never to be an acknowledged
king save within the narrow confines of an exiled
court. In 1720 Prince Charles was the life-blood of
Stuart hopes, their heir to a dream. His birth ensured
the continuance of a royal line; but it also signified the
beginning of the end. When he died on 31 January
1788 the Stuart cause died with him. Charles Edward
died on the anniversary of the execution of his great-
grandfather, Charles I. To the end, the family history

was rife with symbolic accoutrement.

As a cycle of tragedy, the story of the Stuarts was well served by its characters. Their legendary moulds were cast in the face of either death or adversity. In January 1502, James IV of Scotland contracted the fateful marriage with Margaret Tudor which led to a future Stuart occupation of the English throne. Eleven years later, James went to war with his brother-in-law, Henry VII of England, and at Flodden the Scots king secured his place in the family saga with a suicidal charge straight at the English heart. An hereditary audacity remained, and James' granddaughter, Mary, challenged the stature of yet another Tudor. For this, the Scots Queen paid with her head at Fotheringay and earned the sympathy of future generations.

In 1603, the stream of misfortune appeared to be halted; Mary's son succeeded Elizabeth on the English throne. James I was something of a family exception. He managed to die peacefully in bed. But the move to England wrought no lasting alteration in the Stuart fortunes. The example of James was not followed, and Mary's grandson, Charles I, departed in more dramatic circumstances at Whitehall in 1649, eventually achieving the status of a royal martyr. Kings had been assassinated, ill-treated, imprisoned and subdued in the past, but never before had one of the Lord's Anointed been formally tried by his own subjects, with the prospect of his public execution a foregone conclusion. His son was more fortunate. Yet even the Merry Monarch, Charles II, suffered the humiliation of defeat at Worcester in 1650. His escape after the battle became the subject of romantic fiction; hunted by fanatical Roundheads, the young King hid in a hollow oak tree while his pursuers searched feverishly. Ten years later, he returned triumphantly to London.

But after his death in February 1685 good fortune abandoned the Stuarts.

On 2 January 1689 James II 'vacated' the throne and fled to France. The crown now passed to his daughter, Mary, and her Dutch husband, William of Orange. Once he was safely in France, James decided that he did not like this redisposition of his property. He would, after all, contest the claims of his son-in-law. Unfortunately, William was safely ensconced in London with a Dutch army by his side. All James had was the sympathy of Louis XIV, and as he told the Earl of Middleton, the hope that, across the water, there were a sufficient number of '... honest and loyal men (who) will declare for me and stand by me ...'

There were indeed men in Britain, and chiefly in Scotland, who stood by James, and who would continue to stand by his descendants. The history of their organization into a loosely-knit party, and its attempts to effect a restoration of the rightful Stuart king, really begins soon after James landed at Ambleteuse, in France, on 4 January 1689. Others followed the King from England, among them the Duke of Berwick, the Marquess of Powis, the Lords Dover and Dumbarton, and many Roman Catholics. From these was formed the first Jacobite court at Saint-Germain-en-Laye. Right from the start, it was intended to win back the revolted kingdoms. But the King was dependent upon the enthusiasm and efficiency of others. He could neither demand nor buy their support and consequently the organization fell prey to dissension. The movement was always a confederation of divergent interests in which the ultimate aim tended to be obscured by immediate and limited objectives, not all of them selfless. After an initial year of hope had faded with defeat at the battle of the Boyne in July 1690, the Stuart cause was gradually submerged beneath a tangle of personal and party interrelations. Before his death on 16 September 1701, James discovered that he was by now a mere figurehead atop a motley collection of intriguing factions.

11

The situation in which James II left his thirteen-year-old son permanently affected the young King. He spent his entire childhood in the midst of a Jacobite hive and the first five years of his reign in the shadow of a Jacobite regency. That was the only world he ever knew. He had never possessed a kingdom, and his desire for office, always slight, quickly dwindled into cynical disregard. At first he had hoped that his aunt would nominate him as her successor. But the sedate Anne deliberately avoided settling the Stuart future until she was too ill to prevent the throne from going to the Elector of Hanover. In 1708, and then again in 1715, James desperately attempted to regain his birthright by force, only to have both his efforts confounded. The first attempt was wrecked by bad communications, and the King did not even leave ship. Seven years later, he actually landed in Scotland, there to discover that his late arrival and his apparent cynicism made him few friends. After the Fifteen ground to a halt at Sheriffmuir on 13 November, James ceased to regard seriously the possibilities of his return to Britain.

From France, the King was hounded into papal territory at Avignon, and thence to Rome. His health had never been good and under continual harassment he was ageing rapidly. In 1708 he had been prostrated by measles while on the verge of his abortive invasion of England. Three years later he nearly died from smallpox. Before another five years had passed, he was incapacitated by a fistula which engendered a premature debility. James contented himself with his position in Rome. He enjoyed his limited influence there, and was unwilling to risk a loss of the realm he possessed in pursuit of one he did not. In 1719 he preferred to have Ormonde and Marischal lead a two-pronged expedition against Britain rather than go again himself. When the expedition failed and the Nineteen petered out at Glenshiel in June, the King was not overtly dismayed. His attention was occupied elsewhere. For two years James had been looking for a wife. Heirs were essential for the continuance of a Stuart line, and would keep alive the Jacobite dream. In addition, life would be made safer for James. At the moment, he was all that stood between the Hanoverians and complete security of tenure, and thus in danger of assassination. Children would help to remove such a threat. A wife would also bring him the comfort he now desired, in the form of a dowry. On 1 September 1719 James married the Princess Maria Clementina Sobieski, granddaughter of the hero of Vienna, John Sobieski. In semi-retirement he settled down to married life at the sumptuous Palazzo Muti, a wedding present from Pope Clement XI. The King continued to dabble in Jacobite politics, but more out of habit than conviction. By 1743, at the age of fifty-five, James thought himself too old for long journeys. He was prepared to leave the reclamation and enjoyment of the Three Kingdoms to his eldest son.

# I: The Stuart Prince in a Jacobite Court

Charles Edward spent the first fifteen years of his life against the unreal background of émigré life at the Palazzo Muti. The Palace stood in what is now an old quarter of Rome in the Piazza of the Santissimi Apostoli. Opposite it was a seventeenth-century church dedicated to the same two disciples, Peter and Paul. No place name is more evocative of the last days of a royal line than this now rather decrepit building devoted to the business energies of Rome. Here the phantom games of Jacobite losers were played out in all their bitter earnestness. Here King James held court. And here Charles Edward was born. Early in life the Prince must have become aware that his father was the King, and he the heir; but there was no kingdom! In Rome, little care was taken over Charles' academic education, and the young man bore the scars of ill-trained literacy long after his twentieth birthday. What was more excitedly noted was that the boy had an '... over-mastering passion for the profession of arms'. He was a brave hunter and a good shot. Approving courtiers discovered that '... his only complaint was that he had had so little instruction in the school of Mars, the one road to his kingdom'. While James idled at Rome in the winter, and Albano in the summer, his son was tutored carefully by the Jacobite Sir Thomas Sheridan. Through his teacher, Charles learned details of impossible schemes, like that of William Erskine of Pittodrie, who wanted to use Jewish financiers to break the London stock market. The unfortunate Christopher Layer was disembowelled at Tyburn for his part in a hare-brained plot to set the child upon the throne occupied by George I. News also arrived of imminent restoration. But the excitement faded as James once again bowed to the prophets of doom. Both

Sheridan and Charles scorned the King's futile efforts to reconcile Britain person by person. What was required was swift and final action, not petty bribery.

James felt otherwise. Since the demise of Bishop Atterbury in England, Jacobite strength there had declined rapidly. The parliamentary arm of the party was helpless. James blamed this upon hotheads like the Earl of Mar who had seen fit to ignore the King's cautious example. On 21 March 1725, James wrote to George Lockhart. 'It is my friends' business to lie quiet, and to preserve themselves in a condition of being useful on a proper occasion.' But the King was to discover that the rancour borne by men of differing opinions knew no bounds. In March John Hay, later Earl of Inverness, was made Secretary and the isolation of Mar completed. Unfortunately, the Earl still possessed friends at court, one of whom was Mrs Sheldon, a lady of the bedchamber appointed to look after the infant Prince, and of late a confidante of the Queen. As was customary, James had also appointed a governor, under-governor, preceptor and grooms for the Prince now that his age required male tutorage. However, Clementina was reluctant to see her friend depart. Mar seized this minor grievance as a chance to enjoy revenge against both James and Hay.

Mrs Sheldon convinced the Queen that she had been slandered by the Earl and Countess of Inverness. Clementina's complaint to the King was further embroidered as Mar's unhealthy influence took sway, and it was reported that the Queen believed that James sent away her friends lest they disclose his adulterous behaviour with the Countess of Inverness. Eventually Mar played his trump card. Clementina was duped into believing that her son's religion was threatened by the presence of the new Protestant governor, James Murray, Earl of Dunbar. Though James assured his wife that Charles' schooling would actually be the responsibility of the Catholic under-governor, Sir

Thomas Sheridan, Clementina would hear no more. In November she left the Palazzo Muti and took up residence at the convent of Santa Cecilia in the Trastevere in Rome.

Despite the companionship of young playmates, like the daughter of Mr John Walkinshaw of Harrowfield, Charles must have been saddened and perplexed by the departure of his mother. Only later did he appreciate the political ramifications of his misery. But his father well knew that the breach was '... a matter of the last consequence to him and his affairs'. Already he had lost both his papal and his Spanish pensions for refusing to accept the intervention of Benedict XIII. In England the lurid reports sent from Rome by 'John Walton' were doing irreparable damage. Even devoted servants like Lockhart and Atterbury were siding with Clementina. They saw the breach between them only in the light of its effects upon the movement. Lockhart warned James that 'his personal cannot be separated from his regal capacity'. He must place the cause first. James remained obstinate. He recognized the dispute as a further attempt to encroach upon his dwindling authority. In May 1726 Inverness conveyed the King's feeling to Lockhart. 'On the whole you'll find that the separation 'twixt the King and her has been occasioned by a desire of having the entire management of his affairs, which not being able to come at by any other way was at last attempted to be brought about by the Queen's means.'

Only in July of the next year was a reconciliation finally effected. But for Charles, the joy of reunion with his mother was shortlived. From December of the same year, Clementina displayed signs of a religious fervour approaching mania. In March 1728 James wrote to Inverness, 'She leads a most singular life, she takes no manner of amusement, not even taking the air, and when she is not at church or at table is locked up in her room, and sees no mortal but her maids or

17

so; she eats no meat this Lent, but fasts to that degree that I believe no married woman that pretends to have children ever did; I am very little with her, I let her do what she will.' The Queen's melancholy behaviour and diet brought on scurvy, and in January 1735 Maria Clementina died a premature death.

The full effect upon the Prince of the breach between his parents was only manifest in years to come. He blamed his mother's death upon the ridiculous feud between Catholics and Protestants which had conspired to drive Clementina mad. Never did he hold a genuine allegiance to either communion in later life. The Jacobite courtiers, with their interminable intriguing, he held responsible for his childhood suffering and his father's pitiful melancholy. He despised the squabbling and the unrealized fantasy of the court at Rome. Very early in life, Charles Edward decided that the movement would again serve the purposes of a Stuart rather than dictate to him.

In 1734 Charles persuaded his father to permit him the experience of warfare. An opportunity lay at hand in the Neopolitan war being waged between Austria and Spain. Spain had been largely successful, and the Duc de Liria was now stamping out lingering Austrian resistance. Liria was Berwick's son, and therefore Charles' cousin, and he now offered the Prince a chance of taking part in the seige of the last Austrian stronghold at Gaeta. On 27 July Charles left Rome, accompanied by James Murray, Gore, Sheldon, a confessor, a surgeon and four servants. Before departure, he was received by the Pope and given two thousand pistoles. Prayers were said in Roman convents. There could hardly have been greater pomp, even for a distinguished general.

Outside Gaeta, Charles met Liria's master, Don Carlos, son of the Spanish Queen, and styled King of Naples. The Spaniard was so impressed with the Prince's regal demeanour that he thereupon made him

18

a general of artillery. Greater praise was reserved for Charles' behaviour in the trenches. Liria afterwards described Charles' bravery to his brother, the Duke of Fitzjames: '... he made me pass some as uneasy moments as ever I met with from the crossest accidents of my past life. Just on his arrival, I conducted him to the trenches, where he shewed not the least surprise at the Enemies fire, even when the Balls were hissing about his Ears.' This observation led Liria to exclaim, 'In a word, this Prince discovers *"That in great Princes, whom Nature has mark'd out for Heroes, Valour does not wait the Number of Years"*.' Apparently, Charles was 'adored by officers and soldiers', and Liria concluded, 'I wish to God, that some of the greatest sticklers in England against the Family of Stewarts, had been Eye witnesses of the Prince's Resolution during the siege, and I am firmly perswaded they would soon change their way of thinking.'

Charles himself was less enthusiastic about his experiences. The letters he sent to James from Gaeta were merely short messages to confirm his continued survival. On 21 August he wrote, 'Sir, My Lord Dunbar has excused me from not having writ to you hitherto. I have been very good and humbly ask your blessing, Charles P.' The Prince was still only a fifteen-year-old boy, concerned about filial duties which he had failed to perform, and too excited by his situation to waste time over paper and ink in wordy attempts to communicate his adventure. His stay at Gaeta was short and, depite the boasts of Jacobite pamphleteers, the Prince had seen very little action. He left Rome on 27 July, and the garrison at Gaeta surrendered on 6 August. Had he spent a whole week in the trenches, Charles' military education would still have been incomplete. As it was, most of the time was passed in the company of Liria and other notables, high above the action. Nevertheless, the experience heightened the Prince's dissatisfaction with life in Rome.

19

Charles was now in the public eye, and the following year it was suggested to James that the Prince should tour Europe. Charles responded enthusiastically and determined to spend several weeks in Flanders so that Englishmen travelling to Spa or Aix-la-Chapelle might see him. But James rightly concluded that such an excursion was dangerous, and in any case politically impossible. A further two years passed in boredom before Charles was rescued by news of the Porteous riots. His anticipation rose to fever pitch when a determined John Gordon of Glenbucket arrived with a demand for the Royal presence in Scotland. Glenbucket carried a request from Macdonald of Glengarry and General Alexander Gordon of Auchintoul for an independent rebellion in Scotland. All they asked was the King's authority, and they cared not if foreign assistance was unavailable. James refused to be stampeded. He promply sent Glenbucket back with an observer, William Hay. Hay was to scout further intelligence and also try to unite different factions among the Scots. Then he was to gauge whether their combined strength was adequate for independent action. He returned with a guarded report in June 1738 and Charles' dreams faded. But they soared again with the arrival a few months later of Drummond of Balhaldy. Drummond pretended to speak for an association which included the Duke of Perth and Simon Fraser, Lord Lovat. His promises were considerable, and the court hummed excitedly. The catena of circumstances which led deviously towards the events of 1745 was now laid.

For once, the Stuarts were not short of money. Ever since the death of Prince James Sobieski in 1737, there had been a protracted legal tussle between James and his sister-in-law, the Duchesse de Bouillon. The Sobieski estates had been left to Charles and Henry, but the Duchesse pointed out that under Polish law foreigners could not inherit estates in Poland. This James had known, and it had always been his intention to sell the claims of his sons to some Polish bidder. However, he did assert a claim on behalf of his sons for the Austrian portion of the estates at Ohlau in Silesia. These had become Sobieski property in satisfaction for a debt owed by the Emperor and they were clearly not subject to Polish law. The Duchesse nevertheless coveted them, confident in the knowledge that the Emperor would have to decide the case. She well knew that the Stuarts were not friends of an Austria allied with England. James moved astutely. In January 1739 he had the princes surrender their claims to the Pope. Thus the political barbs erected around the Ohlau estates were removed, and the Emperor could only decide against the Duchesse de Bouillon. In return for his gift, James expected papal pensions to be granted by an amenable Clement XII. At the same time, the Polish claims were sold to Prince Radziwill for eight hundred thousand florins. Part of this money was then used to redeem the Sobieski jewels which lay in pawn at Rome. These had also been left to the princes, but until now James had been totally unable to secure their return. With the redemption of the jewellery, the family possessed collateral capable of raising substantial loans. They also had a great deal of ready cash. All they now needed were the opportunities to put their new-found wealth to use.

Chances there were in 1740. Much hope was pinned upon Cardinal Pierre de Tencin. The Cardinal had originally been nominated for elevation by James in 1728, but on that occasion Fleury had blocked Stuart designs. Ten years later, Tencin was raised to the cardinalate and at last there were indications that his favour with Fleury was increasing. Only recently, the Earl of Barrymore had successfully re-engaged French interest in the Stuart cause, and now it was hoped Tencin would convert interest into action. The international situation was set fair for general European involvement in a lingering dispute between England and Spain. Already the Convention of January 1739 between those two nations was in disarray, and France was daily expected to come to the aid of her neighbour. Fleury's first moves were cautious but definite. The Comte de Clermont was despatched to England to estimate Jacobite strength there, while a fleet under d'Antin sailed west to confront and harass the English in the Caribbean.

In January 1740 Philip of Spain asked James to lead an expedition against Britain. Preparations were already under way in Galicia, and an immediate Jacobite commitment was required. James promptly sent Marischal and Ormonde, despite a warning from the former that the main Spanish force was being concentrated at Barcelona, probably with the intention of undertaking a strike against Port Mahon. Marischal's scepticism was vindicated as it became apparent that the Corunna preparations were merely a feint to keep the English fleet from the Mediterranean. No care was being taken to conceal them from Hanoverian eyes, and still the vital subsidy promised to James remained unpaid. Eventually, Philip abandoned the charade when Admiral Haddock entered the Mediterranean and all need for the Corunna decoy evaporated.

Further disappointment followed when Clermont returned to France in September and reported to Fleury. The French agent rejected Jacobite rumours regarding the disaffection of the Duke of Argyll, thus reducing the anticipated loyalist strength considerably. On this basis, Fleury was unwilling to proceed against England. Furthermore, his fears for the safety of the French sugar islands proved unfounded. Fortunately, d'Antin had turned back in awe of an English squadron before reaching his Caribbean goal and the inevitable confrontation had not materialized. War with England had been avoided, and Fleury was only too happy to extricate himself from commitment to the Stuarts. As usual, French designs had been diversionary rather than effective.

Though Charles sulked dejectedly, James expected this sort of abuse, and found it easy to readjust himself to inactivity at the Palazzo. Amidst the surrounding furore, the King's serenity impressed Charles de Brosses, Comte de Tournai et de Monfalcon.

'He does not lack in dignity in his manner, and I have never seen a prince hold a court circle with so much grace and ease. He has occasionally to appear in public in spite of the retirement in which he lives, though he has none of the actual glitter about him apertaining to other sovreigns... He is an ultra-devout, and his mornings are passed in prayer at the grave of his wife in the Church of the Santissimi Apostoli.'

To encourage contentment, the King strove to eradicate the more obvious differences which existed between life at the Palazzo and that of the Hanoverian court in London. He insisted upon the protocol normal at any other British court. Whenever the princes attended their father at dinners and special functions, they knelt to ask the King's benediction when James entered the room. To his sons the King spoke only English although all three conversed comfortably in Italian and French. De Brosses observed that the family enjoyed music, and both princes were proficient musicians. Yet he felt that the provision of musical evenings and concerts was not aimed chiefly at the entertainment of James and his sons. Instead, it must be seen as a normal courtly function, essential for the maintenance of an adequate alternative to St James's.

Despite the regal ease apparent elsewhere, the image which de Brosses retained of Charles Edward was that of a prince discontented with court pleasantries at a time when Europe was crowded with a feverish anticipation of major changes. In 1740 the Emperor Charles VI died and was succeeded by his daughter, Maria

Theresa. Foreseeing that the accession of a woman would be controversial, the Emperor had previously secured international assent to its legality. But both France and Prussia held lightly the Pragmatic Sanction which guaranteed Maria Theresa's position. The Powers were already moving into aggressive alliances when on 16 December Frederick of Prussia invaded Silesia. The War of the Austrian Succession had begun, and Charles Edward was unwilling to let slip such an opportunity for action against England. De Brosses wrote: '... it is commonly reported that he feels his position acutely, and if he does not come to the front it will not be owing to lack of energy'. The Prince was also sensitive to the situation in England, where Walpole's decline promised upheaval. When a general election in 1741 severely reduced the minister's majority, Charles interpreted the event as the evident displeasure of the people of England with an illegal government. According to the Jesuit, Padre Giulio Cesare Cordara, the Prince felt 'that his chance had come'. He would go for long solitary walks upon the Apennines, sometimes barefooted, and caused his family much concern by coming home days late. It appears that he was preparing himself for the ardours of invasion, for Cordara later recorded Charles' conviction '... of the easiness of attempting the enterprise, which then seemed particularly timely'. Only 'the lack of a leader rather than any unwillingness to rise' withheld a general rebellion in Britain.

Spain had already proposed another Scottish descent. However, they promised aid only if France also entered the war against England. French co-operation was not out of the question. Bussy, a French comte in London, had been sending reports which depicted a country on the brink of civil war. The Jacobite office in Paris was optimistic. They assured James that Cardinal Tencin would not disappoint them. But the King refused to become excited. In the autumn of 1742 he wrote to Lord Semphill.

'I take his being called hither (Tencin's summons to the French council) at this time a clear proof that the French stand in no awe of the English government and are not disposed to observe certain managements with them ... (But) ... were Cardinall Tencin actually the first minister, I don't see how he could do great matters for us at this present moment.'

Tencin was a friend, but Fleury was still the power who mattered. If at the time the first minister thought nothing could be done, then nothing must be allowed to upset him. Unfortunately, the King's diplomacy did not extend to his servants. At the end of the year, Balhaldy 'wrote a letter to the Earl of Traquair acquainting him that the Cardinall was then fully resolved to invade England, and desiring the Scots to be in readiness without specifying any particulars'. When James learned of the high-handed action of the Paris office, he placed O'Brien at its head and dismissed the gullible Semphill. But the damage had been done, and agitated Scotsmen, still ignorant of the true state of affairs, and to prevent 'the bad consequences that might follow from a landing without any positive and distinct orders how to proceed', decided to investigate the situation by sending John Murray of Broughton to France.

In February 1743 Fleury died and was replaced by Amelot. So by the time Murray arrived in Paris, the situation had altered. Like his predecessor, Amelot was disinclined to squander French resources upon purely Stuart interests. Only after the battle of Dettingen did he decide to investigate Jacobite claims regarding the state of Britain. In August James Butler was despatched to England on a fact-finding mission.

The Jacobites could scarcely have been displeased with the report with which Butler returned. The man was an equerry of Louis XV and his trip to England was ostensibly to buy horses for the French king. He dined in London, and then prepared lists of his guests which suggested that one hundred and eighty-six gentlemen, including the Lord Mayor Wilmot, out of a total of two hundred and thirty-six whom he had met, were Jacobites. He attended a race meeting at Lichfield and noted that scores of drunken revellers avowed the Jacobite cause. On his return to France, Butler submitted an incredible list of Jacobite sympathizers. Among them he even included staunch 'revolutioners' like the Lords Shaftesbury and Shrewsbury. The English government had known all along that Butler was not really after horses, yet they were content to let him complete his mission. Their confidence was based upon a genuine appreciation of the sympathies of the country. Earlier in 1743 an unknown French agent had also reported to his superiors in Paris: 'The King (Louis) has no party in England. In England there is only an English party, and if French troops landed even the unemployed seamen would rise against them.'

When Broughton saw Amelot later in the year, he was sufficiently impressed by French sincerity to write to James:

> After two weeks' attendance, I had the honour to be presented to M. Amelot, who said in the King of France's name, all that the present situation of affairs would in my humble opinion allow of; which will certainly give great satisfaction to Your Majesty's friends at my return to Scotland.

Either Broughton was deceived, or the French minister preferred Butler's report to the one lodged at the Quai d'Orsay. The decisive factor guiding Amelot's judgement was no doubt the completion on 25 October of the Second Family Compact between France and Spain. (By signing the compact France had committed herself against the signatories of the earlier

Treaty of Worms, one of whom was England.) On 15 November orders were given for the concentration of transports and troops in preparation for an invasion of England.

According to Cordara, it was Tencin who was responsible for French activity. Several years before, he had visited Rome on the business of the French embassy, and there both he and his nephew, the Chevalier de Tencin, had met Prince Charles. The Prince formed a close friendship with the Chevalier, who quickly perceived Charles' desire to retrieve his father's kingdoms. This information was passed on to the Cardinal, and Tencin thereupon resolved to fulfil the Prince's ambition at the earliest opportunity. In 1743 he seized his chance when a threatened alliance between Austria and the Dutch began to worry France. Tencin realized that such an alliance would defeat French attempts to subjugate the Netherlands, for the Dutch had easy access to the coveted area. He suggested to Louis and Amelot that the best means to prevent concerted opposition from the Dutch and English in Flanders was to support a Stuart invasion of Britain. Naturally, Charles was expected to lead such an attempt, for his father was now too old. 'If he landed in Scotland with a reasonable escort of troops to regain possession of his ancient patrimony, all Scotland would fly to arms and a large part of England would come under Scottish rule.' Tencin also emphasized that 'Many even of the English, whether from disgust or from inborn desire for change, were turning to the Stuarts again.' What they desired was '... to be ruled by a Catholic Prince of their own blood'. The policy recommended by the Cardinal was one with which French diplomats had long been familiar. Use of the Stuart diversion in England, or the older Scottish descent, was almost traditional French policy. Even Tencin's reasoning was conditioned by the attitudes which afflicted the mainstream of French diplomacy: '... there was no doubt that at the mere rumour of a Stuart invasion, things in England would take quite a different complexion.' A rumour eagerly spread by Jacobite hotheads may well have been all of which Amelot and Louis had need!

In December 1743 Drummond of Balhaldy was accredited to the court of King James by the King of France. He was sent to obtain leave for Charles to go to France and join the expedition being prepared at Dunkirk. By the middle of the month Cordara reported that two English nobles had arrived in Rome from France. In the presence of James, the Chevalier de Tencin and Charles, the ambassador '... explained that all difficulties had been smoothed away and the whole thing would be quite easy to carry out ... It would be child's play to seize a kingdom thus unprepared, while all the defendants were away, with the support of a number of adherents and friends who were in complete readiness to help.' In addition, Balhaldy promised that France would supply arms, ships and men while Spain provided money.

The greatest speed was essential. The French wanted Charles to be in Dunkirk before 10 January. Yet Balhaldy had only reached Rome on 19 December! Both he and his partner, Sir John Graeme, were anxious to forestall any objections by James. But James knew Balhaldy too well to accept all that he said. Cordara reported that he was reluctant to let Charles leave. 'The idea of risking the life of a son so dear to him, the hope of his royal house, upon a doubtful enterprise was not to be entertained for a moment.' Charles had other ideas, and the Jesuit recorded that the King only relented after his son 'could no longer conceal his disgust, and his knit brows showed his utter disapproval of his father's view'. The Prince blurted out long-suppressed emotions. 'The issues of war are uncertain; but glory is assured and my chances are splendid. What avails hope without daring? For once I shall escape from this inglorious idleness and look fate in the face...' Immediately Balhaldy returned to Paris with confirmation that the Prince would come. James had left the decision to his son and Charles had made it bravely. On 23 December a Declaration was signed making Charles Regent of Scotland.

The negotiations were kept secret, for if any news leaked out, Charles would be unable to make the journey to France. The flotilla at Dunkirk would never be allowed to sail. An English fleet controlled the Mediterranean, and English eyes scoured the Channel. Hanoverian spies roamed Italy, and at the slightest suspicious movement in Rome were quite prepared to use the assassin's knife rather than face the Stuarts across the fields of England. The curiosity of the Palazzo must at all cost be allayed. The Prince would have to make a hostile sea crossing from Liguria to France under the very nose of a watchful English fleet. If word reached their commander, Charles would surely be captured at sea. Such were the dangers that faced the Prince, that Cordara felt they made the mission '... seem almost desperate'. It was mid-winter. Plague was raging in Sicily and consequently the frontiers were heavily guarded. At Genoese borders a compulsory fifteen-day quarantine was in force. The Italian states were at war with one another, and, to top it all, Sardinia was allied to the English.

The date for Charles' departure was fixed to coincide with that of a shooting party arranged for 9 January at Cisterna. About thirty miles from Rome on the Via Appia, the place was a frequent haunt for both Charles and Henry. It afforded pleasant shooting, and no one could suspect that anything out of the ordinary would occur when the princes decided to go there. In fact, even Henry suspected it to be a routine hunting trip. He had been left in the dark lest his brotherly anxiety betray the special significance of the occasion.

At the official leavetaking on the preceding evening, both James and Charles showed great self control. But at a later and private farewell, father and son cried as Charles was commissioned for the task ahead. The Prince left in a state near to hysteria. Besides the grief and the great uncertainty, there was also in him a sense that his destiny was about to be fulfilled. Now was his moment of release, and nothing would stop him except success or death.

Before dawn, Charles Edward left the Palazzo Muti in a carriage, accompanied by Sir Thomas Sheridan. With the servants they left word that Charles had left early in order to make a good start with the day's hunting. Very soon the Prince and his companion drove through the Porta San Giovanni in Laterno. It would be twenty-two years before Charles returned to Rome, and never again would the Prince see his father alive. This fair-haired and rather pretty boy had inherited his mother's Polish beauty and her Sobieski stubbornness. In Europe and Britain he would set many hearts a-flutter. But now, on the verge of becoming a legend, his exterior of easy affability barely concealed the determination within.

The arrangements to have Charles arrive safely in France were undertaken by the Earl of Dunbar. He ensured that adequate precautions were taken in advance to prevent danger or delay. Sir John Graeme had already been sent on to Massa in order to arrange the difficult passage through Genoa. Preparations had been made and parts allocated. Charles would travel as a courier, with no baggage and only one trusted servant. All that Dunbar prayed for now was luck.

Outside the Porta San Giovanni, the Prince's carriage was met by Strafford and an accompanying servant. Both men were mounted, and when he saw them, Charles expressed a desire to ride. He had three saddle horses tied behind the carriage, so there was no difficulty in finding a mount. Once on horseback, Charles challenged Sheridan to a race. The men on horseback would ride to Cisterna on the Albano road, while the coach travelled on the Marino road. The courtier listened to the Prince with visible apprehension. The Albano road was dangerous. Charles should not travel it without the knowledge of his father. But all this was merely an elaborate act to baffle the coachmen, for Sheridan well knew that Charles would never reach Cisterna. The old Jacobite was a game accomplice and at the height of the argument, he pretended to slip in the mud, thus giving Charles an opportunity to ride off. By the time the coachman had recovered his passenger, Charles and Strafford had galloped away down the Albano road and were out of sight. Sheridan then drove to Cisterna via Marino, apparently much vexed by the Prince's irresponsible behaviour.

Several miles from Albano, Charles halted and donned his courier's cap and coat. Strafford went on to Cisterna while Charles and his servant retraced their steps to Rome. They passed under the walls, and then rode towards the Via Flamina. After a while, the two men left the main road and headed for Caparola. There they stopped at a house leased by Cardinal Aquaviva, the Spanish Ambassador to Rome.

By pretending to be servants of the Cardinal the Prince and his companion could obtain fresh post horses at each stop, a service denied to private travellers. The Cardinal had earlier arranged their use of the public posts by informing the post masters that his courier to Spain would soon be arriving and would require a change of mounts ready and waiting at each stop. Charles made good speed. At Massa, Sir John Graeme met the two men and provided them with passports with which to cross Genoese territory. Charles now pretended to be Sir John's servant and thus they arrived in Genoa at midday on 13 January. The journey had taken only four days.

At Genoa, Charles rested at a friend's house for a few hours. Having changed his clothes, he set out the same evening for Savona. Because of internecine disputes in Italy, it was necessary to make a sea crossing to Antibes from Savona. For this purpose, a *speronara* had been hired in advance. But because of heavy seas, the vessel could not leave the harbour at Finale. For a week, Charles fretted. He was in great danger. Across the bay, off Villa Franca, a threatening English squadron under Admiral Matthew rode at anchor. Eventually the Prince could delay no longer. He went to Finale by land and ordered the captain of the *speronara* to slip past the English during the night. He had to reach Antibes as quickly as possible lest his absence from Rome reach English ears and set Matthew on his guard.

At daybreak, look-outs in the English fleet sighted the *speronara* scudding hard against the shore. The discovery of a small boat, butting into the wind after an unsuccessful attempt to steal past the fleet at night, aroused immediate suspicion. A cutter was ordered to bring the *speronara* around for examination. But the Italian boat ignored the English summons and crowded on her sail. A furious chase ensued in which the English were held off until both vessels reached Antibes on the morning of 21 January. In port, English curiosity remained unabated. Repeated demands were made to know the nature of the Italian's business and the identities of the passengers she carried. Charles dared not show his face in case he was recognized. As soon as the captain of the *speronara* requested permission to land, so did the English. Charles naturally refused to walk ashore in the company of an armed body of aggressive English sailors, yet if his ship put to sea again, she would be captured. Nor could the Prince afford to lie alongside an enemy vessel bulging with inquisitive eyes. The harassed port governor was of little use. He could neither force the English to leave, nor forbid them to land. They had not violated the strained peace which still existed between France and England, and he had to honour the international right of asylum in a neutral port. Eventually, the governor decided that he could not allow the Italian to land. Hearing this, the cutter retreated confidently to the outer harbour to await its prey. When the *speronara* emerged, the English bore down greedily.

But Charles was no longer aboard. Once the English sailed out of the harbour, he had been able to reveal his identity to a bemused governor. He was immediately transferred to another boat. The *speronara* then departed to lead the English a wild goose chase all the way to Monaco. At dusk the Prince went ashore and was lodged in suitable accommodation. A few hours later, he took post to Avignon. From there, within the safety of the Duke of Ormonde's residence, Charles sent word to Louis that the journey to the French mainland had been completed successfully. He now respectfully asked permission to enter the territory of the King of France.

That the Prince had reached his destination safely was due chiefly to the success with which his whereabouts had been concealed from Roman society in general. After parting with Charles on the road, Sheridan hurried on to Cisterna. There, his mock anxiety proved so infectious that he succeeded in alarming all with whom he came into contact. Charles should have reached Cisterna before Sir Thomas, so by the time the Duke of York arrived three hours later, confusion reigned. Before his departure from Rome, Henry had read a letter from Charles left for him at the Palazzo Muti. He thus knew that his brother was bound for France and not for a shooting party at Cisterna. The Duke's genuine concern for his brother commingled with his acted distraction to produce a devastating effect among the courtiers attendant. A search for Charles was promptly ordered, but while the search party was still saddling, Strafford arrived at a gallop. He informed Henry that Charles had suffered a fall which had given him a bruised rib. Consequently, the Prince was laid up at Albano and would stay there until the rib was healed. Strafford also warned the party that the Prince was anxious not to trouble his father and had therefore issued strict instructions forbidding news of the accident from being carried to Rome.

On hearing this, Sheridan pretended a desire to go to Albano to be with the Prince. But he was restrained by Strafford, who reassured him that the Prince was in good hands and really quite unharmed. Strafford himself would return and keep the party at Cisterna well informed with news of Charles' health. With this, he returned to Albano, from where he despatched messengers at regular intervals with reports of the Prince's condition. When the longest time possible had run out, Strafford wrote to set a date for the Prince's return. Finally that day arrived, and the party at Cisterna looked forward to Charles' return. But, instead of the Prince, yet another note from Strafford was delivered, containing instructions for the whole party to proceed to the Lake of Fogliano where Charles would definitely meet them.

At Fogliano members of the party became suspicious. Here they were in a remote area, but still the Prince failed to turn up. That very remoteness had recommended the place to Charles and his cohorts. Even the local fishermen were instructed to maintain the fiction of Charles' well-being on the days when they attended the market at Rome. All letters were censored and a false situation was relayed to Rome along with a steady stream of game, reputedly bagged by Charles, and ostensibly gifts for various Roman notables. For eleven days no one in Rome suspected that Charles was anywhere but in Cisterna or Fogliano. Yet by that time the Prince was preparing for his last dangerous run into the harbour at Antibes. Thus communication of Charles' disappearance to the fleet riding off Villa Franca was effectively prevented until the Prince was safely ashore at Avignon. For once, Jacobite security and organization had been successful and one wonders how much of the credit was due to the young man whose determination had allowed no delay. In one of the few well-spelt letters which he wrote, Charles informed his father that his servants were quite 'done in' by the speed with which he had forced them ahead and concluded, 'If I had had to go much further, I should have been obliged to get them tyed behind the chase with my portmantle.'

Slivers of information did in fact reach London from Rome. According to 'An Authentick Account of the Intended Invasion', a pamphlet printed later in the year, the English government had been informed on 14 January of extraordinary activity at the court of the Chevalier. The absence of the Chevalier's son was also noted. But nobody was really sure where Charles was. On 11 February, Horace Mann wrote to the Duke of Newcastle, firm in the conviction that he had seen the Prince at Florence on that very day. Yet the writer of 'An Authentick Account...' asserts that on 22 January, '...the captain of one of the Dover Packit boats brought an Account of his (Charles) being at Calais'. The English government were clearly anxious to play down the rumours that were in circulation. One thing not wanted by George II was a general panic in the face of an invasion. Of course the government was not ignorant of the preparations at Dunkirk. It already had in its possession the examination under oath of Captain Alexander Ridley, master of a Dover packet boat: '... it was the common Talk at Calais that fifteen thousand men were to be embarked on Board Transports, in order to make a Descent upon some part of His Majesty's Dominions ... some said the Landing was to be in Kent, others in Scotland ... there were several Irish officers, and others, in Company with Count Saxe, among which there was a person whom the informant saw upon the Key, and who was said by the French there to be the Pretender's eldest Son, and whom they called publickly the Chevalier, and seemed to pay him a great deal of Respect...' On 3 February Newcastle instructed Thompson, the minister at Paris, to make the strongest protestations to Amelot regarding French intrigues with the Stuarts. Time was running out and George knew it. There were reports that the French Grand Fleet was now fully equipped. Something had to be done. On 15 February George addressed the Lords.

His Majesty having received Undoubted Intelligence that the Eldest Son of the Pretender to his Crown is arrived in France, and that Preparations are making there to invade the Kingdom...

The results of these disclosures in England were not

as Charles would have hoped. There were the customary security measures taken, and these naturally dampened revolutionary enthusiasm. The army was strengthened and troops recalled from Holland. A special oath was circulated in Scotland. Roman Catholics were advised to stay away from London. But these measures were not merely repressive, they were just as much the fruit of nationwide solidarity. Throughout the country, there was a surge of support for the Hanoverian King, not so much anti-Stuart as anti-French. Cordara explained the reaction sensitively.

'A natural rivalry had always existed between England and France, and the English were particularly indignant at the injury she had recently done them; hence though from natural inclination they might favour the Stuarts, they could not endure the thought of this family being restored to the Throne by the French. So with one accord, they set about preparing to offer determined resistance to the attacks of their enemies and forestall any rising at home.'

From the City of London, the Universities, the Bishops and Clergy of Canterbury, the merchants of London, Protestant Dissenters, Ministers of Westminster, Quakers and French refugees, came addresses of loyalty to George II. The City of Exeter gave their '...most unfeigned assurances of our stedfast and inviolable Fidelity and Attachment to Your Sacred Government and Family'. They then went on to exclaim, 'We cannot look upon the Insolence of this Attempt without the Greatest Horror and Detestation.' The attempt which so inflamed the City of Exeter was one which in theory should have placed the Stuarts upon the throne of England. Two armies were to be sent, one to England, the other to Scotland. Charles and Marshal Saxe, the French commander, would lead the main force of twelve thousand French regulars and put ashore at Blackwall near London. Simultaneously, Earl Marischal, with another three thousand regulars, would land in the Highlands. It was hoped that the loyal clans would rally around Marischal until a formidable force was assembled in the north. Faced with a war on two fronts, English resistance would soon collapse, particularly if Charles managed to seize London quickly.

But all this never came about, and the Jacobites were left wondering whether they had once again been duped into serving some obscure French design. That was what Cordara believed. He maintained that the whole operation was merely an elaborate feint designed to frighten George II into recalling his Mediterranean fleet. The departure of Admiral Matthew would leave the Mediterranean free for the French and Spanish fleets now bottled up in Toulon. Cordara was not alone in his suspicions, for all the while at Dunkirk the French displayed a noticeable lack of enthusiasm. Yet the preparations were too thorough to be a bluff. Marshal Saxe was indeed reluctant to embark. But then he had a dispassionate connection with the operation and he saw no reason to allow ardour to obscure the very real obstacles which confronted it. Because of the late arrival of Charles, all advantages of surprise had been surrendered. At regular intervals, snooping English squadrons arrived off Gravelines, and in these circumstances Saxe realized that the flotilla would never reach England without an adequate escort of warships. But most of the Grand Fleet was trapped in Toulon. It could not leave for fear of attack by Matthew before the French ships had time to manoeuvre. The strained peace which existed between France and England would not restrain the English admiral. He well understood that war with France was inevitable. This was the stalemate which delayed Saxe.

In fact, the French commander was given explicit instructions by Comte d'Argenson, the minister of war, to stick to his task as long as there was the slightest chance of its completion. On 11 February the

French and Spanish fleets attacked Matthew in desperation. In early March there was a formal declaration of war between England and France. Within a week, Saxe was allocated his squadron of warships. But now he found that he had no pilots. For a few more days the flotilla rode at anchor while pilots were recruited. Then at last the embarkation began.

All seemed set for success. A protective wedge of French warships cruised off Gravelines, and the sea was beautifully calm. But before half the force had boarded, Sir John Norris and the English Home Fleet appeared menacingly on the horizon. Only the ebb tide and a dead calm prevented Norris from destroying the French warships there and then. Perhaps luck was still with Charles, or so he thought. Under cover of darkness he would be able to slip past Norris. Once this had been done, no serious obstacle would face the invasionary force. Victory would be certain. But luck was definitely not with the Prince on this occasion. During the night, most of the flotilla was either wrecked or dispersed by an aptly named 'Protestant Wind'. Although the French warships managed to evade Norris during the mêlée, they effectively abandoned Saxe by slipping into Brest. Without ships the invasion could not possibly continue, and the French government abandoned the project.

For Charles, that decision was catastrophic. Before his departure from Rome, he had promised his father either to return with three crowns, or die in the attempt. To go back any other way was out of the question. The Prince was desperate. He very nearly embarked upon a solo attempt in a fishing smack and was only restrained by the timely intervention of Earl Marischal. Until the end of the month he remained hopeful, but at the beginning of April he departed for Paris. There, under the code name of Baron Renfrew, Charles lived in the bitter conviction that his association with and dependence upon France had blasted his hopes. In Paris the Prince was virtually ignored by the French court. That suited his mood well. From what he was told by his Jacobite associates, English watchfulness had declined considerably, and George had placed the country under a Council of Regency while he took to the field in Germany. As national vigilance declined, so did antipathy to the Stuarts. Charles hoped that in English minds the name of Stuart would be gradually disassociated from that of France, and so he intended to have only the most casual relations with Louis. Soon enough, the Prince believed, Britons would experience a natural affection for their lawful rulers which would grow into an overwhelming demand for Charles' presence on the other side of the Channel.

Since April d'Argenson had been making peace tenders to the English and had been equally anxious to separate the name of France from that of Stuart. Of this Charles knew nothing. He relied upon Semphill and Balhaldy for information, and they assured him that French devotion to the Stuart interest was unshaken. They also wrote inflammatory letters to Scotland, warning of imminent invasion by the Prince. Of course, they had told Scottish Jacobites of the intended invasion by Saxe. Yet the only concrete information they had offered was on 'How to manage a Conference in London'. After this vital instruction, Semphill neglected to tell the Scots about the cancellation of the venture and Balhaldy continued to forward confirmation of 'the Frenches series intentions ...' Again the agitated Scots had to send Murray of Broughton to clarify the situation.

Murray came via Rotterdam and Ostend and met Balhaldy on the way. Balhaldy admitted that he had not told the Prince of Murray's visit, and during their interview Murray received the impression that Balhaldy was trying to keep him from seeing the Prince. But he pressed on regardless, eventually meeting

Charles secretly in a barn. There Murray learned of the ridiculous promises concerning Scottish support which Balhaldy had made to both the Prince and the French. Regretfully, Murray had to tell Charles that while Balhaldy had promised twenty thousand Highlanders to augment any invasionary force, a more realistic figure would be about four thousand at the outside. Furthermore, Murray discovered that the influence which Semphill and Balhaldy pretended to have at the French court amounted to little. Instead of providing regular troops on demand, France was more likely to prevent the Prince from making an invasion attempt. All this Murray communicated to Charles, along with a warning that he would receive no support either in Scotland or England unless the French supplied concrete assistance.

Charles was thunderstruck. He was now acutely aware that his presence must be a considerable embarrassment to France. It was not that he lived ostentatiously. The meagre pension of three thousand livres per month paid to him by d'Argenson was scarcely enough to maintain his princely estate. His debts accumulated repidly until by the end of the year he owed about thirty thousand livres. In all, he led a quite miserable existence and now it seemed that France was willing to commit him to an eternity of such humiliation. He could not emulate his father and join the army in Flanders, for the French government forbade it. Only occasional weekends at the country residence of his relatives, the ducs de Bouillon and Fitzjames, leavened the Prince's despair. But that was insufficient compensation for a soul consumed with the desire to play a role of destiny.

Charles had entrusted the major part of his business to Semphill and Balhaldy and they had misled him. He blamed them and their entire organization for the plight in which he now found himself. In France Charles had discovered that he received only polite response from the Jacobite hierarchy. They were reluctant to admit him into their confidences, and rarely did they show any enthusiasm for his cause. Now Charles felt that he understood why even men like Earl Marischal treated him indifferently and resorted instead to futile intriguing. His very existence was directed towards a restoration while they had careers and lives not altogether bound to a Stuart return. (In fact, many owed their importance to the existing situation.) They were of no use to the Prince. More and more Charles relied upon the advice of Murray of Broughton. He was a man in touch with affairs in Britain. As a source of information, he could not be matched by the Jacobite bumblers in Paris. He did not claim to have persuasive powers, but the energy and enthusiasm he combined with his realistic representations would probably ensure him more success with the French as well. Murray advised Charles to retrieve his affairs from the incompetent hands of Semphill and Balhaldy and deal directly with the French. In September Charles asked his father to relieve him of further dealings with the creaking Jacobite organization in Paris. James understood the situation and agreed. No more would Charles be misled and disappointed by others. Before Murray departed in October, Charles promised that he would come to Scotland the following summer, 'though with a single footman ...'

Although Cordara asserts that Charles did not make this decision 'till he had spent a year in learning how matters stood', the evidence supplied by Broughton and others suggests that the Prince made up his mind only a few months after the abandonment of the Dunkirk expedition. Furthermore, it was not based upon a careful accumulation of advice from Scotland. Murray and Marischal both warned the Prince against a landing without French support, though Broughton was probably seduced by the Prince's enthusiasm and charm, for he seems quickly to have abandoned his attempts to dissuade Charles. When he returned to Scotland, he communicated the Prince's intention to a few trusted accomplices. Their horrified reaction was recorded by Murray, and contradicts the explanation forwarded by Cordara. Lord Elcho later remembered that 'Most of the Gentlemen of that Party look'd upon it as a mad Project and were utterly against it.' They ordered Murray to draft an immediate reply representing their views to the Prince. Any landing without at least six thousand French regulars and three thousand louis d'or in cash would not be supported at all. Murray entrusted the letter to Lord Traquair who carried it as far as London but no farther. In April of the following year, a horrified Murray learned that Traquair had failed to deliver the memorandum. Nervously, he despatched young Macdonald of Glengarry with a similar warning.

Both Murray and Glengarry said later that the warning arrived too late to deter the Prince. However, more was involved than merely an unwillingness to arrest machinery already in motion. Quite simply, Charles had listened long enough to Jacobite prevarications. He resented the stiff party hierarchy who kept him from the centre of their affairs. On 28 February he communicated his frustration to James.

It would be a great comfort for me to have real business on my hands, but I see little of that at present as I shall explain in another. It is something surprising not to have heard from Lumley (Semphill) this to weeks and even he owe me an answer to one of mine of that standing, but I easily conceive the reason on't, which is that after making such a noise of his being able to do a great deal, he does nothing – or he does not care to let me in the confidence of his manedgements, which I believe has happened before now to more than me, for I see here everybody thinks himself to be the wisest man in the world.

Rather than suffer further indignity, Charles established his own court. It consisted of a few friends, like the young banker, Aenas Macdonald, and several Irish officers, all of them eager for action. The Prince now made the decisions upon which the Stuart future would depend. He had jettisoned the party in Paris, and he was perfectly willing to ignore its Scottish counterpart. For too long Jacobite leaders had stifled the passionate loyalty of people desperate for a Stuart return. In defiance of them, Charles sent Sir Hector Maclean of Duart to Scotland with the pledge that before autumn the Prince would be in the land of his fathers.

In March Charles wrote to James, informing him that he had borrowed money to purchase broadswords and also desiring the King to sell one portion of the Sobieski jewels, 'for the Prince [third person used in cipher] sees almost everything at the French court sticks at the money'. Perhaps Charles was still soliciting fresh help, but it is more likely that he was pretending to do so for his father's benefit. The French victory at Fontenoy in May 1745 convinced the Prince that the Hanoverians were about to topple. On 12 June he wrote again to his father.

In fine our friends without saying it directly have spoke in such a manner that I plainly saw, if the Winter and Spring passed over without some attempt, they wou'd rise of themselves in spite of all I could say or do to prevent it, not doubting that they would succeed if in the least seconded, and that the worst that could happen them was to dye in ye field, which was preferable to living any longer in misery and oppression.

With this in mind, the Prince had accumulated an

arsenal in Paris consisting of fifteen hundred fusils, eighteen hundred broadswords, powder, balls, flints and twenty light field pieces. The money had been raised by two close friends, the Paris banker, George Waters, and his father. All arrangements were kept as secret as possible, for Charles knew that the French were trying to secure a peace with England. The Prince needed to strike quickly and force French hands. Once he was in Scotland, he did not doubt that Louis would come to the aid of his 'cher cousin'. But at no time did Charles receive a definite promise from France; that he did was a fiction concocted later by his defenders. In reality, the French desire for Scottish diversions had spent itself at Dunkirk, and Charles may have suspected this himself. But now he took it upon himself to show the French the way to glory by forcing them into action on his behalf.

With amazing audacity, a French frigate of sixty guns, the *Elizabeth*, had been acquired along with a transport vessel, the *Du Teillay*. The frigate was leased from the French government by a Nantes merchant named Walter Rutledge, who pretended an intention to fit the vessel as a privateer, and then prey on English shipping in the Caribbean. The *Elizabeth* would act as escort on the journey to the Indies, but both vessels needed to be armed and provisioned for so hazardous a voyage. As a further safeguard, it was given out that the weapons being loaded aboard the transport were intended for plantations in the Indies, hence their number, and the generous supply of ammunition. The master of the *Du Teillay* was a Captain Walsh, and on board his ship it was noticed he carried several passengers. Among these gentlemen there travelled incognito Sir Thomas Sheridan, erstwhile tutor to Prince Charles Edward. Also there was Sheridan's brawny son, but few paid him any special attention.

After boarding the *Du Teillay*, Charles sent a letter to his father. He had written it on the journey to

Nantes, but had deliberately held it back until he could be sure that it would not reach Rome early enough for James to halt the venture. Charles expected the contents to come as a surprise to the King, for he included a detailed explanation of his actions and his previous secrecy. The Prince anticipated wide support in Scotland, but from whom this would come he did not say, save that they would be friends. The overall mood was one of desperation. He felt 'obliged in honour, and for my own reputation, to have flung myself into the hands of my friends, and die with them, rather than linger in such a miserable way here, or be obliged to return to Rome which would be just giving up all hopes'. Charles now admitted that the French knew nothing about his plans, but concluded, 'Let what will happen, the stroke is struck, and I have taken a firm resolution to conquer or die, and to stand my ground as long as I shall have a man remaining with me.' On the morning of 5 July, Charles Edward sailed out of the harbour at Nantes.

The expedition was ridiculously underequipped. Of men of consequence on board the *Du Teillay*, there was, besides the Prince and Sheridan, the Marquess of Tullibardine, a veteran of the Fifteen and the Nineteen, and so gouty that he could hardly walk. There were a few men of lesser importance, among them Sir John Macdonald, Captain O'Sullivan, the non-juring parson George Kelly and Aenas Macdonald, a Paris banker and Kinlochmoidart's brother. The sixty guns of the *Elizabeth* afforded a modicum of protection, but even this was eliminated when between Brittany and the Irish coast the *Elizabeth* fell in with a British warship, the *Lion*. Both vessels closed furiously but inconclusively, and eventually limped away from each other. At the height of the battle, Charles wanted to engage his own frigate in the skirmish, and Captain Walsh was obliged to threaten him with confinement lest he stirred the crew of the *Du Teillay* into reckless bravery. When the smoke had cleared, the master of the escort told Charles that his ship could go no farther. Reluctantly the Prince ordered the *Elizabeth* to sail back to Nantes.

Although he had lost half his pitiful force, Charles determined to continue. Now there could be no escape if the Highland reception proved inhospitable, and even before that point was reached, there were other dangers to be faced. Two days later another two enemy warships sailed into view. Walsh feared that all was lost for certain when the timely descent of a sea mist allowed the *Du Teillay* to make a shadowy escape. From now on, they travelled without any navigation lights rather than risk detection from ship or shore. The coastline was treacherous enough, but to complicate matters, violent seas buffeted the craft for two whole days. Weaker men might have broken, but Charles survived his ordeal bravely. Fortune was now with him, and near Barra he picked up the piper of Macneill who piloted the ship into safe harbourage at the island of Eriskay. A few hours before landfall the Marquess of Tullibardine noticed that an eagle was hovering above the ship. Excitedly, he turned to Charles to tell him that the omen was good, for 'The king of birds is come to welcome Your Royal Highness upon your arrival in Scotland.'

Small, roughly three miles long from north to south and a mile and a half in width, Eriskay is part of the fairly numerous archipelago between the eighteen-mile-long South Uist island and the smaller but still substantial Barra. The southern Outer Hebrides of which they are a part are the point of a sword lying defiantly far off the west mainland of Scotland. That sword, known as the 'Long Island', is the whole length of the Outer Hebrides. Save for a few scattered rocks, the remote St Kilda and the even more remote and inaccessible Rockall, there is nothing between them and North America.

Among the Hebrides, Eriskay is unique. It is unique because it is timeless, changeless. History once touched it when on 23 July 1745 the Prince landed there for the first time on the soil of his forefathers. He left a faint and pleasing mark of his landing which still persists for a few yards and then fades into the green and grey of the island's soil and rock. The Prince, it is said, had some seeds of the convolvulus flower in his pocket when he left Nantes in France. In the rough and tumble of climbing over the rocks on landing he spilt them; they took root when he reached the soil and have flourished there for a few yards up the hill ever since. It is easier to believe that this is true rather than dismiss it as a pious legend; the convolvulus grows nowhere else in all two hundred and fifty or so Hebridean islands.

Charles' landing place is still called locally, and so named on the Ordnance Survey Maps, *Coilleag a' Phrionnsa* – the Prince's knoll or landing bay. Until recently the great-great-granddaughter of the man who carried the Prince on his back through the waves and on to the rocks from the landing-boat was still alive and living on Eriskay. That great-great-granddaughter may well have married and now have descendants on the island, for, as has been well said of Eriskay, 'What was, is.'

The Prince landed in pouring rain. None of the pomp which surrounds historic occasions was possible, for the party had scrambled ashore in alarm when two sails were spotted out at sea. Only the immobile Tullibardine remained on board the *Du Teillay*, and it was he who first discovered that the threatening canvas belonged to a pair of French merchantmen. Gratefully, the men ashore emerged from hiding and sought refuge on the island. According to Aenas Macdonald, the Prince and his companions were eventually housed in 'one of the little country houses wherein there were already many others that were weatherbound'. Only a

48

few beds were vacant, and Charles generously offered to do without for the sake of others who had greater need of a night's rest. Hearing this, Angus Macdonald, the landlord of the house, leaned over to Sir Thomas Sheridan and assured him that his beds 'were so good, that a Prince need not be ashamed to lie in them'. The islander had no idea that his guest was indeed a Prince, more used to the finery of a palace than a thatched hut with a hole in the roof through which the choking smoke of an open fire was supposed to escape. Charles kept moving between the fire and the door, alternatively coughing in the smoke and shivering in the rain, until his host could no longer contain his temper and cried out, 'What a plague is the matter with that fellow, that he can neither sit nor stand still, and neither keep within nor without doors?' Thus admonished, the Prince slept.

The next day, Charles met Alexander Macdonald of Boisdale. Boisdale brought bad news. Sir Alexander Macdonald of Sleat and the Laird of Macleod, despite all their previous promises, would not join the Prince. In the light of this withdrawal Boisdale warned Charles that he could expect little support elsewhere. He advised the Prince to go home. 'Home,' Charles replied, 'I am come home.' Still Boisdale was not satisfied, and he prevailed upon his brother, the Laird of Clanranald, to desist from joining the Prince with the assembled might of his clan. Yet Boisdale could not restrain young Clanranald from serving Charles right up until the bloody battle of Culloden. Nor could he offset the influence which Aenas Macdonald had upon the Laird of Kinlochmoidart. Even though he had been opposed to the venture all along, Boisdale himself could not resist giving the Prince shelter when Charles was skulking in the Long Island the following year. He had a peculiar past which was responsible for the dichotomy in his nature.

Born in Benbecula and bred in South Uist, Boisdale, like everyone around him, was a Catholic. One day he took offence at a fancied rebuke from the parish priest about parishioners not attending to their duties. He formally abandoned the Catholic faith and sought what Protestant ministrations he could find from the Reverend Aulay Macaulay. This conversion naturally inclined him to a strong opposition to any form of Jacobitism; and for this he was much praised in Hanoverian circles in Edinburgh and even London. His death in 1768 was dreadful. Perceiving himself to be at his end and in great pain, he was full of remorse, and besought his sons to send for a priest to see him out of the world with the Sacrament of Extreme Unction. They, thinking that he was suffering from a madness in his desire to return to the faith of his fathers (and possibly careful of their own position under the new Establishment), only laughed at him and refused his orders. He died howling in remorse, unshriven.

Boisdale's intransigence was ominous. All along, Charles had expected overwhelming support in the Highlands.

It was natural that the Prince should look to the Highlands to give him back the throne of his fathers; the Stuart tradition was preserved there in the tenacious memory of the Celt. The Highlanders had an extreme hatred of Whiggery as represented in and enforced by the Hanoverian court in London. It was a hatred which outlasted even the eventual failure of the Forty-Five. As late as the early years of the nineteenth century Mrs Grant of Laggan said of the Highlander:

Whig was an appellation of comprehensive reproach. It was used to designate a character made up of negatives; one who had neither ear for music, nor taste for poetry, no pride of ancestry; no heart for attachment; no soul for honour.... A

Whig, in short, was what all Highlanders cordially hated – a cold, selfish, formal character.

In the eyes and hearts of the Highlanders the news of the Prince's birth in far-away Italy came as a revelation of one born to deliver them from Whiggery. Their Gaelic poets sang of it in Messianic terms upon his arrival.

### ORAN NUADH

The deagh-shoisgeul feadh nan Garbhchrìoch,
  Sùrd air armaibh combraig,
Uird ri dairirich deanamh thargaid
  Nan dual ball-chruinn bòidheach;
Chaoidh na seargaibh le cam-earra-ghlòir
  Sluaigh fior-chealgaich Sheòrais –
O's sgeul dearbhtha, thig thar fairge
  Neart ro-gharbh dar fòirinn.

Thig thar lear le gaoith anear oirnn
  Toradh deal ar dòchais,
Le 'mhilte fear' s le armaibh geal,
  Prionns' ullamh, mear, 's è do-chaisgt';
  Mac Righ Seumas, Teàrlach Stiùbhart,
Oighre 'chrùin th' air fogradh;
  Gun dean gach Breatunnach làn-ùmhlachd
Air an glùn d'a mhòrachd.

Nì na Gàidheil bheòdha, ghasda,
  Eirigh bhras le sròlaibh,
Iad 'nan ciadaibh uim' ag iathadh,
  'S coltas dian-chuir gleòis orr';
  Gun fhiamh, 's iad fiadhta, claidhmheach, sgia-
    thach,
Gunnach, riaslach, stròiceach,
  Mar chonfadh leómhannaibh fiadhaich,
'S acras dian gu feòil orr'.*

* Highland Songs of the Forty-Five, ed. and tr. by John Lorne Campbell (Grant, Edinburgh, pp. 62–63).

## A NEW SONG

Joyful tidings through the Highlands,
   Hosts for conflict arming,
Hammers beating making targets
   Of bossy, fine devices;
Never pine, for all the boasting
   Of King George's rascals —
Since 'tis certain that o'er ocean
   Strength comes to assist us.

With eastern winds will come o'er-seas
   One we've keenly hoped for,
With many men, and shining arms,
   Ready, quick, unhindered;
Prince Charles Stewart the son of James,
   The crown's heir from his exile,
Let every Briton homage do
On bended knees before him.

The reckless, active, splendid Gaels
   Will rise with silken banners,
In hundreds they'll encircle him
   Keen to prepare for action;
Fearless, ruthless, sworded, shielded,
   Well-armed, keen, destructive,
Like the wild lion's fearful charge,
   When spurred by ravening hunger.

The song is by Alasdair Mac Mhaighstir Alasdair, the most famous Celtic poet of his era. But its sentiment owes more to tradition than to Jacobite enthusiasm in the Highlands at the time. On the surface, the old ties which made the Highlands a Jacobite stronghold remained. Apart from Celtic devotion to a Scots Prince, there was the additional support of the many Roman Catholics who lived and practised there. But religious connection had never counted much in an area where chief and clan were often of different denominations.

What mattered most in the Highlands was the personal allegiance of the chief, and his ability to rouse his clan when the occasion required.

Having previously based all his hopes upon popular support, Charles now discovered that minor clansmen were little concerned with the injustice of his Stuart situation. Moreover, their individual enthusiasm would have been useless. The Highlandman pulled his broadsword from the peat where it lay hidden only when his chief called, and then not always willingly. Most of the two hundred clansmen who fought for the Prince under Gordon of Glenbucket were pressed into service. Even Donald Cameron, 'Gentle Lochiel', summoned his clan by sending tacksmen throughout Rannoch, 'to intimate to all the Camerons that if they did not forthwith go with them they would instantly proceed to burn all their houses and hough their cattle; whereupon they carried off all the Rannoch men, about one hundred, mostly of the name of Cameron.' This feudal power encouraged a baronial independence among the chiefs which had always been assiduously cultivated by enemies of the central government. Now Charles discovered that the situation was not entirely advantageous. It was virtually impossible to assert his authority among men who cherished their autonomy. They either refused to come out at all or demanded high command appointments, or favoured positions in line of battle. At the smallest slight to their honour, they were likely to leave the Prince and lead all their men back to the glens. Never was this a basis upon which successful armies have been built.

Although the chiefs still held sway in the glens, ever since the Union they experienced increasing interference from central government administrators like Lord Tweeddale, the Secretary of State for Scotland, and his servant Duncan Forbes, Lord President of the Court of Session in Edinburgh. Both men had agents and informers in the Highlands who could make life difficult for a Jacobite laird. On the other hand, conformity promised preferment and easy money in the form of government sinecures. Life away from Jacobite schemes was more comfortable and safe, and many chiefs were simply afraid to hazard their fortunes upon an adventure as risky as that of the Prince. Even Lochiel refused to pledge his support until the Prince promised him security to the full value of his estate. But others remained immovable and some succumbed to temptations held out by the wily Duncan Forbes. Years later, Captain Malcolm Macleod remembered how a letter from the Lord President to Sir Alexander Macdonald of Sleat turned the latter's enthusiasm into brooding abstinence. Despite his relentless efforts on behalf of the Hanoverians, Forbes received no official recognition. But it was largely thanks to his energy that at no time did Charles lead more than six thousand men, even though the Lord President himself estimated the potential Highland strength to be greater than thirty thousand fighting men.

Two days after making land at Eriskay, the Prince began the herculean task of raising an army out of nothing. Already he had made contact with Kinlochmoidart through Aenas Macdonald, and on 25 July he boarded the *Du Teillay* and set sail for the mainland where he landed at Borradale on Loch-nan-Uamh.

An anonymous chronicler noted Charles' arrival on the mainland of Scotland. He was almost certainly Alexander Macdonald, the celebrated Gaelic poet:

> There entered the tent a tall youth of most agreeable aspect in plain black coat and a plain shirt not very clean.
>
> I found my heart swell in my throat. He saluted none of us, and we only made a bow at a distance... At the time, taking him to be a passenger or some clergyman, I presumed to speak to him with some familiarity, yet still retained some suspicion he might be one of more note.
>
> He asked me if I was not cold in that habit (i.e. in the Highland garb). I answered that I was so habituated to it that I would not change my dress for another. At this he laughed heartily and next enquired how I lay with it at night. I explained to him that by wrapping myself in so close in my plaid I would be unprepared for any sudden defence. But that in time of danger or war we had a different method of using the plaid, that, with one spring I could stand to my feet with drawn sword and cocked pistol in my hand.
>
> Then rising quickly from his seat he calls for a dram, when some person whispers to me a second time to pledge the stranger but not to drink with him. By which seasonable hint I was confirmed in my suspicions who he was.

For a fortnight, Charles remained in the *Du Teillay*, anchored off the coast of Arisaig. There he was visited by chiefs and their representatives, many of whom were astonished at the absence of French regular troops among the Prince's party. To their criticism, Charles replied pointedly that he 'did not chuse to owe the restoration of his father to foreigners, but to his own friends, to whom he was now come to put it in their power to have the glory of that event'.

Among the first to arrive were young Clanranald, Boisdale's nephew, Macdonald of Keppoch and Dr Archibald Cameron, servant of the influential Cameron of Lochiel. Both Cameron and Clanranald advised Charles to return to France, and only Keppoch encouraged the Prince's hopes by suggesting that his bravery ought to be rewarded with support. Clanranald eventually altered his opinion, as did Lochiel in August. With these men behind him, Charles had some chance of striking against the Hanoverians. From then on, support grew daily, and on 11 August the Prince decided to go farther south to Moidart, where Aenas Macdonald's brother promised assistance. When he stepped ashore at Kinlochmoidart, Charles observed a young Highlander standing by. 'Will you not assist me?' the Prince asked. The young man, Ranald Macdonald, laid his hand upon his claymore: 'I will. I will, and though no other man in the Highlands should draw a sword I am ready to die for you.' Already the spell was cast, and the fabric of the legend woven.

There was little time for dalliance. As early as 28 July, the Reverend Lauchlan Campbell, Whiggish minister of Ardnamurchan and Eileen Finain, had noticed that 'all my Jacobites were in high spirits'. The following Sunday, when he preached a sermon extolling the virtues of Pauline obedience, his parishioners demonstrated that it was 'quite against their sentiments'. The minister suspected that something unusual was afoot. The same evening in Kilchoan his fears were confirmed by Anna Cameron, a staunch Whig, who told him that the Pretender's eldest son was on board a mysterious ship anchored in Loch-nan-Uamh. She also knew that Charles had only a few men with him, but the clan chiefs had been contacted in the hope of raising an army. That night, Lauchlan Campbell despatched the 'newes frae Moidart' on a journey which ended with the Duke of Argyll on 8 August. But by then Charles was credited with an army of three hundred French troops.

On 2 August Tweeddale wrote to Lord Milton, the Lord Justice Clerk, that, 'the French court was meditating an invasion of His Majesty's dominions, and the Pretender's son had sailed from Nantz in a French man of war, and was actually landed in Scotland, which last part I can hardly believe to be true'. Undoubtedly the government in London believed it to be true, for on 25 July they had issued a proclamation offering a reward of £30,000 to anyone who seized and secured the Prince for the purpose of 'bringing him to justice'. On 10 August Major-General John Campbell was informed by his son that 'there is some design carrying on'. In Edinburgh Argyll fretted that 'nobody would believe anything of it'. Somebody did, for the Duke of Newcastle confided gloomily that 'I was never in so much apprehension, as I am at present'. On Saturday, 17 August, the *Edinburgh Gazette* carried a paragraph confirming the Prince's arrival on the mainland. Nine days earlier, Sir John Cope had arranged to assemble an army at Stirling, and on 13 August Duncan Forbes went to Inverness and succeeded in raising twenty companies for Loudon's regiment among the Highlanders.

On 11 August James heard that his son had gone to Scotland. From Rome, he wrote to Earl Marischal.

What I know of it is very imperfect, but enough to show me that if I had been acquainted with it in time, I had certainly done my best to prevent its being executed. If it was rash, I cannot but say it is a bold undertaking and the courage and sentiments the Prince expresses on this occasion will always do him honour.

The Sheriff at Inveraray was more harsh with the Prince. 'The expedition looks extremely romantick, and to be sure no man in his senses would take up arms.' But audacity was the keynote of Charles' style. From Kinlochmoidart he sent out an order for a rendezvous of all the loyal clans at Glenfinnan on 19 August.

On the seventeenth, Charles left for the rendezvous. Just before his departure he was joined by one hundred and fifty men led by old Gordon of Glenbucket, the Banffshire laird. Glenbucket also brought the Prince news of his first victory. The day before at High Bridge, Major Macdonell of Tiendrish, with only a dozen Highlanders, attacked two companies of Scots militia who were on their way to Fort Augustus. The militiamen scuttled away in the face of the dreaded Highland charge, and their officer, Captain Switenham, was taken prisoner. Charles had no desire to be encumbered with prisoners at this stage and released the captain on parole. A day later, the Prince crossed Lochshiel and spent the night at Glensiarich. The next morning he arrived at Glenfinnan to find the Laird of Morar waiting there with one hundred and fifty clansmen. The Prince now had an army of three hundred men, in addition to his personal bodyguard comprising fifty of Clanranald's. But that was hardly enough for the conquest of Britain.

Where were the rest? Where, above all, were Lochiel and his promised men? 'When God made time He made plenty of it' is a West Highland maxim which does not deter action, ardour or endurance, but it can lower the spirit of those who do not know Celtic ways. For the first time since his extraordinary dash from France to Scotland, Charles may have felt that his intuition had failed him. It had not. With that suddenness of action and the sounds of action which can break into the timelessness of the Celt, the skirl of the pipes was heard, and from over the brow of the hill from Achnacarry there came Lochiel at the head of 700 Camerons. As if at a signal, but really at hazard, other loyal Jacobite followers came from all directions – Keppoch with his 300 Macdonalds, the Marquess of Tullibardine and others, either individually or in crowds. Before he knew where he was Charles was surrounded by a crowd of followers estimated now at over one thousand men in arms.

He in whose cause they had come was alone unarmed, dressed as a civilian in a dun-coloured coat, scarlet breeches, a yellow waistcoat and a scarlet bob to his hat. At first Charles was overcome with emotion, but Major Macdonell later remembered 'that he had never seen the Prince more cheerful than when he had got together Four or Five hundred men about the standard'. The Catholic Bishop, Hugh Macdonald, 'Vicar of the Highland District', was there to bless the Stuart banner which the Marquess of Tullibardine unfurled and raised amidst shouts in Gaelic, *Prionnsa Tearlach Righ nan Ghaidheil* (Prince Charlie King of the Gael).* The Forty-Five had begun.

At Glenfinnan, Charles was joined by Murray of Broughton. Murray automatically assumed the duties of a secretary, although he was not officially appointed until 25 August. Neither the Prince nor his secretary were able to make a decision regarding the command of the Highland army. Charles was badly in need of professional advice, but only Keppoch had seen active service, and his appointment to a senior position would have caused immediate friction among the chiefs. Lower down the scale, the Prince turned to John William O'Sullivan, an Irishman in French service who had accompanied him on the journey from Nantes. O'Sullivan claimed to have some knowledge of staff-work, and on the strength of this he was ap-

* *Tearlach* sounds very like the English version of the name Charlie and has given the phrase Prince Charlie to legend, history, fact and fancy.

pointed Quartermaster and Adjutant-General. It was an unfortunate appointment, and one the Prince would regret. But in his necessity, he had no alternative.

While still at Glenfinnan, Charles learned that Sir John Cope was already moving north. Cope was an industrious leader who had distinguished himself at Dettingen before being appointed to the Scottish command in January 1744. He was not popular in military circles, for his promotion was attributed to other than military qualifications. Under him in Scotland he had about three thousand men and the 'invalid' garrisons at Edinburgh, Stirling and Dumbarton. Of his three and a half infantry regiments, only one (Guise's) could claim to be well established. The others dated from 1741 and had seen no action. Cope's two regiments of dragoons were as inexperienced, and what was more, he discovered that there was not a single Royal Artilleryman in the whole of the land! Nevertheless, on the day that Cope departed for Stirling and the north, he had over two thousand more men than Charles.

Cope was operating on the basis of a contingency plan drawn up earlier with the assistance of the 'King's Servants' in Scotland, chief of whom was the Lord President of the Court of Session, Duncan Forbes of Culloden. Forbes was born in 1685, and was one of a strange breed. He is today venerated for his kind heart, and in particular, for his supposed protection of the true interests of his neighbouring Highlanders (he was an Inverness man). Consequently, not one word of reproach has been hurled against him. But Forbes was one of the heaviest drinkers of the eighteenth century, and that is saying something in an age of heavy drinking. At school in Inverness he and his brother were known as 'the greatest boozers of the North'. His deal tables at Culloden were stained dull red from the spilled claret and burgundy which decorated his daily bacchanalian feasts, and he would point to them with pride. There is no moral objection to his tremendous drinking which was a feature of his century, his class and his country; but it is a trifle hard that nearly every historian of the affair of 1745 should chastise Charles' own drinking during his long years of exile, while saying nothing of Forbes' far heavier and more consistent tippling.

From youth Forbes set out to back what he supposed to be the winning side in his relations with the Highlanders for whom he professed so strong a love. He had seen and tried to damp down the general and understandable disaffection after the massacre of Glencoe, and was active against the Risings of 1715 and 1719. It never seems to have occurred to him to give any advice to 'his' Highlanders other than to obey their new masters. He may well have claimed success after the Nineteen; though what he thought of the steady stream of emigration from the Highlands during all this period is not recorded. The Prince and the affair of the Forty-Five must have meant shocking disillusion.

Since early July, Forbes had heard rumours about the Prince's landing in Scotland which he had respectfully passed on to Cope. From the General they went to Tweeddale and thence to the Council of Regency. The Council ordered Cope to keep his eyes open, but warned him against alarming the country with excessive preparations. In desperation, Cope relied heavily upon the advice of the willing Lord President. Forbes assured the General that the best means of defence against any rising would be swift attack before the rebels had a chance to gather strength. A small Highland body would be easily dispersed and the example would discourage others from leaving the paths of virtue. When confirmation of Charles' presence arrived, Cope decided to march at once.

## 4: The Victory at Corriearrick and the Occupation of Perth

On 21 August Cope reached Stirling. From the castle heights, he had a forbidding view of the sentinel mountains by Ben Ledi. It was now his intention to penetrate those hills and go to the relief of a threatened Fort Augustus. There he would bar the further progress of the rebels. With him Cope had Murray's regiment and five companies of Lee's besides two 'additional' companies of Lord John Murray's Black Watch. The same day Cope marched for Crieff, and reached it the following morning. There he was met by eight companies of Lascelles' regiment and a pitiful detachment of Lord Loudon's Highland militia. All had gone well up to now, but during the night the baggage horses wandered off, and the next morning Cope was left wondering how to carry all his supplies with him. In addition, he was encumbered with a thousand stands of arms which he had hoped to supply to well-affected Highlanders whom Duncan Forbes had promised would rally to the flag. None came, and Cope had to make arrangements to transport the arms back to Stirling. Half the next morning was wasted before the army eventually got under way, leaving behind piles of rotting bread and not a few deserters. On 25 August Cope entered Dalnacardoch and there received his first eyewitness account of the rebel army from Captain Switenham. The Captain believed that his former captors were now at least three thousand strong, and he told Cope that they would very likely ambush the General in the Corriearrick Pass.

Cope had to press on. Although alarming reports of French landings were now reaching him, the General was ordered by Tweeddale to continue 'notwithstanding the Report of the landing of the Troops and even notwithstanding any actual Debarkation of Troops'. He marched north along part of the three hundred miles of road which Marshal Wade had built between 1725 and 1737. At Dalwhinnie, he halted. There he received a letter from Duncan Forbes which added greatly to his fears. The Lord President warned Cope that large numbers of Macdonalds and Camerons were with the Prince already, and it was likely that they would soon be joined by Glengarry and Glenmoriston. He also confirmed Captain Switenham's story: '... they are to wait for you on the North side of the Mountain over which the road of Corryarig leads, in a precipitous or boggy ground where cavalry cannot act.' Forbes was clearly unwilling to advise Cope plainly one way or the other. He concluded, '... if the bushes are well beat, there can be no surprise in daylight and I have no notion that they will look the troops with artillery in the face'. But he added a strange postscript. 'I ask your pardon for the impertinence of suggesting to you, what will certainly occur to yourself, that the Highlanders can at pleasure mar the made roads, and thereby prevent the carriage of heavy artillery over steep or boggy grounds.'

Cope was at a loss. The next day, 27 August, he called a council of war at which he informed his officers that to continue was no longer practicable. But the army had not adequate supplies to remain at Dalwhinnie. Nor could it retreat to Stirling for fear of giving further encouragement to the Highlanders. It was unanimously decided to march for the comparative safety of Inverness, where Forbes had promised a large body of Highland militia (mainly Monroes) to bolster Cope's force and equip it more thoroughly to deal with the rebels on their own terms. The army was then put into line and the General continued towards Corriearrick until he was three miles from Garva Bridge. There he turned off to rejoin the Inverness road and spent the night at Ruthven. He left the barracks the following morning and pressed through the dangerous defile of Slochd, reaching Inverness on the evening of 29 August.

Cope was severely criticized for avoiding an engagement, but his action was based upon a sound appreciation of the dangers involved. The terrain of Corriearrick was ideally suited to sudden and savage ambush by men long practised in such bloody raids. It was eminently unsuitable for regular troops. Moreover, Cope had no idea exactly where the Highland army lay. Neither did he know that Charles' forces had swelled to a formidable two and a half thousand men. The Prince was marching towards Blair Castle, and on 23 August had been joined by another five hundred clansmen. Two days later, a further hundred arrived. At Invergarry, Charles was joined by Ardshiel with two hundred and sixty Stewarts of Appin, and at Aberchalder the Highland army received another four hundred Macdonalds from Glengarry, plus one hundred and fifty from Glencoe. Every day Charles' strength grew as the clansmen arrived, Grants from Glenmoriston, Athollmen and stragglers from Lochaber. Had Cope engaged this host in the narrow passes which led to Fort Augustus, his army would have been decimated.

While Cope's reputation ebbed, Stuart hopes soared. The Highland army was in high spirits and gaining in determination as its numbers grew. On the day that he heard of the enemy's march towards Corriearrick, Charles grandly issued a proclamation offering a reward 'of thirty thousand pounds sterling to him or them who shall seize or secure, till our future orders, the person of the Elector of Hanover, whether landed or attempting to land in any of His Majesty's Dominions'. Charles' humour was not lost among the Highlanders, but it was with greater relish that they heard of his intention to attack Cope in the vicinity of Dalwhinnie.

On the night of 26 August, a detachment was sent to seize the pass and set up an ambush. They had a few swivel guns from the *Du Teillay*, and these they planned to mount in sleeping batteries so as to enfilade the seventeen traverses by which the road wound up the mountain. The final rout would be completed with fierce charges from both top and bottom of the pass. The next day the clans marched over Corriearrick and on 28 August Charles reached Carvamore. But still there was no sign of the enemy. At first the Prince was puzzled, for news of Cope's advance had been trustworthy. Then the situation was explained by a group of men who claimed to be deserters and who now wanted to join the Prince. Charles and his chiefs remained suspicious until at length the story of Cope's retreat to Inverness was confirmed by Gaelic-speaking residents of the town. The frustrated Highlanders immediately offered to follow the enemy and surprise him at night, but Charles would have none of it. He persuaded his army to accept instead the open invitation to the Lowlands so generously left by Cope. Gradually Highland disappointment at not meeting the Sassenach upon their own Gaelic ground gave way to triumph and merriment. They took the affair as a bloodless victory, which indeed it was, a laughably humiliating one for the foe. Report has it that Charles' delighted soldiers made up a number of scatalogical Gaelic verses about Cope's defeat in the hills. The Gaelic language is a particularly good medium for this sort of thing; but unfortunately none of the Dalwhinnie verses survive.

Two days after he reached Inverness, General Cope received a desperate plea for help from the sergeant at Ruthven. The barracks were under attack. In fact, the twelve men at Ruthven were not assailed by the whole Highland might, but by only a small section under O'Sullivan and Lochgarry. Neither side had any cannon, and according to Aenas Macdonald, 'The Highland party endeavoured to set fire to the door, but the soldiers fired through holes in the door, killed one man and mortally wounded another; and then the party returned. All this time O'Sullivan hid himself in a barn.' Charles was anxious to press forward, and the day when news of the attack reached Inverness, he was at Blair Castle. Cope realized that the race for the Lowlands had begun. Hastily he ordered shipping to be sent from Leith to Aberdeen so that he might cross the Forth to Edinburgh. Three days later, the Prince spent the night at Nairne House, and by the time Cope marched from Inverness on 4 September, the Highland army was in Perth.

Audacity had rewarded the Prince. With all his lack of military experience, he had nevertheless made the right decisions intuitively. In fact, his intuitive judgement brought Charles greater success than ever did the informed advice of others. Near Ruthven, Cluny Macpherson was taken prisoner at the head of a company of militia. Charles was convinced of Cluny's loyalty to the Stuarts, despite the compromising situation in which he had been captured. The Prince knew little of the leadership dispute within Clan Chattan which in part accounted for Cluny's questionable position. Others did, yet they advised Charles to keep the prisoner in custody. They could not appreciate that Cluny had contrived to have himself taken prisoner lest an open expression of loyalty to the Prince drove half his company of clansmen into the arms of the rival laird of MacIntosh. Charles simply trusted to his judgement, released the prisoner, gained an additional company of troops and was vindicated in Perth when Cluny joined the Highland army openly. Before he left Nairne on 3 September, Charles had well earned the endearing title of 'Bonnie Prince Charlie', and so named he entered Perth the following morning.

The city of Perth claims, with some justification, to be the ancient capital of Scotland. The historic parish and village of Scone (pronounced Skoon) is so near to Perth that a part of it is within the city boundaries. At Scone the Stuart Kings of Scotland were all crowned; indeed before the Stuarts were heard of, Kenneth Macalpine, the first monarch of Gaelic Scotland received his crown there. Situated where the Highlands touch the Lowlands, Perth contained, and still contains in its people, the qualities of both races. In the Prince's day when he entered it there were plenty of citizens speaking Gaelic; a few still do. Since the Rising of 1715 Perth had been Jacobite and still was in 1745.

The River Tay, the longest in Scotland, flowed by it (now through it owing to its late eighteenth-century extension across the river with a good stone bridge). The river is navigable from the North Sea to only a few miles below the city. To the north lie the Highland hills, to the south the broad champaign of the Lowlands over which stretches a fine view from Kinnoul Hill. With its mixture of medieval wynds and closes and neo-Georgian terraces, rather like those in Edinburgh New Town, Perth deserves its title of 'The Fair City'. But its beauty conceals a turbulent history. Seven times it was besieged, and once it was wrecked by mobs kindled with the fire of John Knox. Even the 'Inches', sedate suburban parks which ring the city, witnessed the fury and clamour of a clan battle.

Perth welcomed the army as no other city did. After the Spartan outline of Corriearrick, the Prince and his Highlanders must have appreciated the hospitable environs of Perth. John Hickson, a native of the city who assisted in the search for billets, and who subsequently forfeited his head at Carlisle, kept a record of the dignitaries who paid homage to King James' Regent at his rooms in the Salutation Inn on the High Street. To this makeshift palace came the Duke of Perth in Highland dress, his cousin, Lord William Drummond, Viscount Strathallan and the laird of Balquhidder. In train with the notables came their proud kinsmen and tenants, some of whom moved to Perth permanently. Even today the descendants of the Maclaurins and Maclarens who came to Perth with Strathallan remain conspicuous in the city. All first came to hail Prince Charles.

One of the visitors to the inn was Lord George Murray, younger brother of the Marquess of Tullibardine. Born in 1694, Lord George held a regular commission at the time of the Fifteen, but with his two elder brothers, William and Charles, he joined the Jacobite army. Four years later, he and William were present at Glenshiel, and only after six years was Lord George allowed to return home. His brother William came back with the Prince to discover that Lord George had settled down to peaceful retirement as a happily married country gentleman. Apparently he had forgotten old enmities, and was on friendly terms with James, Duke of Atholl, the Hanoverian usurper of William's title. Even Forbes of Culloden was counted among his friends now, but for once the wily Duncan was unable to exert his persuasive powers with success. Lord George went to the Prince.

The decision had not been easy. At the beginning of September Lord George wrote an evasive letter to the Duke of Atholl, himself under pressure from Tweeddale to ensure that his neighbour did not join the rebels. That same day Lord George took his nieces to Stirling. There he received a note from Lawrence Oliphant of Gask, a staunch Jacobite who was acting as a self-appointed agent for Prince Charles. Perhaps the memorandum from Gask contained a special communication from the Prince, for it certainly had a dramatic effect upon Lord George. When he returned home, his rational political calm had vanished. He wrote again to Atholl. He had now decided to join the Prince. His friends in Edinburgh credited the change in direction to the evil influence of the Marquess of Tullibardine, but from his letter to Atholl it appears as though Lord George was forced into action by the strength of his convictions. 'My life, my Fortune, my Expectations, the Happyness of my wife and children are all at stake (and the chances are against me). Honour and my duty to King (James) and Country outweighs everything else.'

Lord George was the most distinguished soldier thus far to join the Prince, and Charles hesitated little before making him a Lieutenant-General. To no man would the Prince owe more. He became the mainspring of the Highland army, using it with such dexterity that Horace Walpole seriously considered packing his bags for Holland as the invaders swept towards Derby. But relations between Charles and his commander were not smooth. The twenty-six-year age difference was never bridged, and the Prince often regarded Lord George as a cautious old bigot. For his part, Lord George could not appreciate the reckless daring which drove the Prince along. He lacked the tact with which princes ought to be treated. He was frequently curt when patience would have been wiser. A more insidious thorn in the relationship was the suspicion introduced by diehard Jacobites like Broughton, who believed that because Lord George had devoted so much energy to reconciliation with the Hanoverians, his commitment to the Stuarts must be less than complete. How else could they rationalize his friendship with arch-Whigs like Forbes? Even after resounding victories at Prestonpans and Falkirk, Charles was unsure about his Lieutenant-General. In later life his suspicion became obsessive and he would have nothing to do with Lord George. His personal differences with the General were exacerbated by a clash in military policy ever since the retreat from Derby, and not even the plain fact that Lord George had surrendered his entire estate and the comfort of his family could enable the Prince to recognize where the man's true sympathies lay. He became the scapegoat upon which Charles blamed all his misfortune.

The other Lieutenant-General appointed by Charles was James Drummond, titular third Duke of Perth. The man was a confirmed Jacobite who all along had clamoured for an invasion. Charles had been sure of his support throughout. Perth was only seven years older than the Prince, a Roman Catholic and a man who had spent over twenty years of his life in France. There he had acquired an uneven knowledge of military engineering, but when he returned to Scotland to live with his mother at Drummond Castle near Crieff, he turned his attention towards agriculture and horse racing. He was nevertheless still blatantly involved in Jacobite affairs, and shortly before Charles landed in Scotland Perth only narrowly escaped arrest by Hanoverian agents. A brave but modest man, the Duke easily won the friendship of Charles and the respect of the Highland army. Although not the general that Lord George was, Perth held seniority by virtue of his rank, yet he was astute enough to realize that Charles' best hopes lay with the other commander. Thus he was always prepared to concur with Lord George on questions of strategy, and was sensible enough not to offend the older man's pride. Had Lord George been as affable as Perth, and had the Duke been as able as his colleague, Charles would have found fewer occasions to lament his situation.

For a week the clans stayed in Perth, gradually growing in strength and learning the discipline of an army. The logistical problems posed by daily fluctuations in size were immense. Clansmen came and went and when Robertson of Struan came in with a further two hundred men on 9 September, all previous calculations regarding provisioning were invalidated. So it continued from day to day. Of course there were money shortages as well, and in desperation, Charles levied £500 from the city itself. But this was scarcely sufficient to pay the army, let alone supply it. In addition, the Prince had to contend with inter-clan disputes and the traditions of Celtic warfare. The Macdonalds, for example, demanded a position of honour on the right flank in line of battle. They claimed it as their traditional right, and at Culloden Charles learned how stubborn the clan could be if their claim was denied. Even his commanders haggled over trivial details while the Prince was left wondering whether they would fall out among themselves before the enemy came within gunshot.

But Charles was not dismayed. He regarded the fact that he had a logistics problem at all as a minor victory in itself. From Perth he wrote to James about his popularity in Scotland and claimed to 'have got their hearts to a degree not to be easily conceived by those who do not see it'. Yet the Prince's jubilation was also coloured by a pragmatic realism born out of experience. He credited his success to 'my conformity to the customs of those people'. Not for him the airy dictates of an absolutist prince, for he well understood the continuing frailty of his situation. During the day on which he wrote to his father, news came from Edinburgh of the publication of 'The Speech of Thomas Freeman', archetypal voice of English liberty. 'Freeman' harangued his audience pointedly, reminding them of earlier Stuart reigns. 'Alas! My Countrymen, is it possible that there are any among us, who really wish to see the son of James VII upon the Throne of Britain? Surely no one who remembers those dreadful Times which immediately preceded the Revolution can sincerely harbour such a wish.' Rather than deny the guilt of his predecessors, Charles warned his father against 'the folly of those pious princes' who had gone before. Unlike the theoreticians in Rome, Charles could see that old Stuart sins had not been forgiven. Sadly, he told James that the much sought Duke of Argyll was an implacable foe who would shun any offer put to him by his Stuart enemies. 'What have these princes to answer for,' Charles asked, 'who by their cruelties have raised enemies not only to themselves but to their innocent children?'

The answer was irrelevant and the rhetoric which Charles served to his father must be credited with a practical purpose. Naturally the contents of the letter would be discussed among Jacobites on the continent, and Charles hoped that his stark analysis would impress sceptics like Earl Marischal who had at first regarded the venture as the fruit of a boyish daydream. Marischal's presence in Scotland would not only give weight to the rising, it would also revenge the Prince's injured pride, and Charles confessed, 'I had rather see him than one thousand French.' Against his exposition of the exact situation, Charles set another point about which he was adamant. Again and again he stressed the undesirability of introducing foreign troops into the country. The nation would immediately unite against the invader. Of that Charles was now sure, and he warned James that he could not afford to lose 'one foot of land that belongs to the Crown of England, or set my hand to any treaty inconsistent with its sovreignty and independency'. All would best be left to the Highland army billeted in Perth and the English who had so far concealed themselves.

On the night of 10 September news came that Sir John Cope was nearing Aberdeen. Orders were given immediately, and the next morning the clans marched out of Perth. They travelled south-west to Dunblane, some twenty-seven miles away from the city, where the Duke of Perth joined them with one hundred and fifty men. The Duke also had confirmation of Cope's arrival in Aberdeen, so Charles would have to hurry if he were to reach Edinburgh before the enemy. From what the Prince knew, only two dragoon regiments stood between him and the capital city, Colonel Gardiner's being stationed at Stirling, and Hamilton's at Edinburgh itself. In Cope's absence the dragoon regiments were under the overall command of Lieutenant-General Joshua Guest, custodian of the garrison at Edinburgh. Guest had failed to realize the dangers of leaving his forces divided, and had neglected either to order Hamilton to join Gardiner at Stirling, or recall the latter to Edinburgh. Gardiner was thus stranded alone in the path of the approaching Highlanders.

The prospect of confronting one regiment of nervous dragoons worried Charles little. On the way to Dunblane he paused at the 'Auld Hoose of Gask' to pay his respects to the overjoyed Oliphants, a Jacobite family who maintained their loyalty well into the first half of the last century. The visit was later celebrated in verse by the Edinburgh poetess, Lady Nairne, who also recorded that Charles allowed the Oliphants to clip a lock of his hair and keep it as a relic. The Prince's good humour was not reserved for gentry alone. He often dismounted and walked among the marching clansmen, talking to them in English or the smattering of Gaelic he had thus far mastered. On 13 September he led his clans across the Forth at the Fords of Frew, about eight miles above Stirling. There Gardiner should be waiting.

Charles went immediately to Bannockburn where Sir Hugh Paterson and his attractive niece, Clementina Walkinshaw, entertained him for a few hours. But the Prince did not intend to spend the whole evening at the fireside. With Lord George, Lochiel and a thousand men, he stole under cover of darkness to Stirling to engage the enemy. Though Gardiner had boasted of giving the Highlanders 'a warm reception', not a dragoon was to be seen. They had already retreated to Falkirk. The following morning Charles gave chase, only to discover at Falkirk that the dragoons had once again ridden faster and farther, this time to Linlithgow. That evening the Prince dined with the ill-fated Earl of Kilmarnock, and to him Charles confessed a suspicion that he would travel the length of Britain without having to fire a single shot. However, Kilmarnock assured him that the dragoons were resolved to halt the Highlanders at Linlithgow bridge, so at 1 o'clock the next morning, Lord George again tried to surprise Gardiner. But once more the frustrated clans found that the enemy had slipped away earlier. Hopefully they pursued the harassed dragoons to Kirkliston, but there they discovered that Gardiner was now three miles west of Edinburgh, and entrenched in the little village of Corstorphine.

At Corstorphine Gardiner was joined by Hamilton's regiment, and thus reinforced the dragoons retired for the night to a small field near Colt Bridge, leaving only a small rear-guard to watch for the approaching clans. That same evening, Brigadier Thomas Fowke arrived in Edinburgh from England in order to take command of the Dutch infantry regiment daily expected at Leith. The next morning, 16 September, he reviewed the dragoons at Colt Bridge and left a scathing report of their appearance. Gardiner was at their head, 'muffled in a wide blue surcoat, with a handkerchief drawn round his hat, and tied under his chin'. The rest of the troop were equally sloppy. In fact they appeared to have suffered from their dash to Edinburgh. Fowke found 'many of the Men's and some of the Officer's Legs so swelld, that they could not wear Boots; and those who really were to be depended upon, in a manner overcome from want of sleep'. The horses too had suffered and few were fit to 'receive the Riders'. Moreover, Fowke discovered that the colonel was severely depressed and sincerely believed that 'for his part he had not long to live'.

When Fowke told Guest that his dragoons were unfit to face the enemy, the Commander of the Castle ordered their withdrawal to Leith Links where they would be in readiness for the expected arrival of Cope. But before this could be accomplished, the detail at Corstorphine reported that the Highlanders were ad-

## 5 : Edinburgh and Prestonpans

For many miles Charles must have had a view of what Robert Louis Stevenson once called 'That Precipitous City'. Ever since the accession of James II, Edinburgh had been the capital of Stuart Scotland, and at last it lay before the long-exiled Prince. We do not know what emotions stirred within Charles' heart, but many years later Sir Walter Scott expressed his own impression at the sight of his beloved city.

> *Where the huge Castle holds its state,*
> *And all the steep slope down*
> *Whose ridgy back heaves to the sky,*
> *Piled deep and massy, close and high*
> *Mine own romantic town!*

To have even a faint idea now of the aspect and manner of the capital of Scotland in the eighteenth century it is necessary to have been born in the first years of this one – even before that if you can manage it. I am as old as this century and can, with the rententive memory of childhood, recall certain essential elements of it.

The Castle and its rock were then much as they would have appeared to Charles Edward Stuart The Royal Mile, the sequent streets of the Lawnmarket, the High Street and the Canongate which lead from the Castle two hundred and fifty feet down to the Palace of Holyroodhouse also would, on the surface, have been recognizable to the Prince.

This Royal Mile had decayed during the early years of the nineteenth century into a rotting slum. All the fine folk, the nobility and gentry, had migrated to the gracious neo-Georgian New Town which is still with us today. The Royal Mile, which had once been all of the City of Edinburgh, did retain in its appearance in the earlier years of this century one physical fact which had made it unique; that was the extraordinary height of the houses. Built upon a rock, with the Nor' Loch (now Princes Street Gardens) to the north of it and with the Flodden Wall to the south, the citizens of Edinburgh could only expand by building upwards. They did this even before 1745 and had put up what were known much later as the first skyscrapers in the world.

In the eighteenth century there was, of course, no such thing as running water in houses for washing purposes – it was imported by 'washing-women' and carried up the long, high stairways at one penny a keg. But at the end of the day and when washing-up after supper was finished, the servants would hurl the filthy water on to the streets and pavements with only the warning cry of 'Gardyloo', a corruption of the French *Garde de l'eau* faintly remembered from the days of the Franco-Scottish alliance.

And it was not only filthy washing water that descended from the high upper windows. The contents of the domestic pot and chamber pot would join the general evening cascade. The result was that save for the brief periods after the weekly sluicing down of the street by water, or after a really heavy and long-lasting downpour of rain, the smell of the Royal Mile remained all but permanent.

An added inconvenience of this malodorous smell of the street was that, if you were not careful, it might assail your person too. Should you be coming home from a claret or punch party at a tavern, and your thoughts too happily engaged to hear the cry of 'Gardyloo', you might suffer an inundation upon your fine velvet, silks and feathered hat. Many a young gallant coming from an assignation must have reeled on, drenched and stinking, as he cursed his own and other people's inattention.

78

On 16 September 1745 the absence of a proper sewerage system would have worried the residents of the city but little. Just outside their walls a Highland army was poised threateningly at Grays Mill. The dragoons who should have protected the city were now cowering behind it at Leith, and the rest of the government troops had locked themselves in the Castle. From the safety of the citadel, both army and Crown lawyers urged the beleaguered Lord Provost, Archibald Stewart, to resist the clans. But Stewart refused to make a direct plea for dragoon support lest such action provoked the host outside the city into bloody revenge. In the midst of the uproar an ultimatum arrived from Charles, and a deputation was quickly sent to treat with the Prince at his headquarters near Slateford. The Lord Provost was playing for time and clearly unwilling to throw in his hand with either side until he could be sure which course would prove the less expensive. Already there were rumours that Sir John Cope had been sighted on the Forth, so within a few hours the whole situation might have altered. The citizens of Edinburgh were equally divided about the course of action which ought to be undertaken. A body of militia was raised to defend the city, but while it was being mobilized in the Lawnmarket, a stranger rode up to declare that he had just seen the Highland army and was convinced that it now comprised an irresistible force of 16,000 men! On hearing that, most of the volunteers went home while the more stubborn retired into the Castle.

If Hanoverian supporters were relying on the dragoons being able to recover their order and spirit, they were soon disappointed. Fowke's regiments were unable to obtain forage at Leith and had pressed on to Musselburgh, only to meet with as little luck. Tired and irritable by now, the regiments then rode to Prestonpans which was conveniently adjacent to Colonel Gardiner's estate at Bankton. After supply arrangements had been made, Gardiner was given permission by Fowke to retire to his own house for the night. But two hours after taking to bed, the Colonel was roused by his adjutant who excitedly told him that the troop had again taken fright and were about to ride off. Many of the corps officers were sitting at table in a tavern at Prestonpans when the alarm broke. Though there were no Highlanders within miles of the area, the panic which Gardiner discovered at camp was complete. Most of the troop were already saddled and ready to leave, so all Gardiner could do was persuade a despairing Brigadier Fowke to lead an orderly withdrawal. Once again, the retreat resembled a rout. In the darkness, the regiments were separated into two bodies, one proceeding to North Berwick, the other to Dunbar, where Cope's army was about to disembark. Half the troop gear had been abandoned during the ride, and the next morning amused locals found the roads littered with pistols, packs, swords and ammunition. Why the dragoons believed the Highlanders to be upon their heels was never satisfactorily explained. One story was that the cries of a dragoon officer who had stumbled into a pit were sufficient to convince two regiments that the enemy had sneaked into camp to kill them all with the dreaded claymore. A more likely explanation is that disgruntled locals, anxious to avoid the burden of having troops billeted on their land and consuming their forage, spread false rumours among the scared dragoons with consummate skill. So successful were they that Alexander Carlyle, a minister's son from Edinburgh, later wrote that 'It was vain to tell them that the rebels had neither wings nor horses, nor were they invisible.' Away galloped the dragoons as though every clansman in the land was in hot pursuit.

During the night, while Sir John Cope was inching his way into Dunbar, a second deputation from Edinburgh returned to the city after a fruitless meeting with the Prince. The officials were aware that Charles was tiring of their delaying tactics, but they did not know that his patience had already been exhausted. About nine hundred clansmen under Keppoch, Lochiel and O'Sullivan were hiding by the Netherbow Port when the deputation entered the city via the West Port. Luck was with the Highlanders. The coach carrying the delegates paused for a while to allow its passengers to remove themselves to an inn, and then turned around and headed back to the city walls. The driver was bound for his stables in the Canongate and could not have expected the reception which greeted him as he passed through the now opened Netherbow Port! With wild cries, the lurking clansmen struck. The volunteer guard was easily overcome, and by the early hours of the morning, the entire city belonged to Charles Edward.

When Edinburgh awoke on the morning of 17 September, its citizens discovered that their guard had indeed been changed during the night! Where once had stood nervous volunteers, there now swarmed batteries of nonchalant Highlandmen. The news spread rapidly, and when Charles made his entry, he was greeted by enthusiastic crowds. Accompanied by the Duke of Perth and Lord Elcho, the Prince rode straight to the Palace of Holyroodhouse, where instructions were issued to bivouac the army in the King's Park, by the side of that looming rock called Arthur's Seat. Later in the day, Charles made his first official visit to the city. He was overcome with joy, for he never stopped smiling, and to eye-witnesses he justified his title of 'Bonnie Prince Charlie'. One who saw him that day described the Prince:

He was a tall slender young Man, about five feet ten Inches high, of a ruddy complexion, high nosed, large rolling brown Eyes, long visaged, red-haired, but at that time wore a pale Periwig. He was in Highland Habit, had a blue Sash, wrought with Gold, that came over his Shoulder; red Velvet Breeches, a green Velvet Bonnet, with a white Cockade, and a Gold Lace about it. He had a Silver-hilted broad Sword, and was shewn great Respect by his Forces.

At the Mercat Cross, hard by the Hie Kirk of St Giles and the old Parliament House, heralds proclaimed Charles Prince Regent of Scotland in the name of his father, James VIII, 'King of Scotland, England, France and Ireland'.

Even while the heralds were performing their task, the Union flag fluttering stubbornly above the Castle reminded Charles that as yet his claims had not been consolidated. Sir John Cope was at Dunbar, and by evening, most of his army had disembarked. What was more, Cope would now receive accurate accounts of the size and distribution of the Highland army from government supporters who had recently been in Edinburgh. John Home, the man who later wrote a history of the Forty-Five, turned up at Dunbar with the reassuring news that Charles' army numbered fewer than 2,000 men. He also gave Cope details of their disposition and the state of their armament. Although about three-quarters had swords and firelocks, most of the latter were old fowling-pieces, and the last quarter of the army had only scythes and staves. Cope had sufficient need of such heartening news for he was quite unsure how his own army would react in the face of stiff opposition. The dragoons had already run twice and one of their Colonels confessed in confidence 'that I have not above ten men in my regiment whom I am certain will follow me'. The only comfort enjoyed by Cope was the belief that the Highlanders would be demoralized by bombardment from the pitiful artillery train which his army now possessed. Besides, according to Home, the government troops need fear no retaliation, for the enemy had only 'one small iron gun ... without a carriage, lying upon a cart, drawn by a little Highland horse'. Early on the morning of 19 September, Cope began his march towards Edinburgh.

Charles reacted to the news of Cope's landing with Wellingtonian brevity. 'Is he, by God?', exclaimed the Prince, and then promptly set about remedying his army's most serious deficiencies. Arms and ammunition were urgently needed, so a proclamation for their surrender was issued from Holyrood, and within a day, over one thousand muskets and some powder were deposited in the Highland arsenal. On 19 September the main body of clansmen was moved to a new camp at Duddingston where the Prince and his principal officers also took up quarters. That evening a council of war was held in which the vexed question of battle formation was again raised. Eventually Lord George Murray suggested that each clan should take the right in turn, as they already took it in turn to hold the van of the advancing column. All agreed to this expedient except Sir John Macdonald, and the council next turned to the more weighty consideration of how the Highlanders would behave against regular troops. Keppoch suspected that inexperience would undermine their courage if the clans were subjected to a heavy artillery barrage, but Charles was outraged by this suggestion. He vowed to set his men a brave example by leading them forward in person. The chiefs were horrified at this outburst. They warned Charles that such an action could prove fatal to the cause if the leader were to fall, and they threatened to withdraw their support if the Prince persisted with his pledge. Only under duress did Charles finally agree to remain at the rear of his army, but on one point he would not relent. His army must advance aggressively upon Cope immediately, lest it suffer any deterioration in morale.

During the night, Highland patrols were sent out to scout the roads leading to Musselburgh but found few signs of enemy activity. In the early hours of the following morning, two Edinburgh students who were part of a force of about eighty volunteers serving under Cope were brought back to the Highland camp for interrogation. They had been feasting on oysters at an inn when a patrol surprised them, and they were so terrified of their captors that they could do little except babble incoherently. They were soon released following the intercession of a fellow student serving under the Prince and Charles returned to the more serious business of planning a battle. Orders to evacuate the guardposts at Edinburgh were sent to the city and the detachments which had been holding them joined the main body at Duddingston. Besides the five clan regiments which had joined him soon after his arrival in Scotland, Charles now had companies of Menzies, Macgregors and Maclachlans, plus the Robertsons who had appeared at Perth. In addition there were the tenants of Perthshire landowners like Lord Nairne and Oliphant of Gask. Among the prisoners taken after Culloden were many Lowland men, most of them from Edinburgh, and including artisans, shopkeepers and labourers, who clearly joined the Prince out of devotion to his cause and his person, and not because of the threats of some Highland laird. In all, the force at Duddingston numbered some two and a half thousand men, but among this host were fewer than forty mounted troops.

Against the clans, Cope had mustered an army of roughly the same size (estimates vary from 2,200 to 2,500) at the village of Haddington, some eleven miles from Dunbar. At 9 o'clock on the morning of 20 September, this force set out on the next stage of its advance along the Edinburgh post-road. Halfway between Tranent and Haddington it turned off the post-road and joined the highway running west from Longniddry to Preston. Unlike the other route, the Preston road passed through open, level country, but it involved making a considerable detour. Yet Cope felt the delay to be justified in view of his uncertainty with regard to the enemy position and the necessity of leading his dragoons over ground on which they could act. After marching for eight miles, the army halted at St Germains where a detachment under Lord Loudon went forward to select a camp site in the vicinity of Pinkie. As Loudon approached Musselburgh, the Highlanders came into view, 'in full march towards them'.

That morning, amid the sound of skirling pipes, the clans had gathered into regiments to await their instructions from the Prince. But Charles spoke only to the chiefs and then left it to the lairds to relay his message to their men. The Prince told them that everything which had been previously planned and successfully executed now rested upon the behaviour of the chiefs and their kinsmen. He reminded them of their present slavery and the justice of their cause. Then, drawing his sword, he raised it dramatically and in a loud voice exclaimed, 'Gentlemen, I have flung away the scabbard; with God's help I will make you a free and happy people!' When the chiefs carried this exhortation back to their men, 'all the Bonnets were in the Air, and such a Cry, yt it wou'd be wherewithall to frighten an enemy...' Again Charles raised his sword, and the clans marched off.

Lord George Murray was at the head of the column, with Lochiel and his Camerons in the van, and the rest of the army stretched out behind in a three-mile line. As they wound their way eastwards towards Musselburgh, only a handful of Lord Strathallan's troopers rode ahead as advance guards, and in any case, the speed of the main body was such that it had already crossed the Esk and was just south of Pinkie House when the scouts first reported signs of enemy movement. Parties of dragoons had been observed in the neighbourhood of Preston and Lord George feared that Cope would seize the high ground west of Tranent, known as Falside Hill. Without consulting either the Duke of Perth or Charles, Lord George set out briskly to take possession of the hill before Cope could do the same. Almost at a run, the Highlanders ascended the high ground. Soon they glimpsed stretches of the coastal plain to the northward, and then about half an hour after the enemy had first been sighted, about three-quarters of a mile distant and a hundred feet below, the clans saw Cope's army drawn up in a line of battle. Immediately from both ranks there burst a volley of shouts and cheers. At last the long-awaited moment had arrived.

After sighting the Highland army near Mussel-burgh, Lord Loudon had galloped back to find Cope at the eastern end of a flat and featureless tract of ground lying to the north of the higher ground near Tranent. The General had decided that this area was an ideal field of battle, and even after his salutary defeat he could write, 'There is not in the whole of the Ground between Edinburgh and Dunbar a better Spot for both Horse and Foot to act upon.' The area ran east to west for about a mile and a half, was only three-quarters of a mile wide, entirely open and without cover save for a short corn stubble over much of the ground. It was well protected on three sides. To the north lay the sea, and the villages of Prestonpans, Port Seton and Cockenzie. Along the western boundary were the ten-foot park walls surrounding Preston House, while the whole of the southern edge was flanked by marshy ground known as Tranent Meadows. Most of this was a deep morass from which surplus water was carried in eight-foot-wide trenches, one of which formed a southern boundary of the position for nearly three-quarters of its length.

Cope had picked his position well. Admittedly his eastern flank was fairly open, but from what Lord Loudon had reported, the Highland attack would probably come from the opposite direction. Between the two armies, and through the middle of the bog, ran two tracks. But both were narrow and easily guarded, affording no promise as lines of attack. Cope drew up his army in the centre of the plain, facing south-west, with the baggage in the rear. Thus he was able to command the only two approaches, one to the north of Preston Park walls, and the other along a narrow defile running between Preston and Bankton estates. As he still possessed no regular gunners, the General concentrated all his artillery on the left wing in the vicinity of Gardiner's dragoons. Thus disposed, Cope waited to see what his enemy would do.

When the Highland army appeared on the brow of Falside Hill at about 2 p.m., Cope realized that attack from the west was out of the question. The clans were heading for the high ground to the south, so the government army was wheeled into the position running parallel with the south boundary ditch. But having gained the high ground, Lord George Murray discovered that the no man's land separating the two armies was totally unfit for a swift and savage charge. The Highlanders were exasperated by Cope's expertise, as Murray later confessed. 'We spent the afternoon in reconnoitring his position; and the more we examined it, the more our uneasiness and chagrin increased, as we saw no possibility of attacking it, without exposing ourselves to be cut to pieces in a disgraceful manner.' Tempers became frayed in the Highland camp. Charles feared that Cope would not fight at all, and would instead slip away to Edinburgh during the night. Without consulting his commanders, he ordered Lord George's own brigade of Athollmen to leave the reserve and take up a position on the Musselburgh road. News reached Lord George from unofficial sources and he immediately flew into a rage. According to O'Sullivan, Lord George rode up to Charles and asked him, 'in a very high tone, what was become of the Athol Brigade; the Prince told him, upon which

Lord George threw his gun on the Ground in a great passion, and Swore God, he'd never draw his sword for the cause, if the Brigade was not brought back'. Faced with this outburst, Charles retracted his order, though Lord George himself later asked that it might stand.

After a fruitless skirmish between some Camerons and the enemy artillery in an adjacent churchyard to the front of the Highland line, Lord George became convinced that the only direction from which a successful attack could be launched was the east. Again without consulting Charles or the Duke of Perth, he ordered Lochiel's regiment to march through Tranent and draw up in the fields to the east of the village. However acute Lord George's sympathy for the Highland fighting spirit must have been in the seizure of high ground and his refusal to retreat before a strong enemy position, to professional soldiers like O'Sullivan he was committing the military sin of marching in broad daylight with his flank exposed to the enemy. Cope also noticed the unconventional strategy adopted by his opponent. But he was perplexed by the independent action of O'Sullivan, who had ordered about five hundred Highlanders to move westwards to a position between Preston and Dolphingstone. A two-pronged attack on both flanks appeared imminent. Immediately the government army changed front from south to south-west and the baggage was moved to the east of Cockenzie. However, the westward movement of the Highlanders was shortlived, for they were quickly ordered back to a position upon the ridge above Bankton. By the time they returned it was becoming dark, and both armies were settled down for the night.

Despite what was afterwards said, Cope and his men did not go to bed without first taking adequate precautions against surprise attack. If anything, the General over-estimated the size of his enemy, and behaved as though more than five thousand Highlanders were poised above him on the ridge of Falside Hill. The government army took up a line running parallel with the large ditch and slept in this position. But over a fifth of the force were posted as outguards or kept on patrol throughout the night. Cope himself stayed up to receive the reports that were returned to camp every half hour. More than one hundred men watched the defile between Preston and Bankton, while an equivalent number were posted at the approaches from Seton. Gardiner's reserve dragoon squadron protected the western route between Preston Park walls and Prestonpans, and Hamilton's covered the eastern approaches between Seton and the sea. All along the line large bonfires were lit, and no man was allowed to pass without identification.

At first both armies settled down quietly, but at about eight o'clock the silence of this chilly autumn evening was broken by crisp exchanges of gunfire near Bankton House, where one of the dragoon patrols was attacked by men of the Highland reserve. A little while later, 'all the Dogs in the Village (Tranent) ... began to bark with the utmost fury', and continued to do so for another hour. Cope rightly interpreted the disturbance as the consequence of a large-scale change of position. He knew that the enemy reserve was west of Tranent, so he did not expect that the main Highland body had now joined Lochiel on the east side of the village. Lord George had decided upon his plan of attack, and once the army was in position, he outlined his scheme to his fellow commanders. He intended to go around the bog and fall upon Cope's open flank. Apparently this tactic pleased all the other commanders, Charles Edward included, and the officers returned to their posts to retire for a few hours. Both officers and men lay in rank and file, all of them in high spirits, and with them the Prince joined in a rough meal of bread, beer and brandy.

One of the resting Highlanders was more pensive

than most. His name was Robert Anderson, and he was the son of a local laird. At the recent meeting of chiefs he had kept very quiet, but he afterwards confided to his friend Colonel Hepburn of Keith that he knew of a much less roundabout route to the enemy position. Running through the bog was a track which the young Anderson often used when snipe shooting, and he now wondered whether the path could be made use of by the Highland army. Colonel Hepburn advised Anderson to place his suggestion before Lord George. Murray was duly woken from his sleep. He reacted decisively to the information which Anderson offered. Charles was informed, and an officer council called there and then. At 2 a.m. Lord Nairne marched to join the main Highland body, and shortly before 4 a.m. the army began its advance.

With the Macdonalds in the van, and led by Clanranald's regiment, the first column moved off by the left. Behind Clanranald were Glengarry and Keppoch with their regiments, and the Macdonalds of Glencoe. In the next rank marched the Duke of Perth with the Macgregors, while Stuart of Appin and Lochiel brought up the rear. Perth's seniority entitled him to command the van and Lord George Murray assumed control of the rear. Under Charles and Lord Nairne the reserve closely followed the front-line troops, all of them moving as quietly as was possible. Because silence was essential, Lord Strathallan's cavalry was ordered to remain at the back until all the infantry had passed through the defile. Likewise every officer had to proceed on foot and be prepared to fight that way lest the movement of horses was detected by Cope's guards.

Guided by Robert Anderson, the head of the column crept down the ridge, moving north-eastwards until it was safely through the narrow defile close to the farm of Riggonhead. But before Anderson could enter the morass, he and his comrades were challenged by a dragoon patrol. Though the Highlanders kept quiet, the dragoons suspected their presence and raced back to raise the alarm. Quickly the clans wound their way through the bog to emerge at its eastern end and enter the plain in the cold grey light of a dawn mist. The vanguard had only to cross a four-foot ditch and they found themselves about one thousand yards to the east of Cope's right flank. Moving northwards in the direction of Cockenzie, Perth led the van forward until he estimated the rear to be clear of the bog and then turned to form his line of battle. But he carried on too far. The result was that his wing was separated from that of the rear by a gap of some hundred yards. Lord George perceived Perth's error and briskly ordered one of the reserve regiments to fill the gap. At the head of the reserve, Charles also must have noticed his exposed front. In crossing the ditch leading on to the plain, the Prince had fallen on to his knees, a mishap he plainly read as a bad omen. But even though the flaw in the Highland line could not be corrected in time, Charles need not have worried.

According to the Chevalier de Johnstone, who was with the Prince, the reserve was scarcely out of the bog, 'when the enemy, seeing our first line of battle, fired an alarm gun'. Thus Cope was alerted even before the Highland right had ceased to march towards Cockenzie. He immediately ordered his army to wheel to the left by platoons and face the enemy. When the line turned, the government infantry stood in three ranks, with its right towards Cockenzie and its left protected by the large ditch. All the artillery was concentrated on the right wing and dressed in line with the infantry. Between the guns and the foot soldiers rode two squadrons of Gardiner's dragoons, while Hamilton took the left. The symmetry was classical except for the guns, but the errors were fatal. For one, as Gardiner was quick to explain, his horses were raw and would prbably shy at the sound of the nearby cannon. Secondly Cope failed to take advantage of, or even notice the gap in the Highland line. Instead, he and his staff were overawed by its length and were now convinced that the enemy outnumbered them by at least two to one. Still they would teach the enemy a lesson in warfare today, and as the sun rose, Cope rode along the front of the line, 'Encouraging the Men, begging them to keep up their Fire, and keep their Ranks, and they would easily beat the Rebels.'

While Cope spoke, the Highland advance began. Because of the gap which separated the two wings, it was difficult for the attack to be synchronized, and Lord George Murray found his wing well to the front of the Highland line. Thereupon he ordered Lochiel to incline his Camerons towards the left as they advanced, and in consequence of this direction the Highland charge fell most heavily upon the government army's right wing. There Gardiner's intimidated dragoons, and the motley collection of seamen and invalids who served as gunners, quaked while the clans charged with 'a hideous shout'. As the Highlanders came on, their plaids were discarded and their bonnets pulled low. Very soon Lieutenant-Colonel Whitefoord, the artillery commander, found himself deserted by his seamen gunners and without the civilian carriage drivers who had ridden away all the train horses rather than have to face the edge of claymore or scythe. Whitefoord bravely fired a salvo himself, and this was seen to have an effect upon the charging clansmen. But the Highlanders recovered their momentum, breaking up into several small bodies and running 'with a swiftness not to be conceived'. The largest group, consisting chiefly of Camerons, made straight for the cannons. Desperately, Whitefoord called out for the dragoons to charge, but though their officers advanced, the troopers refused to follow. Most of the rear ranks were already slipping away, and now the infantry as well began to show signs of uneasiness. When ordered to support Whitefoord, the artillery-guard were seen to be 'crouching and creeping gently backwards, with their arms recovered'. Gardiner's squadron vindicated their colonel's gloomy forecast by beating a disastrous retreat despite Brigadier Fowke's assurance that '... We shall cut them to pieces in a Moment.' Things were no better on the other end of the line where the intrepid Lord Drummore, armed only with a riding whip, marvelled at the precision of the Macdonald charge. While they were advancing, Drummore 'could see thro' from Front to Rear, yet to my Astonishment, every Front Man cover'd his Followers. There was no Man to be seen in the Open ... in short, tho' their Motion was very quick, it was uniform and orderly, and I confess I was surprised at it.'

Though many clansmen charged straight through the government lines in pursuit of the fleeing dragoons, some concerted an attack upon the enemy's right flank and succeeded in rolling the line backwards within a few minutes. By the time Cope could ride over to the right, the situation was hopeless, and he endeavoured to gather together as many troopers as possible in order to make a safe retreat. But the General would have done better not to abandon his infantry for the sake of his frenzied cavalry. The narrow defile south of Preston House was choked with swearing, terrified dragoons, all of them trying to force their way through, and few succeeding. Most were caught by the relentless enemy, some of them as they tried to scale the impossible walls of Preston Park. Eventually, in a field at the west end of Preston village, Cope managed to gather about five hundred men around their officers. A squadron was formed, and when a body of Highlanders appeared at the other end of the village, Sir John tried to redeem some of his reputation by ordering his men to attack. But they would not, and the General was forced to ride off at their head along the lane from Preston up the side of Birsley Brae, which is today known as 'Johnnie Cope's Road'.

Although he was well in advance of the Highland reserve, Charles Edward could have seen little of the fighting. The destruction of the whole government front line had taken less than five minutes. When the Chevalier de Johnstone rode up with the Prince, he admitted, 'we saw no other enemy on the field of battle than those who were lying on the ground killed and wounded, though we were not more than fifty paces behind our first line, running always as fast as we could to overtake them, and near enough never to lose sight of them'. Most of the destruction had been wrought by the broadsword, and the battlefield presented 'a spectacle of horror, being covered with heads, legs and arms, and mutilated bodies...' No less effective were the scythe blades of a company of Macgregors in the Duke of Perth's regiment, which 'cut the legs of the horses in two; and their riders through the middle of their bodies'. Although nothing can excuse the butchery which followed the battle of Culloden, it must be seen as the child of a fear first experienced at Prestonpans by soldiers who had never before faced such primitive fury.

The total numbers of casualties on both sides are difficult to assess, for official reports were prone to exaggeration. Murray of Broughton probably came near with his figure of three hundred 'killed' among the government forces, while the Chevalier de Johnstone even exceeded the official figure of 500 with his own ludicrous estimate of 1,300 'killed'. Nearly eighty of Cope's officers were made prisoner, and only the intervention of the Prince and his senior officers prevented more than seven of these men being summarily executed by their excited captors. Still, the percentage of murders on the field cannot compare with that at Culloden. Broughton also suggested that between four and five hundred government soldiers were seriously wounded, and just under two thousand prisoners taken. On the Highland side, the official figure of thirty killed and between seventy and eighty wounded was probably deliberately exaggerated to arouse sympathy. Certainly Charles' losses were minimal.

The Prince, who had wisely left the purely military side of the operations to Lord George, now took command. As soon as his own men who were wounded or dead had been attended to, he commanded that the English casualties, wounded or dead, should receive exactly the same treatment. He remarked with genuine feeling that they were his father's subjects and had merely been imposed upon and misled. Never has Charles Edward Stuart's character shown to greater advantage before a greater number of men. His conduct aroused emotion too deep for cheering or acclamation; it was long remembered of him and inspired lasting loyalty and admiration in all who beheld it.

He spent the night at Pinkie House, Musselburgh, on the route back to Edinburgh. When he reached the capital he discovered that the news of his victory had gone before. Bonfires were lit to welcome the Prince and festivals prepared for him to attend. He refused with graciousness and on 23 September issued the proclamation below.

> We reflecting that, however glorious it may have been to us, and however beneficial to the nation in general, as the principal means, under God to the recovery of their liberty; yet, in so far as it has been attained by the effusion of the blood of His Majesty's subjects and has involved many unfortunate people in calamity, we hereby forbid any outward demonstrations of public joy; admonishing all our true friends to their King and Country to thank God . . .

But whether he liked it or not, Charles was now a hero firmly established in the public eye. In a letter to a friend one anonymous admirer waxed at length on her 'darling theme'. Though her brother had died in Charles' service, the lady appeared to have blamed the Prince little.

> As my Mind is overburthened I must discharge it on some Person like you, who will pity my 'amorous Disposition'; a Fault or rather 'Weakness' you know I always had the Misfortune to be addicted to, and cannot get over it, cannot mend myself even now in my 'Decline of Life'. O! had you beheld my beloved Hero you must confess he is a Gift from Heaven; but then, besides his outward Appearance, which is absolutely the 'best Figure' I ever saw, such vivacity, such piercing Wit, woven with a clear judgement and an Active Genious. ...:
> In short, Madam, he is the 'Top of Perfection' and 'Heaven's Darling' ...

Perhaps more importantly, Charles' demeanour was undermining Whig strength in the Lowlands. In Edinburgh, Mrs Anne Dott confessed to her friend, Mrs Jennett Wilson,

> I am not such a Whigg as you have always persuaded me, for nothing could give me more pleasure than to see this valiant Prince placed upon the Throne of his Ancestors: For I think as he is running the Danger he should have the Reward. Now Madame I engage myself; with you drinking his happy Restoration, the thing which I have often heard you wish for ...

The image of 'Bonnie Prince Charlie' had become a political factor, at least in Scotland, and primarily among women. To his female adherents Charles would owe much during the months of skulking in the spring and summer of 1746.

Only on 7 October did Charles write of his victory to

Prince Charles Edward Stuart as a boy, painted by Edelinck.
*Radio Times Hulton Picture Library*

Charles as a young man, painted by Antonio David.
*Scottish National Portrait Gallery*

Charles 'The Young Pretender'. From an engraving by De Poilly.
*Scottish National Portrait Gallery*

Prince Charles with Captain Walsh, master of the *Du Teillay*. From the painting given by Charles to Walsh.
*Scottish National Portrait Gallery*

Prince Charles entering Edinburgh after the battle of Prestonpans.
From an engraving by J. C. Armytage.
*Radio Times Hulton Picture Library*

Lord President Duncan Forbes of Culloden. Attributed to Jeremiah Davison.
*Scottish National Portrait Gallery*

William Augustus, Duke of Cumberland, the victor of Culloden
(1721–65).
*Mansell Collection*

Rome. Even now, when Scotland lay at his feet, the Prince managed to understate his achievement in a letter devoid of sentiment and excitement.

'Tis impossible for me to give you a distinct gurnal of the proceydings becose of my being so hurried with business which allows me no time; but notwithstanding I cannot let slip this occasion of giving a short account of ye Batle of Gladsmuire, fought on ye 21 of September which was one of ye most surprising action that ever was; we gained a complete victory over General Cope who commanded 3,000 fut and to Regiments of ye Best Dragoons in ye island, he being advantajiously posted with also baterys of cannon and morters, wee having neither hors or artillery with us, and being to attack them in their position, and obliged to pas before their noses in a defile and Bog. Only our first line had occasion to engaje, for actually in five minutes ye field was clired of ye Enemy, all ye fut killed, wounded or taken prisoner, and of ye horse only to-hundred escaped like rabets, one by one, on our side we only losed a hundred men between killed and wounded, and ye army afterwards had a fine plunder.

But by the time this reached James, all Europe had heard of his son's victory.

# 6: The Advance into England

The day after the battle of Prestonpans, Charles despatched a messenger to England to let his supporters there know that, 'there is no more time for Deliberations. Now or Never is the Word, I am resolved to conquer or Perish, if this last should happen, let them judge what they and their Posteriety are to expect.' At first the Prince had wanted to pursue Sir John Cope to Berwick, but this plan was discarded and Charles decided to remain at Edinburgh until his strength was greater. Perhaps Charles should have been given his head, for the delay at Edinburgh gave his enemies time in which to recover from their first shock and organize their defences. The news from Prestonpans had thrown London into chaos, and the Duke of Newcastle confessed to Cumberland that had not three thousand Dutch troops landed, 'providentially the day before the news of Cope's defeat, the confusion in the City of London would not have been to be described, and the King's crown, I will venture to say, in the utmost danger'. As it was, another three thousand Dutch troops were quickly landed and were followed by ten British battalions recalled from Flanders. Immediately further orders were despatched to Flanders to recall still more men and Marshal Wade was instructed to prepare himself for the north. Now Charles would need all the strength he could gather if he were to march into England.

From Edinburgh, urgent appeals were issued for reinforcements. In theory, Charles should have found assistance far more easy to come by than it had been at Glenfinnan. Three days after the Highland victory at Prestonpans, Louis XV wrote to 'mon frère le prince Charles Edouard', informing the Prince that he had engaged the Marquis d'Eguilles and a thousand

99

French regulars to sail for Scotland and join Charles. Louis also assured Charles that he was totally committed to preserve the Prince's person and interests. This was assistance indeed. But d'Eguilles only reached Montrose in December, long after the Highland army had departed for England. Once more, Charles was forced to rely upon the loyalty of the clans and their chiefs.

Although the Prince was ostensibly in control of Scotland, not all Scots were content to enjoy his possession. Behind the protection of Ben Cruachan and Loch Awe, the Argylls remained hostile, while the most northerly clans – Mackays, Sutherlands and Munros – preferred to serve the Lord President rather than any Stuart. Others were divided. Mackenzies, MacIntoshes, Gordons and Grants joined both sides, depending upon the particular allegiances of minor chiefs. As usual, the ordinary soldier, be he from Highland or Lowland, England or Scotland, did not often enjoy any personal conviction. His decision was pragmatic. Either he was coerced, or he joined whichever side promised the greater personal reward. On 26 October, Janett Mill of Aberdeen wrote to her son, James Cummings, who had been taken prisoner at Prestonpans, 'send me word what ye have a mind to do, whether you are to serve the P ... ce Charles or remain a prisoner, or give ye be mind to return to King George or return home'. At that level, the decision was never automatic. Every day clansmen returned to their glens despite the threats of their lairds, or the promises of the Prince.

But notwithstanding the prevalence of desertion, chiefly among Athollmen, the Highland army grew. Three hundred men under Lord Ogilvy came from Angus; one hundred and twenty came with Mackinnon of Mackinnon from Skye; and Lord Lewis Gordon, younger brother of the Duke of Gordon, was raising recruits from among His Grace's tenantry. Daily additions also reinforced the existing regiments, while Lord Elcho found himself with a cavalry detachment which was to serve as the Prince's Life Guard. By the end of October, Charles' army numbered over five thousand foot and about five hundred horse.

At Edinburgh, the Prince strove to increase his popularity among Lowland gentry. He entertained lavishly at Holyrood, but was always careful to pay his bills and avoid city hostility. Unfortunately not all could be satisfied, and one Presbyterian minister used the freedom of his pulpit to petition God that 'the young man who has come among us seeking an earthly crown may soon be granted a heavenly one'. Charles could not afford to deal harshly with such insolence. He was aware of the necessity of cultivating support. On 10 October he issued a proclamation from Holyrood in which he guaranteed the estates and practices of the Protestant churches in England, Scotland and Ireland. He also declared himself against the Union as it stood and would leave its fate to a decision of the Scots parliament. But major constitutional issues were not the only things with which the Prince concerned himself. He also issued temporary declarations of a practical nature, usually designed in response to public opinion. For example, he recalled all Presbyterian ministers in order that they might continue with their work, while knowing that many of them were anti-Stuart. To prevent inflation, and incidentally maintain his own credit, Charles forbade the issue of paper money. He even kept faith with the Bank of Scotland, though it was a post-Revolution agency which had thoughtfully removed its reserves into the Castle. Obligingly the Bank then moved some of its reserves back out of the Castle so that the Prince could pay his troops in hard cash.

But the Castle and its garrison remained a thorn in Charles' side. He could neither capture nor ignore them. For a week after the victory at Prestonpans, intercourse between Castle and city was uninterrupted. Then the Prince decided to adopt a more aggressive attitude. He cut off daily supplies and set a guard of Highlanders around all exits. In reply, Lieutenant-General Guest opened fire on the town with the Castle guns. This continued for five days, and the garrison even made occasional sorties under covering fire directed from the ramparts. Several houses in the city were demolished or set on fire and a few citizens killed. The eighty-six-year-old commander of the castle knew what he was doing, for the townspeople blamed the bombardment upon the blockade set up by Charles. Fearful of inciting a riot, the Prince was forced to call off the blockade. However, feelings still ran high and on 22 October Mrs Betty Leslie wrote to her sister, Mrs Drummond of Logie Almond, to tell her that: 'Yesterday, there was a woman apprehended putting in Poyson in the Well of the Castle amongst the Water.' But at least Charles could now rest easily, for the City's anger was plainly aimed at the garrison in the Castle and not at the Highlanders encamped around Edinburgh. Yet it is interesting to note that Charles still took the trouble to apprehend the mysterious poisoner rather than allow her to eradicate his enemy for him. Charles' humanity had not decreased in the face of Guest's 'real politick'.

The stay at Edinburgh certainly was not allowed to be peaceful. At a later date, James Ray of Whitehaven concocted an amazonian mistress for the Prince while he was at Edinburgh. Ray based his invention upon the daughter of Hugh Cameron of Glendessary. Jenny Cameron was a divorcée who was reputedly present at the raising of the standard at Glenfinnan. This much even Aenas Macdonald admitted. But Ray described a woman who had once bedded with the Duke of Perth, who then lost her to the Prince, and later enjoyed her again in partnership with Charles. Her career of debauchery captured English imaginations. Henry Fielding included an incident in his novel *Tom Jones*, in which the heroine, Sophia Western, is mistakenly identified as the notorious Jenny. In 1746 there appeared upon the London stage a farce entitled *Harlequin Incendiary or Columbine Cameron*. But in truth, though the opportunity for debauchery must have been there for the young hero, he steered well clear of scandal. Above all, he was too preoccupied with his principal task to concern himself with trivial diversions. No doubt Charles enjoyed the attentions and flattery of his female admirers, but that was a traditional facet of any heroic role and entirely acceptable to the Prince.

There were other more pernicious agents in Edinburgh than mere scandal. On 3 October John Murray of Broughton was handed a message by Bishop Keith which warned of an assassination attempt against Charles. 'Ruxby, who wears his own black hair, aged twenty-seven, of a middle stature, and who dined with the Marquess of Tweeddale, the 20th, from whom he got a pass, is in Scotland, with the design of assassinating the Prince. If this do not come too late, for God's sake, stop the blow.' Although Ruxby was never discovered, Charles could not afford to lock himself behind a battery of guards. That would discourage his Highlanders and lend hope to his enemies. Under the guns of the Castle and the shadow of the assassin, Charles Edward continued to display an almost arrogant courage. The only danger was that he would begin to believe himself invincible.

Every day as his army grew, the Prince pressed for an invasion of England. Unfortunately, there was no consensus of agreement among the council that met at Holyrood. Apart from the loyal chiefs, this body consisted of the Duke of Perth, Lord George Murray, Captain O'Sullivan, the Prince's secretary, Murray of Broughton, Sir Thomas Sheridan, and the Lords Pitsligo, Elcho, Nairne, Ogilvy and Lewis Gordon. Charles lacked the experience and statesmanship required to keep such a headstrong collection of men in harmony. For almost eight weeks they argued among themselves, deciding little, consolidating nothing and allowing the enemy to gather his armies. Many years afterwards, both Broughton and Lord Elcho charged the Prince with obstinacy in his desire for an invasion of England. They would have preferred to wait until English Jacobites showed their hands and French troops arrived in strength. But at the time few among the council could have doubted that the French would come.

Others, including the English, definitely did not. At the beginning of November, Janett Gordon of Park wrote to her father: 'Some people is so wicked as to say that there will be no landing from France, but its scarce to be believed that the French King should be such a villain after the many assurances he give the Prince to join him with heart and hande.' Meanwhile, of the three armies which had been mobilized, the government kept one along the south-east coast, reinforced it with county militia and daily expected to use it against a French invader. The other two armies under Marshal Wade and General Sir John Ligonier were despatched to Newcastle and Lancashire respectively where they would be in a position to thwart any descent into England by the Highlanders, be it on east coast or west.

Charles was not overawed by the size of his enemy. He was convinced that his presence across the border would encourage 'a great body' of Englishmen to join him there. He would march straight to Newcastle and attack Wade, 'for he was sure he would run away'. But his Council were less sanguine. They pointed out that the Prince now had many chiefs and clansmen under him who would be loath to leave Scotland. Even if they went into England, it was likely that they would soon tire of that country and yearn for the glens again. If large bodies of men were to desert while the army was across the border, the rest would have little hope of escape from the mighty forces that were being marshalled against them. Perhaps the memory of Flodden still acted as a subconscious deterrent in the minds of Scotsmen, preventing them from visualizing success in England. Whatever it was, the Prince realized that there was a clear division of opinion between him and the majority of his officers.

Nonetheless Charles was adamant. Yet his stubbornness cannot be attributed to an insane conviction of his own invincibility. That was the opinion only of the soured Lord Elcho, still pining for the one hundred and twenty-five pounds which Charles had once borrowed and not repaid. Many believe that the Prince would have stood little chance if he stayed in Scotland while the enemy mounted a careful attack under their best generals. Indeed, one writer has described the whole invasion as a 'reconnaissance in force'. At no time did the Highlanders attempt to consolidate their position; Charles was therefore quite right in wanting to pursue the enemy as far as London if necessary, and as quickly as possible. The Prince's only hope lay in a lightning advance upon the capital which would cause chaos among the Hanoverians, encourage waverers like the Duke of Newcastle to abandon George and join Charles, and perhaps frighten the King into a retreat across the water. Strategists like Lord George Murray never appreciated this style of warfare, and based their hostility to advance upon traditional military principles when in accepted military terms Charles had no chance of success even before he sailed from Nantes.

Scotland has won her major or most important victories by staying within her own boundaries, drawing her enemy to attack her in Scotland and upon ground of her own choosing. Largs and Bannockburn are the best examples. Bruce, after a guerrilla war which had infuriated and damaged his enemies the English, lured them right into Scotland within a mile of their objective and then smashed their superior forces to pieces.

It was the classic example of how Scotland could hold her own. Charles with his Highlanders had already obliterated the English under Cope at Prestonpans *and* on a ground of Cope's choosing. Is it too much to wonder whether, if Charles had waited where he was, lured the might of England towards him and with the military aid of Lord George Murray, had forced them to fight on a ground of Scottish choice, he might have beaten his enemies as effectively as Bruce had done?

However, Charles' aim was not solely to establish Scottish sovereignty. He had come to regain his father's three Kingdoms, and nothing less would suffice. He regaled his Council, threatened Lord George, vowed to enter England alone, pleaded with the chiefs and eventually had his way, though not without permanently alienating his ablest general. From the first it was made plain that the Highlanders would go with Charles, but unwillingly. One more detail had to be established. Charles wanted to advance down the east coast, the fastest route to London. It shows that the Prince, knowingly or not, desired the blitzkrieg that was his best hope. His officers, despite the scepticism which they afterwards claimed to have had, preferred to move down the west coast. It was the longer route, but the wiser if any reliance was to be placed upon an English recourse to arms on behalf of the Prince. According to Lord George the best route was through Cumberland, 'where, he said, he knew the Country, That the Army would be well Situated to receive reinforcements from Scotland to join the French when they landed, or the English if they rose, and that it was a good country to fight Wade in, because of the Mountainous Ground'. It seems that Murray was unable to think outside certain logical premises, even when he had committed himself to an illogical action.

On 30 October news came that Marshal Wade had reached Newcastle, and the following morning the Highland army left Dalkeith in two columns. The strategy which Charles employed was designed to baffle Wade, and that it certainly did. Lord Strathallan was left at Perth to take charge of later reinforcements while the two Highland divisions marched for England along different routes. One, under the command of the Duke of Perth, proceeded by Peebles and Moffat. The other, under Charles Edward and Lord George Murray, took a more easterly road via Kelso and Lauder. Wade was fooled into believing that the Prince intended to enter England by way of Northumberland and therefore waited for them at Newcastle. But after a day's halt at Kelso, Charles swung westwards to Jedburgh, and marching down Liddesdale, joined the Duke of Perth a few miles north of Carlisle.

Much of our information about Charles' movements in Scotland and England comes from John Murray of Broughton. According to Lord Elcho, 'Mr Murray of Broughton, who the Prince had made his Secretary, had gott a great deal of his Master's Ear, and it was supposed he aimed at having the chief direction of all the concerned Military affairs as well, as he had already the Administration of all Moneys belonging to the Prince and everything that concerned private Correspondence.' Murray probably understood Charles best and was certainly in his closest confidence. But much of Elcho's animosity must be attributed to the fact that Broughton turned King's evidence shortly after his capture following the defeat at Culloden. In fact, no one worked harder on behalf of the Prince than this Peebleshire laird. Even after his turnabout he did not betray friends and loyal servants. Instead he turned on the timeservers and ditherers like Elcho, Simon Fraser, Lord Lovat and principally Lord Traquair, the man who had failed to warn Charles against landing in Scotland in the first place. We must bear in mind that all Broughton's papers were destroyed after Culloden and that his *Memorials* were written only in 1757 and were very probably incomplete at the time of his death in 1777. Yet while we may question Murray's factual accuracy, we can still learn from the opinions he passes on characters and events.

At all times the Prince's Secretary speaks warmly of the men whom Charles led: 'There is no instance in the history of any times in whatever Country where the soldiery either regular or irregular behaved themselves with so much discretion, never any rioters in ye Streets, noe so much as a drunk man to be seen.' But what emerges more impressively is the Prince's extraordinary achievement in gaining their admiration and love.

Charles only mounted his horse when it was necessary to emphasize his leadership when entering a town, or upon some such other occasion. For the rest of the time he dismounted and walked with the men in whose native Gaelic he was now proficient enough for general conversation. And what a walker he was! When Charles broke one of his brogues the men were relieved that the pace was now of necessity reduced. But it was still kept up to the rate of a good march. When the brogue was mended Charles was at his old pace again, but, possibly out of consideration for his men, he made it easier for them by going backwards and forwards between the head of the column and the rear, keeping up his flow of talk all the while.

Whether Lord George and other officers approved of this royal fraternization or not we do not know, but the effect on the men was to make them utterly devoted to him. One nobleman who marched with the clansmen was the Lowland Lord Balmerino from Fife. He was to be executed in 1746 and from the scaffold at Westminster, after a reasoned explanation of why he had joined the Prince's army, he said this of Charles:

I must beg leave to tell you, the incomparable sweetness of his nature, his affability, his compassion, his justice, his temperance and his courage are virtues seldom to be found in one person. In short, he wants no qualifications requisite to make a great man.

On 8 November 1745, after a march of about thirteen miles, Charles first placed his feet on English soil. True, it was his father's second Kingdom, but if he expected anything like the popular acclaim that he had met with both in Lowland as well as Highland Scotland he was to be disappointed. There were to be one or two touching examples of individual loyalty in the traditional Stuart district of Lancashire, but for the rest it was to be mostly sullen indifference.

Almost a year later, during his examination in the Tower, Murray admitted that 'during the whole time of their being in England, they received no Application or Message from any Persons in England, which surprised and disappointed them extremely'.

Even today the demarcation of the border between England and Scotland is no piece of artificial cartography. It is immediately obvious in the speech of the people, happily scarcely influenced by half a century of radio and twenty years or so of television. If you cross the Tweed at Coldstream, the most obvious point of national demarcation on the river, people on the northern side of the bridge are talking rich Border Scots, on the southern side the accent is equally rich 'North of England'. If this is so now, what must it have been like in 1745? We are answered by John Murray of Broughton:

> It was remarkable that this, being the first time they had entered England, the Highlanders, without any orders given, all drew their Swords with one Consent upon entering the River, and every man as he landed on t'other side wheeld about to the left and faced Scotland again.

Ahead of the clans lay their first major objective in England, the city of Carlisle. In the days of the Border wars the city had been an important stronghold, the first line of defence against marauding Scotsmen. But in 1745 its defences were obsolete. When Lieutenant-Colonel Durand, a regular officer on a special inspection tour, reviewed the city defences in late October, he was driven to desperation by their inadequacy. The regular garrison of the Castle consisted of eighty 'invalids', most of whom were very old and infirm, a Master-Gunner and four gunners. Of the gunners, two were semi-trained civilians, and one an old man. Reinforcing this meagre force were five hundred infantry and seventy horse of the Cumberland and Westmorland Militia, besides some volunteer companies of townspeople. For artillery, all they could boast were twenty six-pounders and about ten small 'ship guns' hastily installed by Durand.

Besides these physical deficiencies, Colonel Durand had also to contend with ill-discipline and fear among garrison and townspeople alike. They refused to acknowledge his authority, for they were volunteers and he a regular soldier. The Mayor was too nervous to act, and in any case was ruled by his deputy, Alderman Thomas Pattinson, a vain, pompous fool. Such was the Alderman's conceit that he ordered a proclamation to be read emphasizing that his name was thoroughly English and not to be confused with the Scotch Paterson. To endorse his detestation of the Scots he promised to die rather than surrender to the approaching Highlanders. But that was before they appeared above the city. All Colonel Durand could depend upon was the Anglican clergy of Carlisle led by the staunch Whig, Dr Waugh, Chancellor of the diocese of Carlisle. Yet even Waugh was alarmed by the prospect of a meeting with these fearful northern men. Half his anxiety was caused by the absence of any reliable information regarding the enemy. It was the same affliction which troubled his fellow citizens. Waugh readily admitted that 'so many strange Storys have been told us of the Force and Number of the Rebels one post (as that they had 1400 French troops with them, an experienced General, plenty of Money, Arms and Cannon, with twelve Sail of Ships, etc.) and of their insignificance another, that we can make no more guess at the truth than those that are two hundred miles farther off'.

On the morning of 9 November the two advancing Highland columns met at Newton of Rockcliffe and from there a party of horsemen rode up to the walls of

Carlisle. Using a countryman as a messenger they ordered the Mayor to provide quarters for thirteen thousand foot and three thousand horse. The grossly exaggerated figures were intended to shock the city into submission, but as a further precaution the Highlanders threatened to raze Carlisle if the Prince's demand were not met at once. Though Alderman Pattinson was seen to quake, Colonel Durand guessed that the Prince was bluffing. In reply to the summons he opened fire with the Castle guns and the horsemen retreated.

That night Durand sent a messenger to Marshal Wade to tell him that the Highland army was in the vicinity of Carlisle. The Colonel could hardly have expected Wade to come to his relief in time, for the very next morning the enemy columns advanced upon the city. Once more the Castle guns drove the enemy back, and once more a demand for surrender arrived from Charles. The Prince was annoyed at having to invest so paltry an obstacle and endeavoured to obtain its surrender by political means. He called upon the inhabitants to open the gates and prevent 'the effusion of English blood'. He hinted darkly at the savagery of his men if their tempers were roused by confessing that 'it will not perhaps be in our Power to prevent the dreadful Consequences which usually attend a Town being taken by Assault'. And then he gave his words time to take effect by withdrawing eastwards to Brampton, ostensibly to deal with Wade. By 12 November not a clansman was to be seen, and a letter from Wade arrived reassuring the city that Charles would not waste time in a siege. But that same day the Highlanders returned and Lord George Murray blockaded the city while the Duke of Perth set up siege works.

Though Durand opened fire upon the besiegers, he could not comfort his charges, who wilted visibly at the sight of a battery being set up within three hundred yards of the walls. They now knew that Wade would not be coming to their rescue, and were thus resolved to capitulate. In vain the Colonel protested that the Highlanders were not half so strong or terrible as the enemy had given out. Along with his 'invalid' officers, he retired into the Castle after having first spiked the guns on the town walls. There he was joined by some of the city militia, all of them resolved not to surrender. But during the night 'a mutiny begun among the private men of the Militia; who all declared they would do no more duty, nor would they stay and defend the Castle upon any account whatsoever. A general Confusion ensued, numbers went over the walls; others forced their way out...' and by 8 o'clock the next morning not one remained on duty. If Durand had any idea of resisting Charles from within the Castle, he soon had to abandon the notion. Charles had learned his lesson at Edinburgh. He promised to give no quarter unless both the Castle and city were surrendered. Durand was forced to give way in the face of such a threat, and on 15 November Carlisle capitulated before the Prince. Charles Edward had captured his first English town.

The victory belonged to the Prince. He had virtually frightened the city into surrender and was spared the pain of killing his father's subjects, while wasting little of his own precious resources. Yet incredibly, a row had broken out among the Highlanders. Although Lord George had been responsible for constructing the blockade around Carlisle, he had been kept from the negotiations for surrender. These had been handled by Murray of Broughton and the Duke of Perth. Now Lord George pleaded a grave injury at the light way in which he had been treated and kept apart from the centre of negotiations. Before anything could be done to rectify this situation, he resigned his commission.

The reason behind Lord George's action was definitely not the one which he pretended to be at the root of his displeasure. The General was really asking for a vote of confidence. He had been aware of Charles' animosity, and when outside Carlisle the Prince had commissioned Perth to construct the siege, Lord George felt that he was being slowly displaced. His exclusion from the negotiations with the civic authorities was the final straw. Yet he knew that Marshal Wade had marched from Newcastle and was now at Hexham with over six thousand men. In fact all the Highland command knew that Wade was approaching. Lord George simply wished to know what premium Charles placed upon his abilities as a general.

Unfortunately the Prince had neither the patience nor the statesmanship with which Lord George should have been treated. As far as he was concerned, the old man was making excessive demands upon a princely right to commission whomsoever he thought fit for a particular task. Angrily, he wrote rather a foolish letter to the General.

I think yr advice ever since you joined me at Perth has had another guess weight with me than what any General Officer cou'd claim as such. I am therefore extremely surprized you shou'd throw up yr commission for a reason which I beleeve was never heard of before. I am glad of yr particular attachment to the King, but am very sure he will never take anything as proof of it but yr deference to me. I accept of yr demission as Lieutenant General and yr future service as a volunteer.

Though the Prince readily accepted Lord George's resignation, his other officers would not allow him to indulge his personal antipathy towards the General. They petitioned Charles to return Lord George to his command. As a final gesture, the Duke of Perth resigned his own commission for the duration of the stay in England, lest his co-generalship prove a stumbling-block again in the future. Charles had no alternative but to reinstate Lord George after the old man was himself urged to petition the Prince for a reconsideration of his resignation. That Lord George was indispensable Charles already knew. But such an awareness did not alter the disdain with which both men treated each other.

The crisis within the Highland army having been overcome, Charles turned his attentions towards the more difficult problem of what to do next. Carlisle was now safely in his hands and the news was that Marshal Wade had returned to Newcastle from Hexham in the face of impassable snowdrifts on the road to Carlisle. It was also rumoured that Wade was encumbered with more than a thousand sick men and thus in no position to fight. It would be safe for the Prince to remain in Carlisle for at least another week. But that was out of the question as long as Charles had his eyes so firmly set upon St James'. He wanted to forge ahead right away. Others among the Highland Council were less enthusiastic about an advance. The day before Carlisle had surrendered, fresh English troops entered Edinburgh and many Scotsmen feared that the road back home would be cut. They wished to return and reclaim what was theirs. What did the English matter?

About eight hundred soldiers had deserted thus far and more would no doubt follow as news of English revenge in Edinburgh and the Highlands percolated through the ranks. Already letters from the Scottish capital painted a frightening picture.

'... on Saturday the Castle Soldiers were sent down on the Town, and on the collour of searching for Arms they have done great damage and plunder. They have destroyed the apartment the Prince was in, tore down the silk bed he lay in, broke and carried off all the fine gilded Glasses, Cabinets and everything else. They have done the same to the Duke of Perth's Lodging, its entirely ruined. They have visited the Lady Lochyel and used her in the rudest manner calling her Bitch and Whore, and had the impudence to spit in her face... They also went to the infirmary and beat the poor Highlanders, twist about their Arms and Legs that was set after being broke at the late Battle, tore open their wounds so that their shrieks was heard never so far.'

Though he sympathized with his Scottish servants, Charles remained adamant. His army must march to London with all possible speed. Perhaps because of the recent fracas, Lord George supported him and on 20 November the first Highland column left Carlisle. The army marched in two divisions separated by about half a day's march. In most instances, the two columns spent the nights at adjacent villages rather than strain the resources of their reluctant hosts. Nothing was allowed to mar relations between Charles and his English subjects. The Prince ordered his officers to pay '...for everything they gott'. That they did, '...and very often extravagantly which they did rather than disoblige the people'.

Yet the common reaction south of the Tweed remained one of fear. At each town the residents displayed scarcely any sign of enthusiasm as the Proclamation of James III was read, and their disregard quickly turned to animosity when the Highlanders proceeded to make a collection of 'publick money'. On 23 November a nervous citizen of Lancaster warned his friends in safer counties: 'There are eight hundred Rebels within a few miles of this Town and are expected every Moment. I assure you this is the only Express that has arrived since my last I have sat up these two Nights being in perpetual fear of their coming and my Horse is a mile out of Town.' When the invaders did enter Lancaster, they admitted that the town 'testify'd no joy'. The occasion was recorded by John Beynon:

I was determin'd to see some of the Rebels and

today at 12 o'Clock at noon came into Lancr. a Quarter Mastr. 6 Highlandrs, wth Blue Bonnets and Whit Cockades and 6 more Gentn with Blue coats and Scarlet Linings and 2 Sevts for Attendance their Cockades are all White the Quarter Mastr lighted and went to the Town Hall and immediately issued out an Order for the Payment of the Excise and Customs, windo. and Land tax by 12 o'Clock on Monday ... and that order was declar'd in every street by the Bellman. As soon as tht was done, a Body of 30 Horse more came in and rec'ed Billets. The next order issued out was that all Butchers, Bakers, Farmers, etc. sh'od follow their Employment and bring in Provisions for P.C.R. Troops upon pain of military Execution. Between 2 & 3 o'Clock the Foot came in to the no. of 200 headed by Lord Elcho and instead of drums they have Bagpipes to each company. Then the Horse brot up the rear ... By the nearest calculation I co'd make, the Horse amounted to 120. The Foot I observed before was 200, all Brave Men, the Horse poorly mounted but in great Spirits and great plenty of Money chiefly French Guineas and pay for what they have as they go on. Most of the Highlanders have 2 pistols on each side of their Breast and a Musket slung over their Shoulders and a Broad Sword which they carry from the Time they get up till they go to bed.

Only at Preston was there any sign of welcome for Charles, and 'for the first time in England several huzzas'. This was due to an unusually tactful action of Lord George Murray's. He was well in the van of the marching army that entered Preston, and made himself agreeable to the civic authorities. He quartered his men on the far side of the river Ribble just to show that the town was ready for the Prince. It was indeed. This was all the more gratifying because Preston had been associated with Stuart defeats since the days of Charles I and in the Rising of 1715. The Highlanders nurtured a superstition about the essentially friendly town which it was difficult to overcome. Yet even here Charles managed to raise only three recruits, of whom two were Welsh, and the third, Francis Townley, belonged to an old Lancashire family and had himself previously served with the French.

Townley rose to a position of historical significance after the clans reached Manchester on 29 November. Charles expected to receive a warm welcome at the city, and he did. He was met with bonfires, illuminations and the sound of church bells. A cheering crowd escorted him to his lodgings, and 'his Conversation that night at Table was, in what manner he should enter London, on Horseback or a foot, and in what dress'. But despite the Prince's high spirits, the hard facts of his reception were less than encouraging. Rumour has it that the reception was only undertaken upon instruction from Charles himself, and all the Prince gained for his trouble was 'a drummer boy and a whore'. Captain O'Sullivan probably told a truer story. 'We expected yt at least 1500 men wou'd have joyned us here,' he wrote, only to have his hopes dashed by the meagre recruitment of '... about 200 common fellows who it seems had no subsistence...' At the head of this Manchester Regiment was placed the ill-fated Francis Townley.

O'Sullivan was harsh in his description of the unfortunate Mancunians who joined Charles, for they were not merely unemployed seeking the first likely employer. The great majority were weavers, or otherwise employed in the cloth industry, like James Bradshaw, a Manchester man in the check trade whom Charles made a Captain. They were chiefly Protestant and well-off and joined the Prince because they, like Bradshaw, were '... induced by a principle of duty only'. Most of them were captured at Carlisle and punished as traitors.

If Bradshaw was a reliable guide, their horrible fate scarcely altered their deepest convictions. Just before he was hanged, drawn and quartered on Kennington Common in November 1746 Bradshaw declared, 'I have never saw any reason since (joining Charles) to convince me that I was in the least mistaken.'

Somehow, Charles was heartened by what he saw at Manchester. Though his officers fretted at the total absence of any substantial English support while government strength continued to grow, the Prince managed to treat his awesome enemies with courteous disdain. So far, all that they had done to impede his progress was knock down a few bridges, a ploy which was double-edged, for it impeded Charles' pursuers as well. In order to make life easier for them, the Prince graciously offered to repair any dismantled bridges which he might have occasion to pass, and from Manchester he issued the following proclamation:

His Royal Highness being informed that several bridges have been pulled down in this country, he has given orders to repair them forthwith, particularly that at Crossford, which is to be done this night by his own troops, though His Royal Highness does not propose to make use of it for his own army, but believes it will be of service to the country; and if any forces that were with General Wade be coming this road, they may have the benefit of it.

This was the Prince's finest hour. He was within two hundred miles of London and determined to press on to Derby. On 1 December his army left Manchester. On the far bank of the river Mersey, Charles was met by a small party of Cheshire Jacobites. They were accompanied by a Mrs Skyring, a loyal supporter who was nearly 90 years old. As a child she had been held up in her mother's arms to view the arrival of Charles

II on English soil. Her family had strong Jacobite sympathies, and her father had fought as a Cavalier. After the expulsion of the Stuarts and the arrival of the Hanoverian dynasty she had laid aside half her income to send it to the exiled Royal family, concealing only her name. She had now sold all her plate and jewels and gave the money she got for them to the Prince. She kissed his hand saying: 'Lord now lettest Thou Thy servant depart in peace.'

When the Highland army entered Macclesfield, news reached them that the Duke of Cumberland had taken command of Ligonier's army and was concentrating his forces at Lichfield, thus effectively barring the way to Derby. Behind the Prince, Marshal Wade was making heavy work of the chase and had only got as far as Catterick. Nevertheless, the clans were in a desperate situation with armies totalling more than three times their number blocking both the forward and exit roads. When pressed, Lord George Murray agreed with Charles that the only hope of escape lay in advance. Somehow the Highlanders must get between Cumberland and London. Leaving Charles in charge of a division at Macclesfield, Lord George turned off south-west towards Congleton. He hoped that the Duke of Cumberland would interpret this move as part of an advance into Wales, move to block it and thus leave the road to London open.

Posted at Congleton was an advance guard of Cumberland's Light Horse, who hurriedly fell back to Lichfield as the Highlanders approached. By early evening, the Duke was informed of Lord George's manoeuvres. As Lord George had hoped, Cumberland believed that the invaders were heading for Wales and moved his forces to Stone so that he might bar the western exits from Macclesfield. During the night, Highland patrols scoured the area around Newcastle-under-Lyme in order to learn of enemy movements which would indicate the success of Scottish strategy. Confirmation came with the capture of Captain Vere, a government spy who readily told Lord George what he wished to know regarding Cumberland's strength and disposition. One thing was clear. A direct clash was out of the question. Captain Vere estimated the Duke's strength at 2,200 horse and 8,250 foot! Fortunately the road to Derby had been opened and Lord George turned eastwards again. Going through Leek and Ashbourne, he reached the town on 4 December.

Charles marched directly through Leek and Ashbourne without any challenge and arrived at Derby soon after Lord George. Throughout the advance, the Prince had displayed an inspired determination. 'He never dinn'd nor threw off his cloaths at night, eat much at Supper, used to throw himself upon a bed at Eleven o'clock, and was up by four in the morning. As he had a prodigious strong constitution, he bore fatigue most surprisingly well.' Now he was within one hundred and fifty miles of London. His enemies were behind and those who remained in the capital were contemplating flight overseas. The royal yacht was made ready to sail, and the Duke of Newcastle was desperately seeking channels of communication through which to deal with the Prince.

It seemed that nothing could stop the Highland army from sweeping down to London. The clansmen expected to occupy the capital of their ancient enemy within the next few days. Perhaps they would meet resistance, but they had little fear of overcoming that. On the morning of 5 December the narrow streets of Derby were thronged with kilted Highlanders who crowded the cutlers' shops 'quarrelling about who should be the first to sharpen and give a proper edge to their swords'. While the clansmen tended to their weapons, their chiefs and officers attended a special council at Exeter House, the Prince's Headquarters at Derby. The decision reached there marked the first crucial turning-point in Charles Edward's life.

# 8: The Retreat from Derby

When Dr Samuel Johnson and Boswell found themselves in Derby in 1775, the great doctor was heard to muse, 'Ah! It was a noble attempt.' Johnson regarded Derby as the terminating point of the Forty-five. At least that was where Charles Edward's efforts to reconquer the Three Kingdoms effectively ended. From then on, the Prince remained on the defensive, running from his enemies, and preoccupied with self-preservation rather than the establishment of Stuart control in Britain. Thus far he had gambled upon his speed and popularity. The swiftness of his army and the agility of his general saved Charles from an early reckoning with reality at Carlisle and at Derby, perhaps even at Corriearrick. That he was popular in Scotland was unquestionable. But as yet there was no sign of substantial support in England, although Charles was less than three days' march away from the capital. Perhaps he was not wanted, and without widespread assistance the Prince could not hope to hold off the might of Cumberland and Wade. From a military standpoint, Charles Edward had no hope of achieving any worthwhile victory and without that his political aspirations must be doomed.

That was what his Council told the Prince when they met at Exeter House on the morning of 5 December. The debate was opened by Lord George Murray, who explained to Charles that by this time Cumberland would have realized his mistake and would be at Stafford, as near to London as was Derby. What was more, the combined enemy force, including the army hastily assembled on Finchley Common to defend London, totalled almost thirty thousand men. Quite naturally, the Scots chiefs wished to return to their own country, particularly as the Marquis d'Eguilles and one thousand French regulars were now there. The clans had marched into England to support an English rising or a French landing. Neither of these had occurred. Now they wanted to return to Scotland and defend what they knew to be their own.

When his officers had finished, Charles gave vent to his frustration. Early that morning Murray of Broughton had warned the Prince that a retreat was being discussed by the Scots commanders. Since then, Charles had brooded angrily, and he was by now in no mood for formal debate. According to Lord Elcho, he 'fell into a passion and gave most of the Gentlemen that had Spoke very Abusive Language, and said that they had a mind to betray him'. Again and again Charles stressed that if they reached London, all would be well. But his officers were unconvinced. As the Chevalier de Johnstone asked pointedly, 'supposing by a miracle in our favour we should arrive even at the gates of that capital without losing a man, what kind of figure could four thousand five hundred men cut ... in a city of more than a million and a half inhabitants?'

Records of the arguments which occurred that morning in Exeter House show that Charles and his commanders were thinking along completely different lines. In conventional terms of manpower and armament the chiefs were correct. Even the Prince could not deny his military weakness. Yet he had been outgunned and outnumbered all along, and he could not see why this problem should suddenly prove to be a stumbling block. Admittedly, he had previously banked upon expected support from English Jacobites which had since failed to materialize. But even this failure was merely incidental to his overall strategic conception. Before the speed of his advance the enemy had lost their co-ordination. They were hoodwinked and terrified. All semblance of determination on their part had vanished. As long as the image of Highland invincibility was maintained, no one would be able to stand in their way with success. This thesis was justified by Charles' experience so far, and he felt that a bold advance upon London might even be the decisive factor in swinging public opinion his way. The Prince was making an intuitive guess regarding the political climate of England which he could not then verify.

The delay in communication between London and Derby withheld from Charles the facts which could well have altered the opinions of his officers. News of the Highland occupation of Derby reached London only on 6 December, the day when their retreat began. Its impact was tremendous. Fielding's account in *The True Patriot* of this 'Black Friday' is typical of many reports of widespread chaos which reigned in the capital following the arrival of posts from Derby.

When the Highlanders by the most incredible march got between the Duke's army and the metropolis, they struck a terror into it scarce to be credited. The shops were shut up and business everywhere suspended. A rush was made upon the Bank of England ... which only escaped bankruptcy by paying out in sixpences. It was rumoured that the sixpences had been heated to such a pitch that it was all but impossible to handle them. A special prayer was drawn up by the Archbishop of Canterbury to be said by all churches imploring Divine protection ... The guards of the city were immediately strengthened. In the squares and open places soldiers were posted.

The distress and panic of government supporters were aggravated by London Jacobites who openly displayed printed posters welcoming the Prince and his army. George II was, though, less detested than his odious father George I. Despite his many failings he did not lack courage. It gives the best indication of the true state of feeling in London that this vigorous monarch who had led his troops so heroically at the battle of Dettingen had prepared his ships in the Thames and loaded them with all his valuables for a flight to the Continent and his other home, the Electorate of Hanover.

But at the council tables in Exeter House nothing could be known of the confusion which would paralyse London. Charles believed that the opposition would be reduced to harmless oratory, but he was only guessing, though with uncanny accuracy. However, Lord George and the other Scottish commanders would accept only what they could see, and concluded that the Prince was driven by unreasonable stubbornness and pride. 'His Royal Highness,' wrote Lord George Murray, 'had no regard for his own danger, but pressed with all the force of argument to go forward. He did not doubt but that the justness of his cause would prevail, and he could not think of retreating after coming this far; and he was hopeful there might be a defection in the enemy's army, and that several would declare for him.' In reply, Charles may well have asked the General why he had come this far, with no safe line of retreat or communication behind him and in the full knowledge that the enemy was far stronger, if all he intended to do was reteat when the chief dangers now lay behind rather than ahead? For the rest of the day the Prince argued with his Council, eventually suggesting that rather than retreat, they should move into Wales. The Council refused to alter their decision and Charles was forced to consent to their desires, although not without protest. He promised that 'for the future he would ... neither ask nor take their Advice, that he was Accountable to nobody for his Actions but to his Father'.

Charles was not alone in his dislike of the decision forced upon him by his Council. Both Murray of Broughton and the Duke of Perth were willing to go along with the Prince, but they were lone voices in

Exeter House. Murray for one should not even have been there, as he had resigned his Secretaryship at Carlisle. Some of the lower-ranking officers, too, did not care for retreat. The garrulous and not always sober Sir John Macdonald had met his kinsman Macdonald of Keppoch in one of the Derby streets and shouted at him: 'What! A Macdonald turn his back!' Then he turned on Lochiel: 'For shame, a Cameron run away from the enemy! Go forward and I'll lead you.' Murray of Broughton does not record how 'the gentle Lochiel' received this alcoholic sally.

When the retreat began on 6 December, the rank and file of the Highland army were told that they were to march north and attack Marshal Wade. No clansman liked the idea of retreat, and the lie about attacking Wade was devised to keep the men from sinking into abject gloom. But they must have seen through the deception, for they remained 'sullen and silent that whole day'. Charles had been right, their confidence melted away, and soon they found themselves under continual harassment from county militia, mobs of farm labourers and even children. Gone was the awe with which they had been met during the advance south. Although the same route was followed to simplify billeting arrangements, inhabitants along the way proved less hospitable than before. They even waylaid unwary stragglers and carried them off to gaol. At Manchester, the advance guard was attacked by an angry mob, and when the army left the city, the citizens sniped at Captain O'Sullivan, mistaking him for Prince Charles.

With their confidence, the Highlanders also lost some of their self-respect. As they could be seen to be acting like cowards, they saw no reason to keep up a front of noble restraint. Neither the Prince nor his men cared any more about the impression left in England. They retaliated when crowds jeered. They stole at every opportunity. They left bills unpaid. Having abandoned a crown, the invading army made amends with petty theft. Like a band of raiding pirates, they now displayed an anxiety to avoid the forces of law, represented by Cumberland, which had previously been absent. 'We began to behave with less forbearance. And few there were, who would go on foot, if they could ride; and mighty taking, stealing, and pressing of horses ther was amongst us ...'

The Prince, whose splendid youthful spirit was to revive under far greater physical distress, was now sunk in unconcealed gloom. He felt that he had been betrayed by the Council, and bitterly blamed Lord George Murray. He believed that the General's accession to the Stuart army was the prime cause of its failure. He resolved to oppose Lord George at every conceivable opportunity. The affability and perception which had for so long characterized the Prince were now replaced by a childish petulance that was dangerous in one responsible for the welfare of several thousand men. It seems as though the lack of imagination displayed by his officers dulled Charles Edward's own enthusiasm, and throughout the retreat he behaved with a strange, almost suicidal perversity. Whereas before he had risen at dawn and been ready to march before any of his subordinates, the Prince now dallied until late morning before emerging from his quarters. He continually delayed the rear of the army, and allowed dangerous gaps to form between the van and Lord George's rear-guard. When Charles did mount, he rode straight through to the front, upsetting the columns and frustrating the sound military basis upon which the retreat was constructed. At Manchester on 8 December the Prince wanted to rest for a day, just to show that he was not afraid of Cumberland, despite the fact that the enemy was scarcely one day away.

Although the Duke of Cumberland had marched his infantry to a standstill, he was nevertheless in hot pursuit with about three thousand cavalry and a thousand dragoons. He reached Macclesfield while the Highlanders were at Wigan and all the time the gap was closing. Fortunately for the Scots, Marshal Wade's infantry were also exhausted and no considerable challenge was made in Lancashire. Wade retired to Newcastle, but he sent all his cavalry under Major-General Oglethorpe in a flanking movement against the Highlanders at Wigan. Again, luck was with Prince Charles. Icy roads delayed Oglethorpe and he reached Wigan several hours after the invaders had left for Preston. There he waited until Cumberland joined him in pursuit. In all, over six thousand troops were chasing the Scots.

Charles began to be a little worried about the situation he faced. Before leaving Carlisle on the way south, orders had been sent to Lord Strathallan at Perth to bring reinforcements into England. These had not yet appeared and Charles now sent the Duke of Perth to Scotland with instructions to lead reinforcements southwards to meet the retreating army. The Prince appeared to have no intention of abandoning England without a struggle. At Lancaster he ordered his army to halt for a day, despite Lord George's contrary advice, and probably because of it. Abruptly, he instructed the General to reconnoitre a field of battle, but after Lord George's escort captured a detachment of Oglethorpe's scouts, the Prince's yearning for a fight disappeared. Cumberland was altogether too close! When Lord George reported to Charles 'that if our number would answer, I could not wish a better field for Highlanders: he said he was to march next day'. Charles had at last realized that retreat was the only hope of survival, especially as the Duke of Perth had been unable to cross the border into Scotland because of stout militia resistance near Kendal. But still the Prince refused to work in harmony with his General.

Knowing the state of the roads north of Preston, and

fearful lest they had been 'spoiled' still further by partisan Englishmen, Lord George asked Charles for permission to substitute the heavy four-wheeled ammunition carts which the army had acquired in England for the more convenient two-wheeled conveyances found north of the border. Charles ignored this modest request, and by the time Kendal was reached, the ammunition train had fallen to the rear, despite Charles' earlier promise to Lord George that the wagons would be kept in front. At Kendal, Lord George went to see the Prince personally, but could not get to see Charles, who was dining with O'Sullivan, nor O'Sullivan because he was attending the Prince. As Lord George feared, on the next day the rear was unable to march more than four miles before all progress was stopped by 'a water where there was a narrow turn and a steep ascent'. The ground had been churned up by the forward columns, it was raining, the ammunition wagons were stuck and there were not enough men in the rear-guard to get them moving again. Lord George was forced to spend the night in open country and in plain sight of enemy patrols.

At dawn the next morning, the ammunition was transferred to as many small carts as could be found and the march was resumed. Somehow, word reached the Prince that all ammunition was being dumped, and during the morning two messages arrived from him 'not to leave, upon any account, the least thing, not so much as a cannon ball; for he would rather return himself than there should be anything left'. Lord George managed to swallow his anger and promised Charles that he would 'do all that a man can do'. He carried out his instructions to the letter, and when two miles up the road, one of the ammunition carts fell into a stream, the General 'got the men to carry to Shap a good many cannon balls ... I gave sixpence the piece for doing it, by which means I got above two hundred carried.'

At Shap, the Highland rear-guard were joined by the welcome regiment of John Roy Stewart, and on 18 December this enlarged force made its way towards Penrith. All around the Highlanders observed signs of enemy action. Small parties of horse were seen hovering at the rear and at one point three hundred mounted militia drew up ahead, 'but so soon as the Glengarry men threw their plaids, and ran forward to attack them, they made off at the top gallop'. When he reached the village of Clifton, Lord George determined to scour the enclosures of the Whig Lord Lonsdale, where it seemed most likely that the militia were quartered. As a precautionary measure, the ammunition and cannon were sent forward to Penrith to join the Prince and soon afterwards. Lord George's caution was justified when a captured militia officer admitted that the Duke of Cumberland and four thousand horse were less than a mile away. Roy Stewart was sent to Charles to ask for instructions and Lord George led Glengarry's regiment back to Clifton. There he was met by the Duke of Perth, who had returned from Penrith with Cluny's and Arshiel's regiments. Perth immediately offered to ride back and summon the whole Highland army, but Lord George assured him that about a thousand men would be sufficient.

After Perth left for help, Lord George 'caused roll up what colours we had, and made them pass half open to different places'. The Highlanders were cunningly concealed among a network of hedged enclosures, and their General's intention was to give the enemy an exaggerated sense of their numbers. Cumberland was in no hurry, and only an hour later did he order three dragoon regiments to dismount and attack the Highland position. At this moment Roy Stewart returned from the Prince with an order for Lord George to retire to Penrith. Charles himself was making all possible speed for Carlisle. The order was insane. Lord George knew that the retreat down a narrow lane in the darkness, followed by withdrawal from Clifton between high walls, could be disastrous. 'The enemy, by regular platoons in our rear ... must destroy a great many; and by taking any wounded man prisoner, they would know our numbers; whereas ... I was confident I could dislodge them from there by a brisk attack.' Charles was being perverse at a time when immaturity could cost hundreds of lives. Lord Elcho later summed up the Prince's behaviour with customary venom. 'As their was formerly a Contradiction to make the army halt when it was necessary to march, so now their was one to march and shun fighting when their Could never be a better opportunity gott for it ...'

The Highlanders were well hidden in the wan, moonlit darkness, so Lord George and Cluny decided not to obey Charles' instructions. They would mount an attack. The enemy were already firing 'popping shots' which revealed their whereabouts to the waiting Highlanders. Quietly they advanced, Glengarry on the right and Cluny Macpherson with Lord George on the left. There was a sudden sharp exchange of fire during which the Macphersons discovered that they were in the open. With the cry, 'Claymore!', Lord George drew his sword and charged straight at the dragoon lines. Though the Macphersons followed with their customary vigour, dragoon resistance proved stronger than it had been at Prestonpans. Eventually they fell back under the flanking fire of Glengarry's regiment, but their casualties were comparatively light, and the Highlanders were left wondering about the hardness of dragoon heads before they finally found the answer. According to Captain John Macpherson of Strathmashie, 'the poor swords suffered much, as there were no less than fourteen of them broke on the dragoons' skull caps (which they all had) before it seems the better way of doing their business was found out'.

Cumberland had learned from the stories of Prestonpans, and metal skull-caps were just one of the means by which he hoped to lay the bogey of the unstoppable Highland charge. Losses on the Scots side were also light, about a half dozen killed. The main objective of driving the English back had been achieved, but repercussions of the skirmish were severe. In writing his report of it, Cumberland mentioned that when some of his officers were knocked down 'the Rebels cried, "No quarter! Murder them!"' and they received several wounds after they were knocked down. On Drummossie Moor, the Duke avenged his comrades with bloody dedication.

When Lord George reached Penrith, he found Charles waiting. The General observed that the Prince 'seemed very well pleased with what had happened', and was in good spirits during the journey to Carlisle. The reason for Charles' levity was a mystery to Lord George, but had he known that the Prince had ill-advised notions of using Carlisle as a base from which to launch himself again against the English, no doubt his own élan would have disappeared. Charles believed that a large French force was marching to the border, and with this assistance, he saw no problem in mastering the combined might of Cumberland and Wade. In fact there were only a thousand French troops in Scotland, no match for the onrushing enemy. But Charles had faith in his 'cher Cousin', Louis, and felt sure that French succour was at hand.

The army stayed in Carlisle for one day. As the French were probably still north of the border, Charles now altered his plan. He would garrison the city and then take the rest of his army to Scotland, rendezvous with the French and return to his English base in time to deal with Cumberland. With the exception of three Swedish field guns, all the Highland artillery was left at Carlisle under the charge of John Hamilton, the Duke of Gordon's factor, and a garrison of about four hundred men. Most of the garrison came from the

Manchester Regiment, and the rest were drawn from Perth's, Ogilvy's, Glenbucket's and Roy Stewart's regiments.

Charles has been blamed, and rightly, for leaving Carlisle to defend itself. Lord George Murray and the Council were strongly against the move. 'This was done against the opinion almost of Everybody but the Prince said he would have a Town in England and he was sure the Duke could gett no Cannon to take it with.' Charles' error was one of judgement, not, as some have accused him, of wanton neglect. He genuinely believed that the forces he left there were sufficient to hold Cumberland, whom he knew to be in a hurry. They did not, he reflected, have the time to cordon the city off as Lord George had so notably done on the Highland march south. What Charles did not foresee was that Cumberland could bring up guns from Whitehaven. In all, the Duke acquired six eighteen-pounders, and with these he battered the castle at Carlisle into submission exactly ten days after the Highlanders crossed the Esk into Scotland on 20 December.

The Scottish army returned home on Charles' birthday. Crossing the flooded Esk was a formidable business. Lord George subsequently said that there must have been two thousand men in the water as he was making his way over. All eventually got back to Scotland, though the Prince himself had to rescue a man from drowning by seizing hold of his hair. On reaching the farther bank, pipers played and the men danced reels to dry themselves. Five days later, on Christmas Day, the van of the Highland army entered Glasgow.

By the middle of the eighteenth century, Glasgow had changed almost completely from the city which Defoe described in 1706 as 'the beautifullest I have seen in Britain'. Without doubt, it was now the richest and largest metropolis in Scotland, but also less beautiful. Gone was the pleasant little cathedral city set by one of the best salmon rivers in Scotland – the Clyde. In its place was a bustling, growing port. Glasgow had surpassed even Bristol as the 'Gateway to the West' through which all the wealthy trade of the Americas, and indeed of all the West, flowed into these islands. The city had done very well commercially out of the Union, and this affected all classes. The 'Tobacco Lords', the great merchants who had made vast fortunes from the import of tobacco leaf, may have strutted the crown of the pavements, but the lesser citizens who were jostled out of their way had also done well. Even in the past, Glasgow had been something of a state within a state. She was 'Scotch' all right, but had taken little if any part in the struggle for Scottish Independence both before Bannockburn and after. At the date of Charles' arrival in Scotland, Glasgow was a thoroughly Whiggish city.

For those of us who have grown up with a conception of Glasgow as the seat of Scottish national movements, it is odd to imagine anything so frigid as Charles Edward Stuart's reception on Boxing Day 1745. When Lord George Murray and Charles entered the city, the citizens took great pains to demonstrate how unimpressed they were, either with the General's military demeanour or the Prince's more youthful charm. They turned up their opulent, if not well-bred, noses at the Highland rabble who were desecrating their hallowed streets. Even had they appeared at their best, the Highland rank and file would have appalled well-heeled Glaswegians. As it was, they rolled through the town in the same dishevelled plaids which had frightened the scarlet-cloaked dragoons at Prestonpans and in England. Carrying the filth and grime which accompanies any army on the march, the Highlanders appeared more like savages than soldiers to scandalized Glasgow merchants and their wives.

Yet accommodation had to be found for this host, for claymores were arguments which could not be gainsaid; and though Charles specifically forbade looting, the threat of it was enough to effect his wishes. Plainly showing their disgust, the city fathers allocated billets to the Prince's army. But Charles was not satisfied with their ill-mannered methods. He promptly ordered the Lord Provost to provide '6000 short coats, 12000 linnen shirts, 600 pairs of shoes, 6000 bonnets, and as many tartan hose, besides a sum of money'. This cost the city the princely sum of £3,556/10/9½d. Added to the levy of £5,500 which had already been raised, Glasgow suffered to the tune of nearly £9,000. She could easily afford it, but it was the indignity of having to unbelt in favour of a cause which was contrary to respectable Whiggism which hurt most.

Charles did his best to exert his powers of attraction in Glasgow. There he dressed more elegantly than ever he did in any other British city. Twice a day he dined in public, attended by as many Glasgow ladies as were willing to exert themselves. It was a rather odd practice which had been used to good effect in Edinburgh, but at Glasgow it cut little ice. Those who did turn up at these receptions were limited to a narrow circle of the Jacobite families who lived on the outer edge of the city.

We have no definite proof of whether Clementina Walkinshaw was one of Charles' guests at Glasgow. Legend has it that she was. It was quite likely, for her uncle was a Glasgow man who owned a house in the

Gallowgate. If the story about her being a playmate of the young Prince in Rome is true, then her introduction to Charles in Glasgow would probably have followed as a matter of course. But that too is only part of the legend. What we do know is that the Prince definitely met Clementina when he visited her uncle, Sir Hugh Paterson, at Bannockburn, while the Highland army was making its descent upon Edinburgh from Perth. We also know that Charles stayed at Bannockburn again early the following year while he was suffering from influenza, and it was then that the liaison between the two young people may have first become serious. Clementina nursed the Prince through his illness; sick men often fall in love with their nurses. It was quite likely that the Prince did ask Clementina if she was devoted enough to serve him when he called for her. Whatever his meaning, there can be little doubt of the woman's understanding. When Charles summoned her to the Netherlands several years afterwards, Clementina packed her bags and went without question.

Clementina Walkinshaw was the daughter of Mr John Walkinshaw of Barrowfield, a gentleman who acted as James III's envoy to Vienna in 1716. It is not known what part he played in the rescue of Queen Maria Clementina while she was on her way to marry James, but the relationship must have been close, for the Queen eventually consented to be godmother of John Walkinshaw's tenth daughter, and even allowed the child to be given her name. The date of Clementina's birth can only be guessed at. It occurred sometime between 1721 and 1724, either in Rome or Glasgow. So she was roughly the same age as the Prince when they met at Glasgow and Bannockburn. Her portraits reveal that she was attractive, not beautiful, but with dark, hypnotic eyes which convinced suspicious Jacobites that she had a sinister hold over the Prince. But those allegations were yet to come.

Her background is not easily explained. Related to staunch Jacobites, prominent among whom was her uncle Sir Hugh Paterson who first introduced her to Charles at his house at Bannockburn, she yet, without intent, and mainly by force of circumstances, saw a good deal of the other side. Her sister was a lady-in-waiting at the Hanoverian Court in London, and this unconcealed fact was to make many Jacobites suspicious of Clementina and deplore Charles' relationship with her. She had herself seen something of life at the Hanoverian Court when she stayed with her sister in London before 1745. Yet we can confidently assert that the suspicions of exiled Jacobites about her selling secrets of the exiled Court to the government in London were not true. Clementina was not that sort of woman. Moreover the painstaking researches made by Andrew Lang into the details of the traffic in Jacobite secrets from France or Rome to London do not reveal any underhand dealing on her part.

Charles must have felt that he had other more pressing business at hand than secret engagements with Scottish women. Though the city was inhospitable, the army was forced to remain there and collect reinforcements with which to meet a renewed government challenge. A few days after the Highland army had crossed the border into England, Sir John Cope's successor, Lieutenant-General Handasyde, marched from Berwick with two fresh regiments, Price's and Ligonier's, and the remnants of Hamilton's and Gardiner's dragoons. In the north, the companies of Independent Militia raised by Lord President Forbes controlled Inverness, although their influence was limited, having recently been successfully challenged by Lord Lewis Gordon at the 'Skirmish at Inverurie' in the vicinity of Aberdeen. Campbell militia still held Argyll for the government but to the south and west Lord Strathallan had an army of between three and four thousand men ready to join the Prince at Perth. Lord Lovat had finally played his hand and brought his Frasers with him, admittedly only after his wrath had been incurred following his arrest in a ham-fisted government operation. With Simon Fraser at Perth were also the Earl of Cromarty with part of Clan Mackenzie; the Farquharsons; and Lord John Drummond and the French troops who had landed at Stonehaven and Montrose in early December.

In addition, Strathallan had the welcome company of a regiment of MacIntoshes raised by Lady MacIntosh. Although her husband held a commission in the Black Watch, and was incidentally in dispute with Cluny Macpherson over the leadership of Clan Chattan, Anne MacIntosh made it clear where her sympathies lay. While her husband was away, she had raised her clan and given its command to Alexander Macgillivray. She was at Moy when the battle of Culloden was fought, and afterwards was arrested and placed under the custody of Lieutent-General Henry Hawley, an 'honourable' officer who vowed, 'I shall honour her with a mahogany gallows and silk cords.' But Anne MacIntosh survived the blood bath after Charles Edward's final defeat, and died in her bed at Leith in 1787, still a staunch Jacobite.

Charles had need of every MacIntosh and Fraser he could lay his hands on, for about eight thousand English troops were moving up from Newcastle to strengthen the government grip on the Lowlands. Old 'Grandmother Wade' was not in charge of this army any longer, but fortunately neither was the Duke of Cumberland. He had been called south to defend London against an expected French invasion, after first nominating Lieutenant-General Hawley for supreme command in Scotland. In his fifty years of service Henry Hawley had acquired notions which were to be his undoing in months to come at Falkirk. He had been on the victorious right wing at Sheriffmuir and had thus formed the erroneous opinion that Highlanders were unable to withstand a cavalry charge. But Hawley's best-remembered characteristic was a taste for unnecessary severity. On one occasion in Flanders, 'a deserter being hanged before Hawley's windows, the surgeons begged to have the body for dissection. But Hawley was reluctant to part with the pleasing spectacle; "At least," said he, "you shall give me the skeleton to hang up in the guardroom."' It was no wonder that the Lieutenant-General had been given the nickname of 'Lord Chief Justice'.

By 12 January Hawley had assembled twelve battalions at Edinburgh in readiness for a second visit from the Prince. When Charles did leave Glasgow on 3 January, he headed not for Edinburgh, but towards Stirling. Most of Strathallan's army had come to Glasgow from Perth and the Prince discovered that he now possessed an artillery train of two sixteen-pounders, two twelve-pounders and two eight-pounders, all of which had been brought over from France by Lord John Drummond. With these, he planned to reduce Stirling Castle. Charles foresaw no difficulty in taking the town of Stirling, but the Castle he knew would be no easy matter. One wonders why he coveted it. Perhaps he now realized that his continued survival might depend upon a strong base upon which to centre his army in safety. The more likely explanation is that the Prince had at last decided to concentrate his attentions upon Scotland. At least one crown would be returned to the Stuarts. But the repossession of Scotland entailed the weeding out of every single English enclave. No more would Charles Edward stand at the Mercat Cross in Edinburgh, or elsewhere, while the Union Jack fluttered above his head at the top of an enemy bastion.

As Charles had believed, no difficulties were encountered in the taking of Stirling. That feat having been accomplished, the Prince's army prepared to batter the Castle into submission. The chief problem was in finding a battery position sufficiently high for the Scots to dispute artillery control with the Castle guns. According to Colonel Grant, Charles' artillery commander, there was only one suitable site. But to this the townspeople objected and Charles determined to seek alternative advice regarding the battery siting. He turned to a French officer who had come to Scotland with Lord John Drummond. This man, Mirabelle de Gordon, was said to be 'one of the first engineers in France'; but the Highlanders thought otherwise. They resented the Prince's demotion of Colonel Grant and refused to help Mirabelle, or Mr Admirable as they called him. It seems their ire was well placed. Mirabelle decided to open trenches on Gowan Hill, to the north of the Castle, where there was insufficient earth in which to bed the guns. The Highlanders would not carry up sandbags or wool-packs, so the work had to be done by French regulars. Naturally, little progress was made, and all the time the vital understanding between the Prince and his chiefs soured.

At the root of Highland discontent was Charles Edward's refusal to call any councils. Ever since the fracas at Derby, the Prince decided never to endanger his policies by subjecting them to a majority vote. The chiefs, however loyal to Charles, naturally did not like his idea that they should have no voice in the disposal of their clansmen who had followed them. Unfortunately they entrusted the drawing-up of a memorial on this subject to Lord George Murray who worded it as tactlessly as only he could.

He made certain reasonable points in his abrupt manner, pointing with justice to the Prince's error in abandoning Carlisle under the mistaken belief that the unfortunate Colonel Townley could hold the city against all the combined armies under Cumberland. He also was foolish enough to drag in the council at Derby, contending that that had saved the day for the Jacobites. It is extraordinary that Lord George can have been so tactless as to reopen this wound, if not yet healed, at least forgotten in the prospect of action. Charles' reply to this memorial was what might have been expected. It touched him on the raw and he said so. Lord George could do nothing but go to Falkirk and inspect the Jacobite forces there.

To facilitate quartering, the Highland army had again been divided. One part was billeted in the vicinity of Bannockburn, while the rest were at Falkirk, about nine miles away. When Lord George reached Falkirk, he discovered that large sections of men had been deserting. All this he blamed upon the unwise delay at Stirling. He also knew that Hawley would pose a considerable threat if ever he consolidated himself at Edinburgh. A swift attack upon the capital would be just the thing to revive Highland enthusiasm and upset the enemy. But Charles wanted Stirling. It seems as though he regarded the continued defiance of the Castle as an insult to his regal authority. He was settling a personal quarrel with a construction built of rock.

Meanwhile, at Edinburgh, Henry Hawley had not been idle. On arriving in the city he 'caus'd immediately two pairs of Gallows to be set up; one in ye Grass Market, and the other between Leith and Edinr'. The General was less dramatic regarding his military situation. He considered his complement of Gardiner's and Hamilton's dragoons to be useless, while of his 8,000 infantry, about 2,000 were so ill-disciplined and ill-trained that the General thought them 'no better than militia'. A week after his arrival, Hawley wrote to the Duke of Newcastle, 'I only beg of youre Grace not to call this yet a considerable force in the Condition they are in ...' Yet despite the fact that he had no artillery worthy of the name with which to break up a Highland charge, the general continued to hold the poorest opinion of his enemy – 'I do and allwayes shall despise these Rascalls.' But he still took the trouble to issue a memorandum describing the Highland method of attack and the best method with which to deal with it. He advised his troops to fire only when the enemy 'are within ten or twelve paces' and then maintain a steady stream of fire in ranks. On no account should firing commence too early, for that would mean lost time during reloading when the Highlanders would fall upon the front ranks with unabated fury. But even if this should occur, the ranks must hold their ground. 'If you give way you may give your foot for dead, for they being without a firelock or any load, no man with his arms, accoutrements, etc., can escape them...' The General clearly wanted his men to be well prepared for the battle which must inevitably be fought.

Although 'resolved to do nothing rashely', Hawley was keen to come to grips with the enemy. On 13 January he despatched his second-in-command, Major-General John Huske, westwards with five regular battalions, the Glasgow militia, and Hamilton's and Ligonier's dragoons. After diverting some of his contingent to Bo'ness and Queensferry, Huske marched on to Linlithgow, followed shortly by another three regiments. At Falkirk, Lord George Murray heard that provisions were being gathered for Huske at Linlithgow, and on 13 January he set out to destroy or capture as much of Huske's stocks as possible. At Linlithgow, Lord George sent out all his horse under Lord Elcho to patrol the roads leading to Edinburgh. About noon, Elcho reported contact with a small party of enemy cavalry who had then fallen back on a much larger body of combined horse and foot. Two hours later, Lord George received a further report, 'that there was a very large body of horse and foot advancing as fast as they could'. The Scots commander waited until the enemy were just outside the town and then he led his troops across Linlithgow bridge. He planned to attack the enemy while they were in the process of crossing the bridge. But that never occurred. Instead, 'the dragoons who was in the front of the regulars drew up close by the Bridge and very abusive language pass'd betwixt both sides...' Rather than risk a fight, Lord George then withdrew to Falkirk, for he knew that a major engagement was in the offing.

Hawley himself soon arrived to take command of the government forces. He now had with him around eight thousand men. He caught up with Huske by the evening of 16 January when the army was encamped in a field to the west of Falkirk. For two days now, the Highland army had drawn up in line of battle on Plean Muir, two miles south-west of Bannockburn. But the enemy remained motionless. On 17 January the Highlanders once more took their positions on Plean Muir. Because they spent their nights in innumerable small units, it took the Scots until midday to assemble. But fortunately Hawley did not take advantage of such an ideal opportunity for defeating the Highlanders piecemeal. It seemed that he still had no intention of stirring, and in desperation Charles decided that the enemy must be roused into action. He reviewed his troops, and then called a Council of War in which the relieved chiefs found that their opinions did in fact still hold weight with the Prince. Eventually, Lord George Murray proposed that his army should move to high ground known as the 'hill of Falkirk'. This ridge of bare moorland lay less than a mile above Hawley's camp.

The Highlanders received with relish the news that at last something was going to be done. According to John Goodwillie, 'This two days drawing up and expecting an engagement and being disappointed gave great discontent to the private men, who told their officers if they were drawn out again they would engage at any event even altho' without a commander.' One detachment of troops under Lord John Drummond took the main road from Bannockburn to Falkirk, where it would come in plain sight of Hawley, while the main body under Lord George crept up unseen until it was less than two miles from the town. In all, only between six and eight thousand Highlanders were involved, because about a thousand had been left to continue the siege of Stirling Castle under the Duke of Perth.

Lieutenant-General Hawley spent the night at Callander House, the seat of the Jacobite Earl of Kilmarnock, where the genial hospitality of his hostess must have lulled him into a false sense of security. On the morning of 17 January, he rode out to his camp at about 5 o'clock. A few hours later in the day he went to reconnoitre ground between his camp and the Torwood through which some of his officers thought they could discern enemy movements. Hawley saw nothing and returned to Callander House. The last thing he expected was for the enemy to attack him.

Less than two hours later, Lord John Drummond's decoy force was seen moving about to the north of the Torwood, and the government army stood to arms. But after a quarter of an hour, the men were allowed to rest and go in search of lunch. One of the Glasgow Militia officers present, William Corse, later remembered that food was hard to find. He had barely finished his meal when an excited countryman rushed into camp shouting, 'Gentlemen, what are you about? The Highlanders will be immediately upon you!' Anxiously, some of the men scampered up trees from which they confirmed the warning that the enemy was approaching to the south of the Torwood. But still Hawley considered himself safe and did not even return to camp.

His negligence allowed Lord George to cross the river Carron without hindrance, and incidentally avert a change of plan by the Prince. When the Highland army had only gone about half a mile, 'Mr O'Sullivan came up to me (wrote Lord George) and told me he had been talking with the Prince, and that it was not thought advisable to pass the water in sight of the enemy, and therefore it was best delaying it till night, and then we could do it unperceived.' A little later, Charles himself rode up to have a word with Lord George. Wisely, the General kept on with the march while arguing with the Prince. He disliked the idea of passing the night out in the open at this time of the year, for he knew that if this was attempted, the men would probably disperse and go looking for shelter. Either the advance should be continued, or the army should return to quarters. When one of the Irish officers accompanying Charles reflected upon the danger of the Highlanders being spotted by the enemy and then challenged while they were crossing the Carron, Lord George assured him that they would not be noticed until they were too near the crossing for the enemy to dispute it. This reassurance appeared to settle the Prince's mind, for he then ordered the advance to continue as planned.

At about 2 o'clock the government army received confirmation that the enemy were about to ford the Carron at Dunipace Steps with the obvious intention of making for the high ground on Falkirk Muir. Immediately Major-General Huske ordered the men to form their lines, a movement which was carried out with such precision that William Corse later admitted, 'I was surpriz'd to see in how little time ye regular troops were form'd.' Hawley was summoned from the comfort of Callander House. He arrived at a gallop, without his hat, and 'the appearance of one who has abruptly left a hospitable table'. Realizing the situation, he frantically ordered the cavalry, followed by the foot and artillery, to make for the high ground before the Highlanders could reach it.

The field upon which Hawley chose to fight was thoroughly unsuitable for regular troops. Falkirk Muir was a hill which rose steeply to a moorland plateau of scrub and heather. Its face was made up of irregular folds and ridges, intersected by a deep ravine running half-way up the hill. To have the wind behind him, Lord George was climbing the hill from the south-west, while Hawley's dragoons hurried up from the opposite direction. Only when the two sides were very near the summit did they come in sight of each other.

At first the Highlanders thought the dragoons were just a scouting party, but changed their minds as more and more cavalry rode into view. For a while the dragoons tried to draw the clans out of line by riding temptingly close. But the Scotsmen knew all about delaying tactics and pressed forward resolutely till they reached the top where Lord George formed them in line, the Macdonalds on the right, the Stewarts of Appin on the left and between them the Camerons, Frasers, MacIntoshes, Mackenzies and Farquharsons. The second line regiments were those of Lord Lewis Gordon and Lord Ogilvy, and the Atholl Brigade. The third line reserve under Prince Charles consisted of the troops whom Lord John Drummond had led in the successful decoy along the Falkirk road, and the French regulars, flanked by the Highland cavalry. Lord George himself had chosen to fight on foot, and he walked up and down the line, armed with broadsword and targe, speaking to the men, desiring them 'to keep their ranks, and not to fire till he gave the order'.

But there was one serious omission. Though Lord George had repeatedly asked Charles to nominate commanders for various parts of the line, this had not yet been done. Even the General had no particular position allocated to him! All he knew was that he was in charge of the front line. He took that to mean the right wing, and so no officer was placed on the left. Throughout the battle this position was never filled, and only some extempore execution on that side by Lord John Drummond saved complete disaster. To add to the confusion, Charles sent Captain O'Sullivan over 'to arrange' the front line. The Irishman proceeded to criticize all Lord George had done. The ground nearby was 'full of old stone walls, & ... some of them just at the heels of the last rank'. Therefore, the line should be moved forward to another wall. Patiently, Lord George agreed to this first suggestion, but when O'Sullivan wanted to have the Atholl Brigade moved up in column to cover the right flank, the General would hear no more. As far as he was concerned, the right flank was adequately protected by a small morass. A disgruntled O'Sullivan rode back to the Prince complaining that the General was being stubborn again.

Charles had no time to intervene. Government dragoons had reached the crest of the hill and were making repeated attempts to either outflank or dislodge the Highland right. Fortunately Lord George was right. The morass which O'Sullivan had scorned effectively prevented the enemy from outflanking the Macdonalds. Try as they might, the horsemen could neither draw their enemy out of line, nor break through them. Most of their comrades on foot were still toiling up the hill and as yet of no help against the resilient Highlanders. The artillery, too, was bogged down along the way, and would remain out of the engagement. To add to the misery of the government soldiers, a storm broke in their faces, arresting their progress and drenching their muskets sufficiently for one out of every four to be of no use when the action began.

The lines formed in haste. According to Corse, his Glasgow Militia marched straight up the hill in fine manner and took up a position to the left and rear of the dragoons, too far out to be of any use to Hawley. The other militia regiment from Argyll placed themselves in an even more useless position at the bottom of the hill on the extreme right of the government line. In between, the regular regiments stood where they found themselves when they could no longer march farther up the hill. Hamilton's was the first to reach the top, so it held the right, followed by Wolfe's regiment and the rest of Hawley's army. The other wing, the government right, was manned by Price's, Batterau's and Ligonier's regiments. There Hawley's forces easily outnumbered the enemy. The Highlanders neglected to balance this discrepancy by moving up reserves, but Hawley could not take advantage of their mistake by moving around and behind them, for he found himself thwarted by the ravine which traversed the hill. His exposed left wing enjoyed no such natural defence. Wolf and Price found themselves outflanked by nearly half the Highland front line regiments. Then at about 4 o'clock, Hawley perversely decided to take the initiative for a change and begin the attack. A nervous Colonel Ligonier pointed out that half the infantry were not yet in line, but Hawley remained adamant. The dragoons were to advance immediately. The Highlanders would crumble under the first cavalry thrusts.

On the other side, Lord George Murray waited patiently. The dragoons 'came on in good order' and only when they were within pistol range did the first Highland volley ring out. At less than ten yards, its effect was devastating. Nearly eighty dragoons fell dead on the spot, and most of their fellows promptly turned tail and fled. Only a small party under Lieutenant-Colonel Whitney continued to press forward. Whitney had been wounded at Prestonpans, and when he recognized his old enemy, Colonel John Roy Stewart, among the Highlanders, he called out a challenge. Stewart greeted him and promised him a warm welcome. A few moments later Whitney fell dead. His fall seemed to inspire his men, who drove through into the midst of Clanranald's regiment. There the Chevalier de Johnstone recorded the fight. 'The most singular and extraordinary combat immediately followed. The

Highlanders, stretched on the ground, thrust their dirks into the bellies of the horses. Some seized the riders by their clothes, dragged them down, and stabbed them with their dirks; several again used their pistols; but few of them had sufficient space to handle their swords.' But the cavalry attack had been repulsed. Though Lord George ordered the Macdonalds to stand and hold their ground, he could not prevent Clanranald's and Glengarry's men from giving chase. In blind panic, Hamilton's and Ligonier's troopers fled through the government ranks, some of them over the unfortunate Glasgow Militia. Others plunged into the infantry left wing, scattering men in all directions, while Cobham's dragoons cantered down the no man's land between the two armies, despite heavy fire directed from the Highland centre and left.

Yet this very victory caused Lord George some disquiet. Those who had pursued the dragoons were beyond recall, and the left and centre regiments had expended most of their fire upon Cobham's dragoons. Reloading was out of the question. The heavy rain and the fact that the Highlanders did not use cartridges made that impossible. There was only one way out of this predicament and Lord George took it. With the cry 'Claymore!', his clansmen threw aside their muskets and charged, sword in hand. In what O'Sullivan called 'perhaps one of the boldest and finest actions, yt any troops of the world cou'd be capable of', the Highlanders swept down upon Hawley's mesmerized infantry.

The government left wing was capable of little resistance. Four of the six front line regiments broke ranks and ran before the first shock hit them. They were soon followed by the second line. So unexpected was their cowardice, that Lord John Drummond exclaimed: 'These men behaved admirably at Fontenoy. Surely this is a feint.'

General Hawley himself appeared to be in a state of

shock. John Home, one of the Edinburgh volunteer company, seeing his commanding officer 'involved in a crowd of horse and foot', asked 'if there were any regiments standing? Where they were? The General made no answer, but pointing to a fold of cattle which was close by, called to him to get in there with his men. The disorder and confusion encreased, and General Hawley rode down the hill.' Only Hawley's second-in-command, Major-General John Huske, retained his calm. He directed the three regiments who had stood their ground to fire into the flanks of the advancing Highland regiments. Slowly, Huske moved up the hill towards the left in a determined bid to halt the rampant clansmen. But the battle was over. Even the Highland second line, consisting of the Atholl Brigade (all the rest had advanced with the front line), had set off after the enemy. Though the field was abandoned to Huske, there could be little question of who the victors had been.

Eventually Huske retired towards Falkirk in good order, protected only by the unnerved remnants of Cobham's dragoons. Stragglers and refugees from the other regiments joined Huske in the town, and there he determined to resist the enemy till the last. Lord George, however, could not challenge Huske's resolve. He had only his own Brigade and the reserve with him, and as it was now growing dark, the first question was whether to quarter the army for the night. His own preference was to gather his forces and chase the English out of Falkirk. If Huske and Hawley were given time 'they might line the houses, and clean their guns, so as to make it impossible' for the Prince to regain possession of Falkirk without another major battle. Charles agreed with his General, but before the Highlanders could be formed for the attack, up rode Lord Kilmarnock to tell the Prince that he had just seen the enemy scurrying down the road to Linlithgow in full retreat.

The Highland army divided into two divisions before it entered Falkirk from opposite ends of the town. Despite this precaution, they found few government stragglers remaining. The Highland entry was marred only by the wounding of Lord John Drummond as he attempted to capture a lone English soldier. But the injury was comparatively minor, and when Charles Edward rode into the town soon afterwards, he 'profited of General Hally's supper wch he wanted very much'. No doubt Charles also relished the 'great many hampers of good wines & liquors & other provisions which were found in the Town'. On a more important level, Lord George could tell him that the enemy had left all their ammunition and several carts. However much Hawley may afterwards have denied it, the evidence suggested that he abandoned Falkirk in a rush, with little thought beyond the immediate preservation of his life.

Yet the battle which preceded his retreat had been far less bloody than that for which Sir John Cope was forced to stand before a Court Martial. As at Prestonpans, the action had lasted not much more than twenty minutes. Highland casualties were light, involving only some sixty dead and about the same number injured. Hawley himself claimed to have extremely light losses – twelve officers and fifty-five men killed, and a total list of two hundred and eighty 'killed, wounded and missing'. The true figure must have been somewhat heavier, though probably nowhere near Lord Elcho's ridiculous estimate of thirty officers and between five and six hundred men killed.

About four hundred prisoners were also taken by the Scots, most of them on the day after the battle while they skulked in the villages around Falkirk. The greater part were released on parole, including two of Hawley's hangmen. The one Scotsman to be taken prisoner by the English was less fortunate. He was Macdonnell of Tiendrish, a major in Keppoch's regiment, and the man responsible for Charles' first victory in Britain at High Bridge on 16 August 1745. Tiendrish had become separated from his regiment when in the half light he came upon a group of men from Barrel's regiment whom he mistook for Lord John Drummond's reserve. He rushed up to the cowering government soldiers and ordered them to pursue their comrades. Too late he realized his mistake. As soon as Barrel's men discovered that the Major was alone, their presence of mind returned, and they arrested him. Tiendrish was brought before Major-General Huske when his captors returned to camp. There he insisted that he was a Campbell Militiaman, whereupon Huske ordered him to be shot as a spy. Only the intervention of Captain Lord Robert Kerr saved Tiendrish's life, but not for long. He was hanged at Carlisle later in the year.

Hawley's first reactions to the battle of Falkirk were rage and vexation. He is said to have broken his sword against the market cross as he retreated through the town. From Linlithgow he wrote to the Duke of Cumberland in a more reflective vein. 'Sir, My heart is broke. I can't say We are quite beat today, But our Left is beat, and Their Left is beat. We had enough to beat them for we had Two Thousand Men more than They. But suche scandalous Cowardice I never saw before.' The next morning, a visitor noted that the General 'looked most wretchedly; even worse than Cope did a few hours after his scuffle'. By the time he reached Edinburgh on 18 January, Hawley was again himself. Ten days after his return to the city, he wrote to the Duke of Newcastle to tell him that 'thirty-two of the foot (are) to be shot for cowardice'. Defeat, it seems, sharpened the General's appetite for brutality.

Success at Falkirk reinvigorated Charles Edward. Unlike Lord George the Prince was not dismayed because a total victory had not been achieved. He refused to countenance his General's repeated recriminations concerning the lack of a commander on the Highland left wing. If Lord George wanted someone to blame, then Charles suggested he should chide himself for fighting on foot when a swift pursuit on horseback might well have destroyed Hawley's army for good and all. As to future plans, Charles found his army divided. Lord George wanted to make for the safety of the Highlands, but others talked of a second march on London. Strangely, very few suggested following Hawley's demoralized army to Edinburgh, and eventually it was decided to concentrate again upon the siege of Stirling Castle.

On 19 January Prince Charles ordered the garrison at Stirling to surrender. They refused, and their commander, Major-General Blakeney, told the Prince 'That he had always been looked upon as a man of honour, and that the rebels should find that he would die so.' Charles was incensed. He urged 'Mr Admirable' to greater efforts so that the Castle walls could be knocked down forthwith. Secure within his fortress, Blakeney must have smiled. Not once did he attempt to sabotage the Prince's gun emplacement. He knew that the idiotic Mirabelle was wasting precious energy. The longer the Highland army was detained in futile sieges, the more time Blakeney's superiors would have to catch the rebels before they could retreat into the Highlands. At last, on 29 January, Mirabelle was ready to begin his cannonade. He promised a gullible Prince that the Castle would fall in fewer than eighteen hours. The actual course of events witnessed by the Chevalier de Johnstone was somewhat different.

M. Mirabelle, with a childish impatience to witness the effects of his battery unmarked it ... and immediately began a brisk fire ... but it was of short duration and produced very little effect on the batteries of the Castle, which being more ele-

vated than ours, the enemy could see even the
buckles on the shoes of our artillerymen. As their
fire commanded ours, our guns were immediately
dismantled, and in less than half an hour we were
obliged to abandon our battery altogether ...

With that, the siege of Stirling effectively ended.

During the last week of January Charles had been
suffering from influenza, albeit in the comfort of Bannockburn House under the gentle ministrations of
Clementina Walkinshaw. Although he must have suspected that Mirabelle's attempt to batter the Castle at
Stirling was doomed, the Prince showed few signs of
misgiving. Fortified with lavish doses of cinnamon, he
quickly recovered from his illness. Whatever news of
his progress he had sent to friends abroad must have
been almost entirely optimistic. From Nantes, Abbé
James Butler wrote to Secretary Edgar at Rome in
January:

> We have all the expectations possible of our dear
> Prince's conquest in England this year, and have
> so many flying letters of late that we cannot tell
> what to think of them. Some doe Assure us that the
> Prince had bet Ligonier and routed all his army;
> and that he took the Duc of Cumberland and
> remitted him to the Towne of Liverpoole ...

Butler's information was simply untrue, and one can
only conclude that he read too much into the excited
despatches which arrived from Scotland. The Duke of
Cumberland was not held prisoner in Liverpool. On
30 January he had entered Edinburgh to take command of government troops in Scotland, leaving a perplexed Charles wondering how to obviate the threat
posed by this most esteemed Hanoverian General.

Cumberland's appointment was announced on 25
January, and ever after that day Charles Edward

found himself under increasing pressure to act determinedly, one way or the other. Either the Highland army must retreat across the Forth to the safety of its own ground; or, the government force stationed at Edinburgh must be destroyed before Cumberland took control. Charles preferred the latter course. His General and chiefs thought otherwise.

In my opinion a descent on Edinburgh while Cumberland and Hawley were there would have stood a fair chance of success. The hilly, indeed near mountainous nature of the ground by and in Edinburgh would have suited the Highland troops, and if the Scottish army had approached stealthily and unperceived (a movement in which they were expert) they could have surprised and obliterated the occupying forces.

After that, the speculation about Charles increases. He had had his bellyful of English lukewarmness in his Cause on his march to Derby and back again to cross the Border. Unless he had been presented with the extremely unlikely event of a spontaneous uprising in his favour in England, he would surely have remained in Scotland. That is where the family should have stayed at the Union of Crowns, 'the source of all our woes' as that patriotic Scot, Sir John Clerk of Penicuik, had well put it.

A decision was reached on the morning of 29 January at a council meeting in Falkirk between Lord George Murray and the chiefs. The clans wanted to withdraw to the Highlands immediately, and Lord George was appointed to communicate their desires to the Prince. Murray made his point in the form of an address, evidence of which is provided by the accounts of Maxwell of Kirkconnel and Hay of Restalrig.* Owing to widespread desertion among the Highlanders, and the increasing might of the government army, the

* *Narrative of the Prince of Wales' Expedition to Scotland*: Maitland Club Publication, 1840.

chiefs felt that their army was in no fit state to meet the enemy. Furthermore, if His Royal Highness 'should risque a Battle and Stirling Castle be not in your hands', the clans foresaw nothing but disaster and destruction. Rather than chance his hand against Cumberland, Charles was advised to spend the winter based in the Highlands, where complete dominance would be won with the eventual reduction of all government forts in the area. By springtime the Prince could have an army of ten thousand men, plus the inevitable French regulars. Then he could think again of a descent through England. Lest Charles think ill of their motives and devotion, the chiefs added a postscript:

> We whose names are hereunto subscribed do hereby solemnly and in the Presence of God declare that tho' for reasons which seem to us of the greatest weight, we have advised His Royal Highness to retire beyond the Forth, we are still firmly resolved to stand by him and the Glorious Cause we have espoused to the utmost of our lives and fortunes.*

This depressing and uncharacteristic document was carefully sealed and sent by a special messenger with due caution to the Prince at Bannockburn House where he was still lodging with Sir Hugh Paterson. Lord George Murray who put the 'Memorial' into the messenger's hands gave him explicit instructions and a letter to Hay of Restalrig, who at this time was acting as the Prince's secretary. In the letter to Hay, Lord George entreated him to place the document before the Prince without a moment's delay; he added: 'We are sensible that it will be very unpleasant, but in the

* *Itinerary of Prince Charles Edward Stuart's Wanderings* by Walter Biggar Blaikie: Appendix, p. 76; Edinburgh University Press, 1897.

name of God what can we do?' Hay of Restalrig took the packet, read the instructions written to him, but would not allow the Memorial to be put at once before the Prince, who was still asleep.

At length, after some uneasy waiting and listening the messenger and Hay heard sounds of stirring from the Prince's room. Hay then went in and, without a word, handed the sealed Memorial to the Prince. It took a moment or two for the newly-awakened Charles to master the contents of this momentous document; when at last he did he seemed to lose all control of himself. 'Good God! Have I lived to see this?', he said, and started so violently that he struck his head against the wall of the bedroom.*

The Prince was convinced that retreat 'would result in nothing but ruin and destruction', and would only raise the morale of the enemy. His Highland army would lose all the advantages so recently won, besides most of its heavy artillery. In addition, retreat would end hopes of receiving substantial aid from France. But having made these objections, Charles realized that they carried little weight with his chiefs. He was helpless. There was nothing he could do except record his disagreement on paper.

Predictably, the Prince blamed Lord George Murray for the truculence encountered among the clans. He guessed that desertion was no higher than it had been all during the campaign, and he saw no reason why a confrontation with Cumberland should be delayed until the following spring. What Charles failed to appreciate was that his officers were inventing excuses to conceal qualms regarding the reliability of their kinsmen. The days of idleness which accompanied the

* The incident is described in Home's *History of the Rebellion in the Year 1745*. Home, the minister-playwright, was on the Whig side, but took great care to be accurate. He verified his sources, especially in the appendices from which this is taken. He must have had it verbatim from Hay or the special messenger.

siege of Stirling had eroded discipline among the men and reduced the confidence of their officers. According to contemporary accounts, the Highlanders 'sauntered about all the villages in the neighbourhood of their quarters', paying scant regard to strategic deployment in hostile country. Their behaviour was careless. They were tiring of regimented life. Lord George and the chiefs secretly felt that the security of the entire army, and of the Prince himself, was at risk. The pride of centuries prevented them from communicating their apprehensions to Charles, but their reasoning was clear. If the men were made to move, they would remain alert. On the first day of February the Highland army began the short march which was intended to return the clans to the safety of their glens.

## 10: The Retreat from Stirling and Disaster at Culloden

The exchanges between Charles and his chiefs prior to and during the retreat from Stirling mark the beginnings of an Irish–Scottish rift that was to culminate in disaster a few weeks later. During the arguments at the end of January, the Prince employed Sir Thomas Sheridan to represent his own views against those of Lord George Murray and other trusted Scottish leaders. Lord George resented Sheridan's intervention in affairs of which he had little experience. He also disliked the arbitrary manner in which the courtier treated the Highlanders and he reminded the Prince: 'It is to be considered that this army is an Army of Volunteers, and not Mercenarys, many of them being resolved not to continue in the Army, were affairs once settled.' To this cautionary hint Charles reacted angrily. 'When I came to Scotland I knew well enough what I was to expect from my Enemies, but I little foresaw what I meet with from my Friends.' The Prince reserved the right to invest his authority in whomsoever he chose. At least his friends knew better than to challenge his authority, and Charles warned Lord George, 'my Authority may be taken from me by Violence, but I shall never resign it like an Idiot'.

The root of the difference between Charles and his Highland officers was strategic rather than personal, though the matter soon became submerged under a deluge of bitter recrimination. For Charles and the Irish, their best hope lay in maintaining a vigorous presence at the heart of the enemy. Action like that would be widely publicized even if militarily unsuccessful. Victory would be political. French and Spanish regulars would land and the Prince could enter London. Lord George and the chiefs understood the situation differently. Experience taught them that all they could rely upon was the clansman's broadsword. Thus, preservation of Highland resources was crucial. Weeks before the fatal decision to fight at Culloden, Charles had made up his mind that there would be no complete retreat into the Highland fastnesses. At Drummossie Moor, he accepted the advice of O'Sullivan and Sheridan and rejected that of Lord George. The result of the battle vindicated the Scots general, but it cannot be seen as an outright condemnation of the Prince. It is well to remember that ever since the retreat from Derby, overall strategy had been contrary to his wishes. At Drummossie Moor he found himself up against the wall, and by no means in the position he himself had advocated. In ordering Lord George to face Cumberland, he did not act along his own intuitive lines, for he could not, placed as he was in a situation novel to his temper. He turned to his Irish friends and acted on their advice against the Scots who had this far pushed him against his wishes.

In one respect, Charles was at one with his clansmen where their officers were not. The Highland army was not made for retreat, they may have gone back from Derby in England with some mixed feelings, but at least they were getting out of what was to them a foreign country, and they could do it with some semblance of order. But retreating in Scotland itself was a much more distasteful and therefore less easily organized business. A general rendezvous of the army was ordered at St Ninians on 1 February. There, a rearguard was to be selected and left under Lord George Murray. But on the morning, before daybreak, the Highlanders began streaming westwards towards the Fords of Frew. 'Never was their a retreat resembled so much a flight, for their was no where 1000 men together, and the whole army passed the river in Small Bodies and in Great Confusion . . .'

As he had been ordered, Lord George proceeded

that same morning to St Ninians, but while still several miles away from the village, he was startled by a loud explosion. He arrived at his rendezvous to find not a man in sight, and the village church blown up. The church had been used by the Highlanders as an ammunition store, and while gunpowder was being removed, some of it was accidentally exploded, leaving only the church tower standing.

The Highland army quartered for the night at Doune and Dunblane, and the next day the major part, consisting of the clan regiments, marched for Crieff, while the remainder headed for Perth. Charles stayed with the clans until he reached Crieff, and there he held a general review. Feeling ran high at a council of war held that night. '... Never had there been such heats and animosities as at this meeting...' Lord George Murray demanded the name of the man who had advised the hasty and ill-ordered retreat from Stirling. 'It was,' he said, 'worth the Government at London's while to have given a hundred thousand pounds to anyone who would have given such advice and got it followed.' Charles refused to join in this exhibition of 'high feeling' and took the responsibility for the retreat on his own shoulders. But inevitably an acrimonious discussion ensued as to the route that the army should take to Inverness – obvious point for the regrouping of the retreating forces when they had made their way north. The Chiefs wanted to take the rough-going direct route through the *massif* of the Central Highlands – a formidable undertaking. Charles more prudently suggested the east coast road via Aberdeen.

They took a vote which showed that the large majority favoured the Central Highland way. The wranglings which had now become an endemic complaint in the Jacobite command ever since their return to Scotland inevitably broke out. Murray of Broughton who, with the gentle Lochiel, was all for pouring oil on troubled waters, achieved a compromise by getting hold of the Prince's old tutor Sir Thomas Sheridan. Sir Thomas managed this to the extent of persuading Charles that his Highlanders needed his presence on their march and eventually it was decided that the Lowland regiments and what French there were should take the east coast road under the command of Lord George, while the Prince led the clans over the mountains. On 4 February the two divisions took their separate ways. That same day the Duke of Cumberland left Stirling with an army of twenty thousand men. A 'Highland Chace' had begun.

The two Highland armies reunited at Inverness on 21 February. The retreat had been successful, but not without incident. Five days before entering the Highland capital, Charles was entertained at Moy Hall by Lady Anne MacIntosh. He was alone, except for a small bodyguard, for he knew Cumberland to be taking the seaboard route northwards and he expected no trouble from ill-organized Campbell Militia. Somehow, news of Charles' solitary visit reached Lord Loudon, one of the Campbell commanders based at Inverness, who hatched a plan to capture the Prince at Moy.

Campbell security was no better than that of Charles Stuart and unfortunately for Loudon, the Dowager Lady of Inverness, also in Inverness at the time, came to hear of his intention. She immediately despatched a hasty warning to her daughter at Moy. The message was carried with extraordinary speed by a fifteen-year-old lad named Lauchlan, who warned Lady Anne of the danger to the Prince's life. Yet Lady Anne was reluctant to wake an exhausted Charles and alarm him lest the story prove exaggerated. Instead she turned to Donald Fraser, a local blacksmith, and ordered him to take two servants and stand watch beyond the line of Charles' own sentries.

Fraser and his companions saw nothing in the vicinity of Moy, but as they advanced beyond the hamlet, they discovered Loudon's men stealing through the shadows. There was no time to warn Charles, and in the situation, Fraser acted with great presence of mind. He ordered his comrades to spread out until the three men formed a line of regiment width. Then he fired his musket straight into the heart of the Campbells, killing one of them immediately, and halting the others in their tracks. Seizing the advantage, Fraser called out loudly to his companions, ordering them to 'Advance, advance, my lads, advance.' The Campbells feared that they had stumbled upon the main Highland force, for the blacksmith proceeded to name individual Highland regiments as his friends ran back and forth, imitating the noises of a large army. That was too much for Loudon's men. They turned and ran with Fraser in hot pursuit, bellowing confidently, 'Advance, advance, my lads, advance, I think we have the dogs now.' Three of his followers had won yet another victory for the Prince, even while he was asleep!

The way was now open for the Prince to Inverness, the historic county town of the largest shire not only on the mainland of Scotland but containing within it more Hebridean isles than any other. Loudon, the recreant Macleod of Dunvegan and the Lord President Forbes, retired across the ferry into Cromarty. Forbes and Macleod took refuge in Skye and awaited the arrival of Cumberland. This, however, was to be delayed; and the Prince settled into Inverness where he was warmly welcomed, soon to be joined by Lord George.

The ancient town of Inverness has always been of importance in Scotland. Situated near the mouth of the river Ness and at the north-east end of the long clean-cut divide of Scotland known as the 'Great Glen' which splits Scotland from the North Sea to the Atlantic, its position alone gives it status; like Edinburgh it has an adjacent port still operating, but in the eighteenth century it was much used for connection with the continent of Europe.

Today it is trim, clean, neat and prosperous. When Charles entered it it was neither trim, neat, nor particularly clean (another similarity between it and the Edinburgh of the Old Town). But it was fairly prosperous and had a 'style' about it. It had and has some agreeable half-country, half-suburban seats of the gentry clustered round it. It was the capital city of the north of Scotland, and still is. Its religion was officially that of the Presbyterian Church of Scotland, but there must have been Episcopalian meeting places if not churches; and the Catholic Mass was certainly celebrated, though only privately.

Inverness even more than Perth was a strongly Jacobite city, and its politics in this matter were widely considered worthy of respect. Inverness on the north side of the Grampian *massif* was too far away for government agents to be active there; only a few nearby notabilities such as Lord President Forbes thought it might be worth while keeping in with the Elector while professing a strong love for the Highlanders.

'Inverness Castle', known as Fort George (not to be confused with the present military establishment of Fort George on the Moray Firth to the east of Inverness), held out as a Hanoverian stronghold. Though the Castle had been established by Wade during his road-building 'pacification' of the Highlands, it easily surrendered and upon its evacuation Charles blew it up.

Here the present writer can from a knowledge of his own family history add a few details. The Prince certainly visited Kingsmills and its policies* just southeast of Inverness town where my great-great-great-grandfather lived. Besides being the laird of Kingsmills he owned a vessel at the port near Inverness in

* The Scottish word for the property cultivated or uncultivated immediately surrounding a small or moderate 'landed estate' and house. Kingsmills was sold between the last two wars and is now an hotel.

the Moray Firth called *The Pledger*. There is a strong tradition in our family that *The Pledger* was used by the Prince for communicating with France. Whatever services we rendered the Prince were certainly recognized by him, for he presented my forebears with a handsome silver-headed walking cane, now alas lost.

The stay at Inverness was punctuated by events more significant than an occasional Regent's ball. In the Highlands away from Inverness, in Cromarty and farther south, there was a good deal of Jacobite activity in reducing, sometimes successfully, government strongholds such as Fort Augustus and Fort William. Lord George Murray conducted these operations with his usual military skill. He was successful at Fort Augustus but not so at Fort William. He moved into his own country of Atholl with dazzling success. But he was pressed for time and realizing that the Prince was only enforcedly wintering at Inverness, knew that he had to be back again for the early spring to take part in the certain and imminent encounter with Cumberland and Hawley.

The Hanoverian generals were in no hurry to reach Inverness. Cumberland realized that he had no hope of catching Lord George, so he proceeded at a leisurely pace to Aberdeen. His most pressing task was to raise the morale of his troops. Thus far they had known only ignominy against the rebels. As soon as the government army entered Aberdeen, a detachment was despatched to seize a cache of Spanish arms and ammunition which the enemy had stored in Corgarff Castle. This raid right into the heart of Jacobite country was successful, and Cumberland rewarded himself and his men with illicit plunder, despite the many stern edicts against looting which the Duke penned at regular intervals. By the middle of March the government army was truly ready to begin operations against Prince Charles.

The Duke of Cumberland was a thorough administrator rather than a brilliant general, but he made few errors. He knew that the rebels had to be crushed, and he knew the means by which that end could be reached. After a raid by a party of Highlanders on Campbell barracks at Kynachan, Captain John Macpherson of Strathmashie recalled an order 'subscribed (if I well remember) by General or Colonel Campbell, setting forth that it was the Duke of C......d's peremptory orders if they could meet any party of the rebels whom they could at all expect to overcome, to engage them and give them noe quarter...' Whether Cumberland actually issued such an order does not really matter. His men appear to have followed such instructions, and the Duke did precious little to stop them.

On 12 April Cumberland reached the Spey. Here the Duke expected the enemy to dispute his crossing, but he was unaccountably allowed to ford the river in three places without the least resistance from the Duke of Perth's 'Army of the Spey'. The Spey crossing was the Rubicon of Cumberland's campaign; Lord George recognized this and subsequently said: 'Had the rest of our army been come up we were all to have march'd there,' implying that the Prince had intended to meet Cumberland's advance but had failed either through the absence of his best troops or because he was beginning to lose his initiative in attack.

For Charles Edward the consequences of retreat had been more severe than they had been for his men. At Inverness the Prince paid scant attention to military affairs. Partly this was because of illness, but apathy and foreboding also played their part. When Murray of Broughton became ill, the handling of Charles' affairs passed almost entirely to his Irish favourites. They issued orders without consulting their master and against the better advice of his Scottish servants. Cumberland's undisputed crossing of the Spey was the direct result of an unreal attitude towards logistics possessed by the Prince's advisers. Perth and the 'Army of the Spey' were in no position to offer resistance. The war chest was empty, the men without pay; clothing and food were scarce, supplies haphazard. Moreover, every effort made by the chiefs and Scottish nobles to organize their army was liable to be countermanded. With the command split, it was no wonder that the rank and file ignored orders, refused watch duties and generally deteriorated into a rabble.

Only when Cumberland unexpectedly appeared before Nairn on the evening of 14 April did the Highland army pull itself together. Perth had barely enough time to vacate the town and was forced to leave behind most of the Prince's grain supplies. That evening the Prince dined at Culloden House, the home of Lord President Forbes. He was joined there by Lord George and the other Scottish leaders. Although the General had recently surveyed the ground between the two armies, and come to the conclusion that the best defensive position lay near Dalcross Castle, Charles preferred to listen to the wisdom of Captain O'Sullivan, who had himself conducted a survey which showed a strip of open moorland a mile to the south-east of Culloden House to be eminently suitable for any battle with Cumberland. At Culloden House on the evening of 14 April the chiefs pressed Charles to reconsider his choice of ground, but to no avail. The next morning at dawn, the Highland army drew up on the field which O'Sullivan had chosen, 'a plain moor where regular troops had ... full use of their cannon so as to annoy the Highlanders prodigiously before they could possibly make an attack'.

All day long the Highland army stood in line of battle. While the men waited for food and relief, their leaders reopened the vexed debate about positions in the line. The previous night Lord George insisted that he should hold the right with his Athollmen. Too often in the past he had been accused of shielding them from danger, and now he was resolved to rescue their reputations from further abuse. Rather than in-flame the argument over the battle site Charles agreed to the General's request. But the Prince's tact did not suit the Macdonalds. A deputation consisting of Clanranald, Keppoch and Lochgarry pressed Charles to 'give us our former right'. Charles bravely refused to waver and the Macdonalds were left smarting under imaginary insults.

Only late in the afternoon were the men dismissed. They had lasted the day upon a meagre ration of a biscuit apiece, and now they split up and set off in search of food. Within half an hour, the army was virtually beyond recall. John Hay, Charles' replacement secretary during Murray's illness, had proven himself totally unable to cope with the usual problems of supply. The commissariat had broken down completely and with it went the order of an army whose soldiers were dangerously near their homes. Many clansmen returned to their native glens for food and rest during the weeks spent near Inverness, but their return was hopefully expected within the next few days. The fiasco of the army dispersal at Culloden was part of the process which had already seriously depleted Charles' forces. Most of the men went to Inverness where they knew that ten days' provisions had been left behind for want of transport horses to take them to the vicinity of Culloden. Some of the clansmen believed with Lord George that the lack of sufficient provision had been contrived out of the mistaken belief 'that the Highlanders would not fight except they were obliged to do it for want of provisions'.

Lord George laid all the blame squarely at the feet of Charles' Irish friends, who he was convinced 'dreaded a summer campaign in the mountains', and wanted to reach a conclusion with Cumberland as soon as possible, win or lose. Charles Edward also wished to reach a conclusion, but not for the same reasons. He was impatient with endless manoeuvring and petty skirmishes. He wanted a decision, yet he held no fear of defeat. Indeed, the notion of defeat appears rarely to have entered the Prince's head. His General, on the other hand, was preoccupied with avoiding defeat and rarely imagined outright victory over Cumberland. Lord George wanted to fight a long war of attrition against the Hanoverian, gradually wearing him down in strength and confidence, striking only when the conditions favoured the Highlanders clearly and never committing his whole army in any one sweep. That no doubt was the wiser policy. It could never be Charles Edward's method.

The Prince had another scheme up his sleeve. He knew that 15 April was the Duke of Cumberland's birthday, and reports had reached Culloden confirming celebrations among the government army at Nairn. Charles and O'Sullivan solicited individual chieftains to consider the merits of a surprise dawn attack upon Cumberland's camp at Balblair. Most of them refused even to consider the proposal until reinforcements arrived. Lord George only learned of the scheme upon his return, and he expressed grave doubts regarding its efficacy and wisdom. Yet he also disliked the idea of fighting upon so open a field as Drummossie Moor, and when Keppoch arrived with reinforcements, Lord George endorsed the Prince's plan.

It was essential that the march should be kept as secret as possible. In order to mislead the enemy, fires were lit on the moor and small patrols combed the roads, giving the impression that the entire Highland force was encamped for the night. Men whose county it was were appointed to guide the columns through the dark to Nairn and it was resolved that the attack would be launched before 2 o'clock in the morning. Surprise was all that could guarantee success against Cumberland's strength. The odds were stacked against the Highlanders, and to make matters worse, over a third of the Scots army had not returned from foraging. Officers set off to round up the hungry men, but few were successful. Less than four and a half thousand clansmen were finally available for the march against an army which O'Sullivan estimated at some 18,000 strong.

The attack started off in good style. It was misty, dark and moonless; everything including the drunkenness of the foe augured a successful surprise. Lord George led the van at a spanking pace, and he soon outdistanced the clansmen in the rear. Charles, as at Prestonpans, was in the middle of the column and had to send a message forward asking his General to halt.

The accumulated delay, rounding up the army, waiting for reinforcements, and now the sloth of the rear of the column, convinced Lord George that the Highlanders would not reach Nairn before daybreak. There would be no surprise, the men would be tired and Cumberland would destroy them. Lord George ordered his men to turn back. His column met the middle and rear marching the other way, and for a time confusion reigned. Lord George was for retreat; then a message from O'Sullivan arrived to say that the Prince was anxious to attack, even if dawn broke. A few Life Guards who had marched with the van strongly supported the Prince's views, but the General had to be obeyed. They retreated. On the way back they encountered Charles who asked: 'Where the devil are all the men going?' On being informed that they were retreating by Lord George's orders the Prince after a conference with the Duke of Perth said 'There's no hope for it my lads, march back to Culloden House.' He had given in.

Opinions still differ as to the necessity for this retreat only four miles away from the objective. It would be evasive for the present writer to refrain from stating what he believes. All are agreed that the long night march was a disaster; it exhausted the men and largely contributed to their loss of the Battle of Culloden on the next day. Would it necessarily have been as great a disaster to go on and surprise the enemy in the twilight of dawn? I think not. The worst that could have happened would have been a complete defeat. The men would have been killed on the spot and none escaped into the hills. At best the Highland Jacobites not yet exhausted might have given Cumberland a hard drubbing and given themselves time for regrouping and planning. If the victory at Falkirk over the allegedly unbeatable Hawley had scared the London Government more than Prestonpans, a severe beating of Cumberland might have thrown them into a state of indecision verging on despair.

At about 6 o'clock on the morning of 16 April, the main body of Charles' army returned to Culloden. According to Lord Elcho, 'Everybody seemed to think of nothing but sleep.' The officers entered Culloden House and threw themselves on beds, floors, even tables in order to snatch some rest. The Prince was the last to return. On the way back he became aware of growing discontent among his men. They were hungry enough to desert. About three thousand had already gone in search of food, and lest he be left with no army, Charles decided to go on to Inverness in order to have the food stored there despatched to Culloden. But before he had gone more than three miles, he was halted by an anxious Duke of Perth who warned him that any absence from his army would be construed as abandonment. Wisely, Charles returned to Culloden after first ordering Fitzjames' Horse to fetch food from Inverness. By the time the Prince reached the house, he was very tired and irritable, besides being a little worried by the sullenness of his men.

The first person Charles Edward encountered when he entered Culloden House was Lord George Murray. The General was tired too, and certainly in no mood to contend with Charles' rancour over the abortive night march. If the Chevalier de Johnstone is to be believed,

Charles, 'enraged against Lord George Murray, publickly declared, that no one in future should command his army but himself'. Lord George retired rather than argue, although O'Sullivan maliciously accused the General of laying the blame for the retreat upon Lochiel. Charles had already decided that the General was to blame for all his misfortunes. He is even said to have told some Irish officers 'to watch Lord George's motions, particularly in case of a battle, and they promised the Prince to shoot him if they could find he intended to betray him'. Whether Charles actually believed Lord George to be a traitor is doubtful. At the time of the retreat from Nairn, the Prince was merely exasperated and at the limit of his patience. However, by the next year, this unjust suspicion again reared its ugly head when Lord George decided to visit Charles' father in Rome. From Paris, the Prince wrote hastily to James warning him that: 'It would be of the most dangerous consequences iff such Devill was not secured immediately in sum Castle wher he might be at his ease but without being able to escape, or have ye Liberty of Pen or Papers.' By then Charles had contracted acute paranoia, and was convinced that Murray of Broughton and Lord George had been 'in a click' against him since the beginning of the invasion.

On the morning of 16 April 1746 Charles made no such accusation. He was determined to fight the Duke of Cumberland that day, partly because he wanted to settle the matter quickly, but also to spite Lord George and the other commanders who had continually challenged his plans and desires. It was an unpopular decision with all except Charles' most sycophantic servants. In a private letter written to the French King, the Marquis d'Eguilles told of a private interview which he held with the Prince that morning: 'In vain I represented to him that he was still without half his army; that the greater part of those who had returned had no longer their targets; that they were all worn out with fatigue ... and for two days many of them had not eaten at all for want of bread.' D'Eguilles pleaded with the Prince to retire beyond the river or into Inverness. That way the battle with Cumberland could be postponed for a day, allowing the Highland army time to recuperate. But Charles, proud and haughty as he was, could not bring himself to decline battle even for a single day.

When Lochiel and Keppoch joined the voices against him, the Prince lost his temper completely. 'God damn it!' he screamed at the top of his voice, 'Are my orders still disobeyed?' The chiefs would have remained stubbornly aloof but for the idle sneer of Walter Stapleton, commander of the Irish Picquets, who turned to Charles and declared that, 'The Scots are always good troops till things come to a crisis.' That was too much for the Highlanders. There was only one answer for it – they would demonstrate their valour in spite of their better judgement. Charles would have his fight that day.

The army was not given much time to rest before the fight. The Duke of Cumberland had heard of their night march and intended to give them no opportunity to recover. At Culloden House the Prince was roused from his bed before he could enjoy an hour's sleep. Cumberland's cavalry were only four miles distant and closing rapidly. On the way downstairs, Charles was told that a breakfast of roast lamb and chicken had been prepared. But he refused to eat when he knew that his unfortunate soldiers could not have had the opportunity to kill and prepare the cattle which had been rounded up from the surrounding country during the morning. He turned angrily upon his dumbfounded steward to ask. 'Would you have me sit down to dinner when my enemy is so near me? Eat! I can neither eat nor rest while my poor people are starving.'

The Prince's soldiers had neither time to eat, nor

dally over positions in line of battle. The orders of the previous two days had to stand. The Duke of Perth would command the left wing, Lord George Murray the right and Lord John Drummond would take the centre. 'The men were mustered with the aid of pipes, drums and the occasional boot. Officers ran about on all sides to rouse them ... some were quite exhausted and not able to crawl, and others asleep in coverts that had not been beat up.' Many who had slipped off to the village to find food and shelter were surprised in their beds and killed within the hour by Cumberland's marauding troopers. Although on paper, Charles led some nine thousand men, only about seven thousand were in the vicinity of Culloden. When the alarm was raised, fewer than one thousand men were ready to take the field.

So great was the hurry that Charles did not even take time to view the moor upon which his men were forming. His haste proved fatal, for nobody noticed the boggy nature of the ground over which the High-landers would be forced to travel in a charge. Both the Prince and O'Sullivan apparently thought Cumber-land to be far nearer than he actually was. The Irish-man therefore refused to alter the order of battle, or to place the Camerons on the right, whose turn it was to occupy that position of honour. When the battle was over, Lord George passed judgement upon O'Sulli-van's fitness for command. He 'had forty-eight hours to display his skill, and did it accordingly'. He had chosen a battlefield which Cumberland's experienced artilleryman, Brevet Colonel William Belford, would have been pleased to select himself. He had not recon-noitred the ground upon which he had rushed his men in the morning. He had failed to appreciate the poli-tical delicacy with which positioning in the line had to be treated. When the battle began, all these points were driven home in blood within half an hour.

On the other side, the Duke of Cumberland was

'mightily pleased' with the belated birthday present Charles and O'Sullivan were handing him. He had treated his soldiers to a feast of brandy and cheese the previous evening. All nine thousand of them were fed and fit. One clear talent Cumberland possessed; he could inspire confidence. The English army was convinced, with their leader, that 'we have but one march more and all our labour will be at an end'. They went to bed at 10 p.m., with their arms stacked at the ready, and their horses saddled. At 5 o'clock the next morning Cumberland led his soldiers out of Balblair in hot pursuit of their erstwhile attackers. The whole army had taken less than two minutes to draw up in regimental order following the first alarm, and within three-quarters of an hour the host was on the move. In gratitude for their superb manoeuvring and discipline, Cumberland ordered an extra ration of bread and brandy to be distributed to each of his fifteen infantry regiments and cavalry.

So easy was Cumberland's progress that he suspected an ambush somewhere along the road. He could not understand why his previously canny enemy neglected to send out scouts, and it took several local sympathizers and a militia patrol to convince the Duke that the Highland army were not in hiding among the dark heather. Eventually, 'we discovered the rebels formed in a moor'. In ten minutes Cumberland's troops moved from column formation to line of battle and waited for the expected Highland charge. The front line was commanded by the Earl of Albemarle and consisted of the Royal Scots, Cholmondeley's, Price's, the Royal Scots Fusiliers, Munro's and Barrell's regiments, in that order from the right. Major-General John Huske was in charge of the second line. Under him, he had Howard's, Fleming's, Conway's, Bligh's, Semphill's and Wolfe's. Behind Huske, bringing up the rear under Brigadier-General John Mordaunt, were Pulteney's, Battereau's and Blakeney's regiments. In each of the five spaces between the battalions of the front line, Cumberland ordered Colonel Belford to mount two three-pounder guns – ten pieces which all but won the battle for the Hanoverian Duke by themselves.

Cumberland's royal opponent sat determinedly on the other side of the moor astride a grey gelding at the head of the clan Cameron. He wore a cockaded bonnet upon his head and a light broadsword at his side. On his back hung a ruffled tartan jacket and buff waistcoat. Turning to his men, Charles Edward cried in his lisping Italian voice, 'Go on my lads. The day will be ours!' Those of the clans who possessed enough energy raised their bonnets in a hoarse cheer. As the Prince had dictated two days before, the Highlanders were all in kilts, burning scarlet or faded green, with their clan badge freshly placed in their caps alongside the white Stuart cockade. Lord George Murray commanded the right wing of their first line, comprising Athollmen, Camerons and Stewarts of Appin. Lord John Drummond held the centre, consisting of Frasers, Clan Chattan, including Lady Anne MacIntosh's regiment, and several mixed clan units among whom were John Roy Stewart's Edinburgh regiment. The left wing was composed chiefly of Macdonalds, and was commanded by the Duke of Perth. This side of the Highland line was more than eight hundred yards from the enemy formations, but Lord George's right wing was approximately half that distance from Albemarle's line. Though it was longer than Cumberland's the Highland front line boasted less than half the troop content! On and on it stretched for more than a thousand yards, an oblique line which refused to be altered despite shouts of 'Close Up' from worried captains. Behind the front was an unhappy second line of unhorsed cavalry and Lowlanders.

The clans were ready. Their kilts were pulled high between their thighs and their plaids were thrown free. Despite the challenge of the pipes and the occasional roar, the Highlanders could elicit no response from their enemy save the beat of battalion drums. For two hours the two armies waited for a sign of movement. Cumberland expected a sudden charge, the swish of steel which had scattered armies at Prestonpans and Falkirk. Slowly the Duke rode along his lines, coaxing, pleading, threatening and advising. He reminded his men of the special tactic he had developed for use against the charge should volley firing prove ineffective. Each man must rely for protection on his left-hand neighbour. The bayonet thrust must be made to the right, under the Highland shield of the attacker to the right. Charles had no similar advice for his soldiers. Cumberland's troops cheered him with the cry, 'Flanders! Flanders! We'll follow you!' One clansman slipped into the government lines, pretending to be a deserter. Mistakenly, he took the elaborately uniformed Lord Bury to be Cumberland himself. Wrenching a musket from the nearest soldier, he fired at Bury and missed, whereupon he was shot dead by a trooper named Newman from Semphill's. The first victim of the battle of Culloden had fallen in a suicidal attempt to serve the Prince he loved.

Ten minutes later, Colonel Belford gave an order for the government artillery to open fire. The ground shuddered as the ten guns exploded in one great roll. The Highland lines were immediately obscured by smoke as the first shot came bouncing along the heather. Belford's gunners poured cannonballs into the clan formation with a continuous roaring that was itself terrifying. The effect was devastating. Great holes were cut in the Highland lines within the space of a few minutes. Desperately the chiefs shouted to their men to close ranks. The men, in turn, begged for the order to charge; they were expected to stand and be killed for no reason except that someone had not given the command that could stop the carnage. Most of those who died in the battle were killed at this time, their limbs parted from them and hurled among their fellows. For nearly half an hour Belford's guns thundered, destroying a third of the Highland army before Clan Chattan broke line and charged. Athollmen and Camerons suffered most under the bombardment, but Lord George would not advance until Charles gave the order. The Prince had made it clear that this was to be his battle. Desperately, Lochiel asked Lord George for the necessary command. Lord George sent a messenger to Charles. Charles gave the order, but a cannonball killed his messenger before he could return to the front lines. At last O'Sullivan himself begged Lord George to begin an attack. It was then that Clan Chattan broke and the Highland charge began.

Before the clansmen could negotiate their own dead, the government infantry began their musket roll. Of twenty-one officers who had run forward with Clan Chattan, only three survived the first volleys. When they got to close quarters, the Scots fared no better. For once, government lines held, and the clansmen stood about ten yards away, shouting like enraged animals, unwilling to risk the musketry but too proud to retreat. They were shot where they stood. Thirty-two officers of the Atholl brigade fell under the volley-fire of Barrell's regiment. Lochiel had both his ankles broken by grapeshot, fifty yards from the guns. There he leant on his elbows and watched the behaviour of his kinsmen. He at least may have felt proud, for his Camerons extracted the highest toll from among front line government battalions.

To the rear of Lochiel's Camerons, Charles Edward watched the destruction of his dreams with increasing detachment. The Prince placed his command on a rise behind the right wing of his army. For protection he had only a guard of horse. During Belford's cannonade, Charles was shocked by the dreadful impact of the shot among the Highland lines. Fifteen minutes passed before a messenger from Lord George arrived to shake the Prince out of his stupor, and within the next few seconds Charles fully appreciated the impatience with which his general appeared to behave. The English artillery commander had noticed a small knot of men around the Stuart standard, and now he ordered his gunners to raise their elevation in order to disturb what he took to be Charles' command post. The first cannon shot aimed at the rear decapitated one of Charles' servants, less than thirty yards away from where the Prince stood. The barrage continued with accuracy, and eventually Charles was induced to move to the right. As he turned his horse, a ball landed to one side of him, covering him with earth. Weeks later, while hiding in Glenmoriston, Charles recalled the incident vividly. 'I was riding to the right wing, my horse began to kick, at which I was much surprised ... and looking narrowly to him to see what was the matter with him I observed blood gushing out of his side. "Oh, oh!" says I, speaking of the horse, "if this is the story with you, you have no less reason to be uneasy." Whereupon I was obliged to dismount and take another.'

As he rode off, Charles made frequent turns 'to see how his men behaved, but alas! our hopes were very slender'. He had barely gone ten yards when the Prince ordered his standard bearer to return to his former position, 'lest the sight of my standard going off might induce others to follow'. Shortly afterwards, the clans charged. Led by Lord George Murray, and out-flanked by Campbell Militiamen and dragoons, the right and centre of the Highland army made the first move, charging and shouting until they could advance no farther, and then dribbling back in ones and twos, and finally in a frightened mass. The left wing, consisting chiefly of Macdonalds, only began their advance after the right had started to retreat. Although the Chevalier de Johnstone was to claim that his wing very nearly broke the enemy, their actual charge never got within fifty yards of the government line. The Macdonalds had to run for more than half a mile, in the face of unwavering fire, before they could respond to the Duke of Perth's futile cries of 'Claymore, claymore!' Their opponents refused either to run or be drawn out of line and were content to slaughter Scotsmen at will, safely outside the reach of frantic broadswords. The Highlanders danced and threatened, roared and fumed in frustration while their comrades fell by the dozen.

What close action there was had been fierce. A sergeant of the Buffs remarked to his wife that 'the Rebels, I must own, behaved with the greatest resolution. It was dreadful to see the enemies' swords circling in the air as they were raised from strokes, and no less to see the officers of the Army, some cutting with their swords, others pushing with their spontoons, the Sergeants running their halberds into the throats of the enemy, while the soldiers mutually defended each other, and pierced the Heart of his Opponent, ramming their bayonets up to the socket. But still more terrible to hear the dying groans of either party.' A captain in Munro's regiment underlined this description. 'No one that attacked us escaped alive; for we gave no quarter nor would accept it of any.'

Hanoverian supporters, Cumberland among them, later declared that the refusal of quarter was only undertaken in retaliation for an order issued by Lord George Murray on 15 April. Yet the battle orders issued by the Scots General on that day make no reference to the refusal of quarter.

It is His Royal Highness's posetive orders that every person attach himself to some corps of the armie, and remain with that corps night and day untile the Battle and persute be finally over. This regards the foot as well as the Horse.

The Order of Battle is to be given to evry Ginerall officer and evry commander of a Regiment or Squadron. It is requir'd and expected of each individual in the Army, as well as officer or souldier, that he keep the post that shall be alotted to him. And if any man turn his back to run away the nixt behind such a man is to shoot him. No body upon pain of Death to strip slain or plunder till the Battle be over.

The Highlanders to be in their Kilts, and no body to throw away their Guns.

By His Royal Highness's Command

George Murray

Lieutenant Ginneral of His Majestie's forces.

That this is the verbatim order as issued by Lord George there can be no doubt. Two copies of it are in possession of the Duke of Atholl and can be seen at Blair Castle. There is, or was until recently, one in the Hardwicke collection of Jacobite MSS; it is authentic. It is then crystal clear that a copy taken from a Jacobite prisoner was deliberately tampered with by adding after the 'Battle be over' the words *And to give no quarter to the Elector's troops on any account whatsoever*.

This defaced and libellous copy found its way into the hands of the editor of the Edinburgh Whig journal *The Scots Magazine* in April 1746. No sooner was this slander sanctified by being in the newspaper than it was seized upon and reprinted over and over again.

Charles Edward himself saw hardly any of the desperate fight in which his soldiers were engaged. He had been forced to retire to a spot about a mile away from the field. His closest advisers, and his most devoted chiefs had warned him not to risk his life in the heat of action. Without the Prince all would be lost. Charles was reluctant to wait so far from the field and had to be forcibly restrained from joining his men.

According to Sir Thomas Sheridan, the Prince found it impossible to accept that his clans were being routed. 'He could scarcely believe he was struck with so severe an affliction.' Desperately, he tried to rally the left wing regiments that were streaming from the field even before news of defeat had been confirmed. His Italian valet, Michele Vezzosi, described how Charles 'saw with astonishment these troops which he had looked upon as invincible, flying before the enemy in the utmost disorder and confusion. In vain did he strive to reanimate and persuade them to return to the charge. . . .'

It is unlikely that Vezzosi was present on the field, and there are other stories which suggest that the Prince was elsewhere during the battle. Mr John Cameron, Presbyterian preacher and chaplain at Fort William, stated that Charles 'was in the heat of the action'. A sour Lord Elcho presented the image of a cowering boy, muttering incoherent Italian gibberish. But Vezzosi's description appears to be authentic and probably derived from eyewitnesses. Charles was finally led from the field by Lochiel's uncle, Major Kennedy, who seized the Prince's bridle and forced him to retire with two left wing regiments, Glenbucket's and John Roy Stewart's. This suggests that Charles did not flee the field. If anything, he remained too long, hopelessly trying to retrieve a lost cause.

Eventually, accompanied by Hay of Restalrig, Sir Thomas Sheridan and a detachment of Irish picquets, the Prince rode towards the Ford of Faillie over the River Nairn. There he was met by Lord Elcho and Captain O'Sullivan. Elcho remembered that the Prince seemed obsessed with the notion that the Scots intended to betray him. He 'neither Spoke to any of the Scots officers present, or inquired after any of the Absent . . . !' Apparently Charles decided to proceed into Fraser country with his favourites and he instructed the Scots to go to Ruthven, where they would receive further instruction. However, a few minutes later, another message arrived from the Prince telling the Scots to disperse and head for their homes. For Charles the battle was over. Though the charges which Elcho lays at the Prince's door cannot be trusted, he was perhaps correct in assuming that the young man held the Scots responsible for his defeat. They had forced him to retreat from Derby. They had refused to complete the ambush of Cumberland at Nairn. Now they had lost his most important battle. That was the way Charles reasoned in the snatched moments after Culloden. In the next few months he was to again realize the magnitude of his debt to Scotland.

The Scots paid dearly for their devotion to Prince Charles and the House of Stuart. In all, about two thousand men fell during the battle on Drummossie Moor. During the following three months nearly three thousand prisoners were taken and sent to England. Cumberland's aim all along had been the pacification of the Highlands, and with this he now proceeded by systematically destroying the economy of the region and the society upon which the army of clans was founded. He killed and deported the men, stole their possessions, burnt their houses, drove away their cattle, and imposed his martial law throughout the land with savage rigour. The victor of Culloden achieved his ends not by a single brilliant military victory, but through the extirpation of the human material of the Highlands.

The brutality which followed the fight on 16 April remains inexcusable. Wounded Highlanders were butchered on the field. Drummossie Moor was surrounded by sentinels during the night. There helpless unfortunates died of exposure, or else were impaled on the end of some guard's bayonet. The day following the battle was reserved for the final rounding-up of those who survived on the moor. Few prisoners were taken at the time, only about four hundred actually on the field. Most were killed within minutes of their capture. General Henry Hawley revelled in the mire. On the day of the battle, a few hours after the last of Clan Donald had quit the field, Hawley rode over to where the Frasers lay thickest and there came upon young Charles Fraser of Inverallochie. The laird was half dead, but Hawley was not satisfied with his suffering. Turning to one of his staff officers, reputedly James Wolfe, he ordered the man to pistol the rebel dog. Wolfe refused, preferring to resign his commission instead. Still Hawley would not be thwarted. He quickly found another soldier who was willing to kill Inverallochie without hesitation.

Henry Hawley was not alone among the government army. While riding home along the Inverness road on 16 April, the Rev. James Hay discovered the fury with which the victors had behaved. By Kingsmills, Hay was horrified to find the body of a child with 'his head cloven to his teeth'. Farther along the road, the minister came upon 'a woman stript and laid in a very indecent posture, and some of the other sex with their privities placed in their hands'. A few miles hence was a similar pile of bodies, 'not all of them Rebel soldiers'. Such horror proceeded not from a direct order, but from a collective desire for revenge expressed by another soldier in Cumberland's army. 'This rebel host had been most deeply in debt to the publick for all the rapine, murder and cruelty; and since the time was now come to pay off the score, our people were all glad to clear the reckoning, and heartily determined to give them receipt in full.' This sentiment may have been common among the eighteenth-century armies, but usually it was held in check by a more educated and authoritative humanity. This time, directly and indirectly, unmitigated savagery received the blessings of the High Command.

The victory at Culloden and the activity of the months that followed sealed the fate of the young

Stuart Prince. Never again could he rely upon the traditional support of the Highlands. Not that the men were unwilling. It was simply that too few remained, and for that the Forty-Five was to blame. Yet, although one vision had faded for Charles Edward, it was in the coming months that he entered his name among the legends which enrich Scottish history.

No one in Charles' camp had foreseen complete disaster at Culloden. Consequently the routed Scottish army had no emergency instructions to follow after the flight from Drummossie Moor. Most clansmen carried on running until they reached their native glens. There they told only of disaster and death. Some of their Lowland brethren made the error of returning to Edinburgh prematurely before the battle of Culloden actually began, and succeeded in exciting the capital with wild stories of Charles' overwhelming victory. Some Highland leaders, like Lochiel, apparently regarded the defeat as a temporary reverse. Donald Cameron and his brother hid in Callich for three days after the battle, waiting for news of a rendezvous with the Prince and his army. On the fourth day Lochiel crossed Loch Arkaig and took shelter amid a cluster of huts on the loch side. There he was joined by Murray of Broughton and Sir Thomas Sheridan. Murray firmly believed that Charles' single hope lay in regrouping his forces, and was horrified to discover a few days later that the Prince was about to depart from the mainland.

Perhaps Charles now felt that with Highlanders alone he could accomplish little. His aim would then be to get to France as quickly as possible. With that intention, the Prince should have made straight for the western coastline along which he first landed in Scotland at Loch-nan-Uamh. But Charles went instead to Cortuleg House, where Simon Fraser, Lord Lovat, was resident. Pages could be devoted to analysing the motives and character of this man who had been called 'the fox of the Forty-Five', the most brutal nobleman of the north, the most learned, cultured and well-mannered as well as villainous and deceitful. He was a

189

mass of paradoxes; on his better side he was animated by genuine Scottish patriotism, a curious devotion to the Catholic faith (which did not seem to hamper his more unscrupulous actions) and above all a brave determination and undaunted physical courage. He was at heart a Jacobite sympathizer.

Lovat at once set himself to inspiring Charles with a continued determination. He reminded the Prince that Bruce had lost eleven battles only to win at Bannockburn. This homily delivered by a man old enough to be Charles' grandfather cannot have failed to cheer the young man. Indeed, we know it did, for Charles dictated a letter to Cluny Macpherson from Cortuleg referring to 'the ruffle we met with this forenoon' (Culloden) and speaking of a rendezvous to reassemble the clans.

The rendezvous never occurred. The Reverend John Cameron suggested later that Charles was misled by supporters at Invergarry Castle. 'He was made to believe his loss was much greater than it was; that Lochiel, Keppoch, and other leading men of the Highlanders were killed, and was advised by O'Sullivan, O'Neil, and John Hay to dismiss all that were then with him for greater security of his person, as in that situation he could trust none....' According to Cameron, in response to the advice of his ill-informed, Irish pessimists, Charles abandoned all notions of reassembling his army.

What Cameron fails to add is that at Invergarry the Prince also received a letter from Lord George Murray in which the General resigned his commission and proceeded to blame the young man for the disasters which had lately befallen the Scottish cause. However much Charles may have disliked Lord George personally, he still respected the old man's military judgement, and the knowledge that the Scot had given up hope of reviving the campaign eroded the Prince's own assurance. He immediately made plans to leave the mainland. Unfortunately, the Prince decided to go to the Western Islands, and thus missed the French ship which arrived shortly in Loch-nan-Uamh. It would be several months before a similar opportunity for escape presented itself to Charles Edward.

While wandering along the western seaboard, the Prince met Donald Macleod of Skye, a man of whom he had already heard. 'Are you Donald Macleod of Guartergill in Skye?' Charles asked him. Donald, recognizing him, replied: 'I am the same man, Your Majesty.' Charles then told the honest old man in what distress and perplexity he was and asked him if he could convey him to Skye to seek refuge with Sir Alexander Macdonald of Sleat or Macleod of Dunvegan. It shows the distress and confusion that Charles was suffering that he could bring himself to make so extraordinary a suggestion – Macdonald and Macleod had let him down at the beginning of his campaign. What could he expect from them now that he was beaten, hunted and on the run?

Donald was appalled by this suggestion, and implored the Prince to seek further and more remote safety in the Outer Hebrides. The old man offered to procure a boat and go with him to the Outer Isles. Charles agreed; but before venturing on the perilous crossing of the Minch (the wide channel between the Outer and Inner Hebrides) he dictated a letter to the chiefs.

FOR THE CHIEFS, –
When I came into this country, it was my only view to do all in my power for your good and safety. This I will always do as long as life is in me. But alas! I see with grief I can at present do little for you on this side of the water, for the only thing that can now be done is to defend yourselves until the French assist you, if not to be able to make

better terms. To effectuate this, the only way is to assemble in a body as soon as possible, and then to take measures for the best, which you that know the country are only judges of. This makes me be of little use here; whereas, by my going into France instantly, however dangerous it be, I will certainly engage the French court either to assist us effectually and powerfully, or at least to procure you such terms as you would not obtain otherways. My presence there, I flatter myself, will have more effect to bring this sooner to a determination than any body else, for several reasons; one of which I will mention here; viz. it is thought to be a politick (policy), though a false one, of the French court, not to restore our masters, but to keep a continual civil war in this country, which renders the English government less powerful, and of consequence themselves more. This is absolutely destroyed by my leaving the country, which nothing else but this will persuade them that this play cannot last, and if not remedied, the Elector will soon be as despotick as the French king, which, I should think, will oblige them to strike the great stroke, which is always in their power, however averse they may have been to it for the time past. Before leaving off, I must recommend to you, that all things should be decided by a council of all your chiefs, or, in any of your absence, the next commander of your several corps with the assistance of the Duke of Perth and Lord George Murray, who, I am persuaded, will stick by you to the very last. My departure should be kept as long private and concealed as possible on one pretext or other which you will fall upon. May the Almighty bless and direct you.*

* This is from the Stuart papers at Windsor marked on the back in Charles' own handwriting: 'The Letter to ye Chiefs in parting from Scotland, 1746.'

*Top* The Duke of Cumberland with his army crossing the Spey at the battle of Culloden. From an engraving by T. Bakewell.
*Radio Times Hulton Picture Library*

*Bottom* The battle of Culloden, 16 April 1746. After H. Heckel.
*Scottish National Portrait Gallery*

*Top* After the battle of Culloden. The survivors were shown no mercy by the Hanoverian troops. From an engraving by H. Griffiths.
*Mansell Collection*

*Bottom* The first meeting of Prince Charles with Flora Macdonald on South Uist. From the nineteenth-century painting by Alexander Johnstone.
*Radio Times Hulton Picture Library*

Flora Macdonald, the heroine of the Bonnie Prince Charlie legend.
From the painting by Richard Wilson.
*Scottish National Portrait Gallery*

Charles disguised as Betty Burke, the maidservant of Flora Macdonald.
*Mansell Collection*

Charles with Flora Macdonald taking refuge in a cave. From an engraving by J. Rogers.
*Radio Times Hulton Picture Library*

*Top* 'Lochabet No More' by J. B. Macdonald. A romantic nineteenth-century view of Charles's final farewell to Scotland.
*Radio Times Hulton Picture Library*

*Bottom* Charles arrested in Paris, 10 December 1747, on the orders of the King of France.
*Radio Times Hulton Picture Library*

Princess Louise of Stolberg, Charles's wife.
*Scottish National Portrait Gallery*

Charles in old age, probably painted by H. D. Hamilton in Rome, *1775*.
*Scottish National Portrait Gallery*

Deliberately, the letter was post-dated by about a week to prevent Highland attempts to dissuade the Prince. Charles was determined to secure French assistance and would not allow a prolonged stay on the mainland to jeopardize his chances of success.

Crossing the Minch even by modern steam-boats can be an unpleasant experience. The Atlantic swell which sometimes gets round the top of the Hebrides to heave and dip in the wide channel is uncomfortable; when added to this there is storm and rain, the visitor to the 'Long Island' is tempted, when he gets there, to stay there for the rest of his life, or at least until all weather forecasts combine in promising several placid days. As it so happened, the crossing that Donald had arranged for Charles in a six-oared boat on 26 April was unusually vile. Only luck and the skill of Neil MacEachain* enabled them to survive when they were driven ashore at Rossinish, in the north-east part of Benbecula.

The Reverend Aulay Macaulay, who was Church of Scotland 'Preacher' to the minute Protestant flock of South Uist, was at Rossinish. Both these islands are predominantly Catholic today, especially South Uist, so Macaulay's job must have been something of a sinecure. Mr Macaulay happened to be dining with one of his Catholic neighbours in Benbecula when the Prince arrived and sought shelter in the house. Tradition has

* Neil MacEachain Macdonald, upon fleeing to France, married there and begat Napoleon's famous Marshal Macdonald. He brought up his son in the home to speak only Gaelic. This language and French were the only two that the Marshal could speak. In 1825, ten years after the defeat of Napoleon, the British Government generously invited the Marshal to visit the land of his forefathers and sent him in a frigate, *H.M.S. Swift*, out to South Uist. The Marshal visited his father's homestead, dug up with his own hands some of the earth there and took it back with him in a 'fine French jar', which was later buried with him in France. Before leaving South Uist he addressed six hundred men, all called Macdonald. He was much moved and spoke (so it is reported) 'fine accurate Gaelic but with a French accent'.

it that Mr Macaulay mentioned the possibility of the Prince's arrival in the Outer Isles and spoke of the reward for informing or capturing which he declared himself anxious to earn from a grateful government in London.

The Prince and his boatman, Donald Macleod, had fortunately decided in advance to assume the name of Sinclair. Donald was Sinclair Senior; the Prince was his son. It is said that the 'Sinclairs' discussed the question of the reward with Mr Macaulay most amicably. It must have chagrined the reverend gentleman deeply when he learned (as he must have done when the Prince escaped to France) that he had met the Prince and might have won the reward.

As soon as he gained privacy from the inquisitive Macaulay, the Prince was able to receive the legal Chief of Clanranald who, though he had large territories on the western mainland, also held sway in the southern Outer Hebrides. He approved of the scheme that Neil MacEachain and the other followers of the Prince had devised. This was that a story should be spread throughout the islands that a ship bound for the Orkney Islands had been wrecked on the Minch – the Prince (a merchant) and his followers, the only survivors, had got ashore at Benbecula. But they wished to go north to Stornoway (the only real town in all the Outer Isles) for the purposes of their business.

At six o'clock the next morning on 29 April, with old Donald at the helm again, the party set out for Lewis, the large island containing Stornoway. Once again the weather proved treacherous. Moreover, they became aware of Government ships which were scouring the seas and lochs of the Outer Hebrides, not so much to look for the Prince whose presence they did not suspect there yet, but for the Jacobite leaders fleeing to France. The Prince and some of his companions were put ashore first at the small island of Scalpa off

Harris (known as a separate island, but in reality con-
joined with Lewis), then at Arnish on Harris, while
Macleod continued to Stornoway to charter a ship.

Donald returned from his voyage to Stornoway in
high spirits having succeeded in hiring a vessel there
that might even be of a size sufficient to take the
Prince to France. The Prince was much cheered by this
news, though a little worried by Macleod's obvious
inebriation. But he soon forgot Donald's drunkenness
and concentrated upon the arduous forty-mile march
to Stornoway.

The party did not have to cover the whole forty
miles but only thirty-eight; for when they reached Kildun they learned that poor old Donald's alcoholic in-
discretions the night before had alarmed the inhabitants of Stornoway. Rumour had it that Charles was
advancing on the town with five hundred well-armed
men. The people of Stornoway did not wish the Prince
ill, but they were fearful of his possible presence
among them. All they wanted was for him to clear out
of the Long Island as soon as he could, and above all
not to endanger their town by coming in to it, with
armed men or alone.

Clearly it was dangerous and impracticable to go on,
so they stopped two miles short of Kildun where they
had received confirmation of the news from Stornoway. Most fortunately for them the Lady of Kildun,
Mrs Mackenzie, was a Catholic, sympathetic to the
Prince. This was a real stroke of good fortune for two
reasons. Firstly, Catholics and Jacobites were rare in the
northern Outer Hebrides, particularly near Stornoway.
Secondly, by the time they reached Kildun House, the
whole party, including Charles Edward, were nearly at
the end of their tether from exhaustion and hunger.

Those who love the Outer Hebrides know that when
the summer weather is fine and beneficent, there is no
more gently exhilarating walk than that which you
can take up the west side of the islands by the 'mac-

hair', the grass-tufted sand by the Atlantic shore. They also know that nothing in all the British Isles is more arduous than walking even a few miles in the teeth of a raging Atlantic gale, a gale of a kind unknown anywhere on the mainland of Great Britain. Yet the Prince and his companions managed it – not a few miles, but thirty-eight of them, sustained only by draughts of brandy and a few dry biscuits.

The lady of the house did all she could do to comfort the beaten and bedraggled travellers; she provided meat, bread, cream, whisky and brandy of which last two the Prince partook heartily. Perhaps this is the place for a short digression on the much-disputed subject of Prince Charles' drinking habits. In France he had been as temperate as the ordinary bourgeois Frenchman. In the campaign on the mainland of Scotland and England no one noticed his drinking. Not even the lying and malicious tongue of the disappointed Lord Elcho who had joined the Prince outside Edinburgh and who subsequently did all he could to damage the Cause by scandal, says anything about his use of wine or spirits during the campaign.

But he did drink in the Outer Hebrides and in quantities that seem staggering to us. Yet one must quickly add that no one ever records that it had any effect on him. It must have ultimately had its effects, but not there in the Hebrides where his prowess with the bowl was much admired. He would take his 'morning of brandy', that is a large quaich or shell containing spirits before breakfast and would go on with it throughout the day till the bottle, or two bottles, were finished – this apart from any other sociable drams he may have partaken of in company. On one occasion he drank Macdonald of Boisdale,* known as the greatest

* Boisdale, as we have seen, was against the Prince's venture, but to do him credit he helped the Prince when he was on the run and skulking in the heather. It would never have occurred to him to insult island hospitality by giving the Prince away either

bowlsman in all the Hebrides, under the table and even helped to put him to bed.

The eighteenth century was one of heavy drinking and nowhere more so than in Scotland. Judges drank heavily; Braxfield, the hanging Judge, and model for Stevenson's *Weir of Hermiston*, could drink all night and preside in Court in the morning with a clear head and unimpaired judgement; Henry Mackenzie, the author of *The Man of Feeling*, one of the most tearful of any sentimental novel in our language, was a noted Edinburgh toper; Porson combined great Greek scholarship with stupendous drinking; and so on.

It should be remembered, however, that these legendary drinkers mostly used wine. In the Hebrides Charles drank nothing but brandy and whisky on a scale which certainly did not shock the islanders, especially of South Uist, but did surprise them. They had never seen anything like it before, which is remarkable when one considers the reputation of South Uist not for drunkenness but for hardness of head.

For six days, Charles stayed on South Uist, but it now appeared that snooping government ships, particularly one commanded by the notorious Captain Ferguson,* suspected that the Prince was on the Long Island. Rather than risk Ferguson's repeated intrusions upon the fretted coasts of Benbecula and the north end of the Long Island, Charles decided to go to the Orkneys in another six-oared boat. Unfortunately, his crew were frightened by the sighting of an English flo-

---

for money or because of his new-found loyalty to the Protestant régime in London.

* Ferguson, a Scotch Whig, was an atrocious sadist. As an officer he was not allowed to soil his hands by actually administering floggings himself, but insisted on being present at such punishments and gloating on them. He liked not only to see blood run upon the backs of his victims but to note the ribs sticking through the lacerated flesh. He had members of his own crew flogged regularly and, of course, anyone faintly suspect of Jacobitism or of helping to hide the Prince who fell into his hands.

tilla and Charles was rudely dumped upon the desert rock of Iffurt. There he stayed until 10 May, living on salt fish, until he was able to set sail for Harris on 11 May. But again his enemies appeared and Charles was driven back to Benbecula.

At last it was decided to remove the Prince from within telescope range of his seaborne enemies, and on 14 May Charles entered the Mountains of Corodale. Glen Corodale is on the west side of South Uist, lying between two big mountains, Ben More and Ben Nella, and there Charles installed himself in a grass-cutter's cave. Till the 18th the Prince seemed completely at ease. Here he enjoyed shooting; deer were plentiful and so in those days were grouse. Charles aroused much admiration by bringing down an occasional grouse on the wing with a single ball. None of the islanders had seen such a thing done before, and were filled with astonishment. But the hardy crofters of the island were more surprised by the Prince's generosity. Once after he had shot a deer, Charles sat down to enjoy his prize when a young lad came up and stared at the Prince's meat with evident hunger. Servants sprang up to chastise the boy severely, but Charles stopped them, saying he could not see a Christian perish from want of food. To the delight of all present, he gave the boy most of his meat.

The stay in Corodale was shortlived. On 17 May a party of Militia landed on South Uist and began to search the island thoroughly. It was apparent that Charles' presence in Corodale had been reported, for the Militiamen acted with great determination, closing rapidly on the Prince's position. Ahead of them, Charles and his companions fled to Ouia and from there took a boat to Loch Boisdale. However, the sea was no safer than land, and rather than risk capture by one of the several English warships in the area, the fugitives landed at Loch Karnon. There the party hid for twenty-four hours before they were able to continue towards Loch Boisdale. Even at Boisdale, the Prince found no peace. The area was crawling with Militia. Charles could neither make for the open sea, nor hide inland. Instead. he took refuge upon a rock in the Loch. For eight days he lived on what fish he was able to catch, with only a tattered sail to keep the rain and wind from his back.

Charles had journeyed to Loch Boisdale hoping that the once sceptical Macdonald of Boisdale would be able to negotiate a safe passage to France. Surprisingly, Boisdale himself had been transported to London for interrogation, notwithstanding his earlier disassociation from the Prince's affairs. He could be of no use to Charles now. The Prince was trapped in the Loch with little idea of where his friends might be, and where his enemies. When news came from Loch Arkaig of the arrival of two French ships loaded with money, he decided that a trip there might prove fruitful.

But the Prince saw neither treasure nor French ships. He and his guide were trapped in the mountains near Boisdale. To one side the Militia stationed at Kilbride waited expectantly for Charles to betray his position. Across the way, at St Kilda, General Campbell himself conducted the search for the Prince. Yet Charles' inactivity scarcely mattered. Firstly, there were no French ships near Arkaig. There never had been. Two ships, the *Bellona* and the *Mars*, had indeed put into Loch-nan-Uamh several days before, but they had been forced to return to France almost immediately following persistent attention from British naval sloops. The story of treasure at Arkaig was nonetheless true. The French had landed nearly 35,000 louis d'or in six casks before their departure. The money was received by Lochiel's brother, Archibald Cameron, who the next day transported the casks by boat to the head of Loch Morar and from thence to Arkaig. There Cameron buried the treasure in the presence of Major Kennedy and Alexander Macleod of

Neuck. No other person was present.

In fact, only five of the casks were buried. Already one part of the accursed treasure had been stolen or mislaid, and for this error two clansmen faced a court-martial. The next day most of the missing gold was recovered, but Cameron also learned that Macdonald of Barrisdale, accompanied by two hundred kinsmen, had only been minutes late in preventing the treasure from being transported out of Macdonald country. For another seven years Cluny's treasure, as it came to be known, fired desperate allegations among the Prince's followers. After Charles returned to France later in 1746, the money, or what remained of it, was entrusted to Cluny Macpherson. Despite the heavy inroads made upon this fortune, in accordance with Charles Edward's own promises to several chiefs, and to meet the expense of services undertaken for the Prince, Cluny and Cameron were afterwards accused of theft and embezzlement. The charge was never levelled by Charles, but rather by disgruntled Highlanders like Glengarry, himself the least innocent of those concerned with the money. Both Cluny and Cameron were destitute by the middle of 1753, a poverty which suggests that neither had feathered his nest with money intended for Charles Edward.

In May 1746 the Prince must have been less worried about money than an opportunity for escape so narrowly missed. On board the vessels which called at Loch-nan-Uamh, the Duke of Perth, Lord John Drummond, Lord Elcho, Sir Thomas Sheridan and several lesser personages had sailed to France and safety.

His escape from almost certain capture on the Long Island was engineered by Neil Burke and Neil Mac-Eachain, but legend has concentrated attention upon Flora Macdonald. She was born in 1722, the only daughter of Ranald Macdonald of Milton and Bale-vannich in South Uist. Her father died before she was two years old and her mother than married Hugh

200

Macdonald of Armadale in Sleat. She had a brother, Angus, whose house in Milton Flora made her headquarters. Not only was she a kinswoman of Clanranald's, but also a close friend of the laird's children. Thus her connections and influence were invaluable to Charles Edward at a time of special danger.

Flora must have had sympathy for the hunted young man of royal blood; and she may very well, though there is no indication of this, have when she met him felt the influence of his still potent charm. Charles, who was at this age singularly heart-free for a young man, admired Flora for her distinguished lady-like qualities, and above all for her courage. But although her Celtic name was *Fionnghal*, 'the fair one', it is impossible to weave any story of a romance (in the usual sense of that much misused word) about Flora's relationship with Charles. There is little substance in the suggestion made by some historians that Flora met Charles at Holyrood and was there captivated by his charm. Her devotion was more probably inspired by her friend, Lady Margaret Macdonald, a fervid Jacobite.

Early in 1746 Flora was at her brother's house at Milton. She knew that Charles was in the area, and so did her stepfather. Hugh Macdonald was a government man, and commander of a Militia contingent, who nonetheless sympathized with the Prince. At some time he must have confessed his sympathies to Flora, for she was never in doubt about his assistance when the occasion to help the Prince arose. Late in June, one of Charles Edward's companions, Captain O'Neil, visited Angus Macdonald at Milton and there told Flora of the predicament in which the Prince found himself. According to the lady herself, O'Neil then took her to meet the Prince. She then returned to Milton, and from there got in touch with Lady Clanranald to ask her advice. Together the two women concocted a plan to disguise the Prince as Betty Burke, a maid in Flora's service. That very evening, Flora procured a boat with the intention of taking Charles Edward to Skye. But, as the Prince was to travel as 'Betty Burke', maid's clothing had to be obtained from Lady Clanranald. While on the road to her house, Flora was arrested as a matter of course by a Militia patrol acting under instruction to bring all travellers into camp for interrogation. Fortunately the girl did not lose her head and make a premature confession, for her interrogator turned out to be the district Militia commander, Hugh Macdonald of Armadale, her stepfather. Armadale released her after giving her passports for herself, her maid, 'Betty Burke' and her servant Neil MacEachain. He even wrote to his wife to tell her that their daughter was returning home. 'She has got one Betty Burke, an Irish girl, who, as she tells me, is a good spinster. If her spinning pleases you, you may keep her till she spins all your lint.'

With Neil MacEachain, Flora arranged to meet the Prince at Rossinish. As all the fords on the island were guarded, Charles had to make the journey by sea, and so was obliged to wait a long time for a homeward-bound fishing vessel. He finally persuaded a wherry to land his party on the rocks near Rossinish on 26 June. From there the Prince traversed moorland until he reached a place of rendezvous outside Rossinish at 5 o'clock the following morning. Although Charles was to meet Flora at a shepherd's hut, he could not make use of the shelter because MacEachain discovered that the hut was frequented by militiamen in search of fresh milk. Instead, the Prince had to hide among rocks at the water's edge where '... there lay such a swarm of midges upon his face and hands as would have made any other but himself fall in despair, which notwithstanding his incomparable patience, made him utter such hideous cries and complaints as would have rent the rocks with compassion'. For two days Charles Edward suffered this discomfort, until on 28 June Flora

Macdonald arrived with Lady Clanranald and sufficient woman's clothing to disguise the Prince. Clad in
a flowered linen gown, a light-coloured quilted petti-
coat, a white apron, a mantle of dun camlet and with
two pistols in his pocket, Charles left the Long Island
in an eight-oared boat, accompanied by Flora Macdonald and his other servants, and bound for Waternish in Skye. Soon the wherry was caught in a storm,
but at Waternish Charles discovered the landing area
swarming with Skye Militia who immediately fired
upon the boat when it failed to answer their chal-
lenges.

Eventually the boat made land at Kilbride, very
near the seat of Sir Alexander Macdonald. Flora hid
the Prince amidst some rocks and then hurried to see
her friend, Lady Margaret Macdonald. At Lady Margaret's house, Flora was horrified to discover that a
lieutenant of the Militia was at dinner with Sir Alexander. She also learned that Lady Clanranald and
her husband had been arrested and transported to
London to await trial for their part in the Forty-
Five. Lady Margaret Macdonald was no easier than
Flora upon hearing of Charles Edward's proximity. She
herself sought the aid of Alexander Macdonald of
Kingsburgh, her husband's factor, who from that moment assumed responsibility for Charles' welfare.

Kingsburgh decided that Charles should cross to the
Isle of Raasay, where the owner, Macleod of Raasay,
was a sympathizer who had served the Prince at Culloden. The party immediately set out for Kingsburgh's
own house, with Charles striding forward boldly as an
Irish maid. Neil, who walked a little behind Macdonald of Kingsburgh, was much amused by the comments of the people they met or passed on the road.
This is what he says in his unfinished narrative. It is a
narrative written almost *viva voce* in the characteristic
Highland Celtic style. Such narrators usually refer to
themselves in the third person by their own Christian

names because the idea is to give the narrative a saga-like quality.

> They spoke of the impudence of Miss Burke who was not ashamed to walk and keep company with Macdonald of Kingsburgh. The people were no less vexed than surprised how he (Kingsburgh) took so much notice of her. Betty, very easie of what would be said of her went always at such a rate (the Prince always walked rapidly) that she very often got before her fellow traveller, 'Curse the wretch', they shouted out, 'do you observe, Sir, (meaning Neil) what terrible steps she takes, how manly she walks, how carelessly she carries her dress' and a hundred such like expressions which they repeated over and over again.
>
> But what they took most notice of was when Kingsburgh and his companion was come to a rivulet about knee deep which crossed the high road, to see Burke take up her petty coats so high when she entered the water. The poor fellows were quite confounded by this sight ... and asked if Neil was acquainted with her. Neil told them that he knew nothing about her further than to hear she was an Irish girl who was with Miss Macdonald in Wist (Uist), and upon a report of her being a famous spinster of lint had engaged her for her mother's use. The honest people soon after parted with Neil and Miss Flora and made for their different homes full of astonish.

Here Neil's narrative ended, but Flora, riding on horseback, had caught the travellers up and overheard more of the people's comments. They were to the same effect.

Macdonald of Kingsburgh and his companions arrived wet, weary and late at his house. His wife Mrs Macdonald had gone to bed.... Presently her daughter rushed in to say that: 'a very odd, muckle, ill-shaken up wife' was with him. Later Kingsburgh came into his wife's bedroom and told her to dress, get up and make supper ready. Whn Mrs Macdonald got up and came downstairs she met the 'odd muckle trallup of a carline' striding about the hall.

The 'carline' saluted Mrs Macdonald who felt the bristles of the Prince's beard upon her chin. She was alarmed and drew Kingsburgh aside and asked who this peculiar stranger might be.

'Why, my dear,' replied her husband, 'it is the Prince.'

'The Prince! Oh Lord, we are all ruined and undone for ever!'

'Hout good wife,' said Kingsburgh, 'we will die but once, and if we are hanged for this, I am sure we die in a good cause.'

Mrs Macdonald of Kingsburgh then moved into action in silence and without comment to arrange things. She prepared a good supper of roast eggs, collops, bread and butter. At the end came the brandy. The Prince poured himself out a large helping of it into a tumbler. 'I have learned in my skulking,' he said, 'to take a hearty dram.' He certainly had.*

Soon after this Kingsburgh called upon the Prince

* The frequent references to brandy rather than whisky (now Scotland's national drink) may puzzle some readers. The present writer does not know when nor to what extent whisky became 'Scotch'. Brandy, however, was easily procurable in Scotland (so was claret) in the eighteenth century. The reason was that, by an odd freak in the Act of Union of 1707, Scotland was still permitted to import certain French wines and spirits duty free. This happy state of affairs lasted until the 1780s. Then the English made a special commercial treaty with 'their oldest ally' Portugal, and let in port all but free of duty. They compelled the Scots to follow suit. Hence John Home's well-known quatrain:

> Firm and erect the Caledonian stood;
>   Old was his Mutton, and his claret good.
> 'You shall drink port' the Saxon cried;
>   He took the poison and his spirit died.

and asked him how he had rested: 'Never better' was the truthful if laconic reply. In order to stop the servants from gossiping the Prince came down from his room in the clothes of Betty Burke, but soon left to assume the usual dress of a Highland gentleman and made his way to Portree, the only town (and still the capital) of Skye.

At Portree, Charles bid Kingsburgh farewell after thanking him for his assistance and then turned to Flora Macdonald. It must have been a touching moment, but the Prince's adieu was an optimistic exhortation to a faithful follower rather than the tearful goodbye of a lover. 'For all that has happened, I hope, madam, that we may meet at St James's yet.' With that, he climbed into his wherry and departed for Raasay.

Flora was later arrested and taken to London on 8 November 1746. There she was imprisoned first on board the *Royal Sovereign* in the Thames, until 6 December, when she was taken to the Tower. In accordance with the Act of Indemnity, she was released the following July. Her stay had not been as unpleasant as it might have been, thanks largely to the propriety with which her stepfather had appeared to behave during the previous year, but also because her story had fired the imaginations of romantic Englishmen, one of whom happened to be the King's son. Although Flora was permitted to return to Scotland, she remained in London for a while where she was the guest of the notorious Jacobite socialite, Lady Primrose.

While making the crossing back to Skye in June 1748 Flora very nearly drowned, but the next month she reached Armadale to discover that her fame at home far outstripped the admiration she had won in the south. Two years later, at the end of 1750, or perhaps the following January, she married Macdonald of Kingsburgh's son, Alex, to whom she bore ten children over the next sixteen years.

After their marriage, husband and wife emigrated to

America. But in the American War of Independence Flora took the British side and was wounded. She returned to her native Skye at the end of her life and died there in March 1790, when nearly 68 years old, and is buried near the place she was born, Kilmuir. 'Her name,' to quote Dr Johnson's celebrated remark, 'will be mentioned in history, and if courage and fidelity be virtues, mentioned with honour.' This is engraved upon her tombstone.

Charles was able to stay only two days on Raasay. His host, Macleod, was under constant surveillance, and therefore advised the Prince to head for Mackinnon country in the south of Skye. Whatever the privations he had so far suffered, Charles Edward remained undaunted. Macleod noted his determination and optimism even while the Prince was being forced to run before his enemies. Of his host and guide Charles asked:

> Macleod, do you not think that God Almighty has made my person for doing some good yet? When I was in Italy and dining at the King's table, very often the sweat would have been coming through my coat with the heat of the climate; and now that I am in a cold country, of a more piercing and trying climate, and exposed to different kinds of fatigues, I really find I agree equally well with both. I have had this philibeg on now for some days, and I find I do as well with it as any of the best breeches I ever put on. I hope in God, Macleod, to walk the streets of London with it yet.*

Having reached the Mackinnon country, they found their expectations of the grand old laird of Mackinnon fully justified. He himself, assisted by four boatmen, rowed the Prince to the mainland at Knoydart which

* Malcolm Macleod's *Narrative of his adventures in the Forty-Five*, quoted by W. D. Norrie.

he reached on 6 July, despite an encounter with a militia boat. By various routes on land and in boats, including a perilous hiding under rocks at Borodale, the Prince was passed from one devoted adherent to another until he reached the hiding place where he was to rest for the longest period of his mainland flight.

Before we come to this life-saving interlude at Glenmoriston, I must mention poor Charles' physical condition while hiding at Borodale protected only by a heavy rock. He (and this is scarcely a minor point as any traveller today in the West Highlands can vouch for) was tormented by midges. He was also covered with lice and suffered much from that revolting and painful inflammation of the bowels we now call dysentery. All this makes Charles' powers of endurance the more remarkable.

In July, John Cameron, a messenger from Lochiel, met Charles at a place near Loch Arkaig, and later described the Prince's appearance at length. 'He was bare footed, had an old black kilt coat on, a plaid, philabeg and waistcoat, a dirty shirt and a long red beard, a gun in his hand, a pistol and dirk by his side.' Cameron noted that Charles was still cheerful, despite his obviously desperate condition. 'He was cautious when in the greatest danger, never at a loss in resolving what to do, with uncommon fortitude. He regretted more the distress of those who suffered from adhering to his interest than the hardships and danger he was hourly exposed to.' Charles Edward's princely disposition cannot be ignored. We know that he could outwalk in speed and distance the best Highland troops; we know he could endure despite his weak point, his bronchial tubes, hours of inactivity in hiding and under drenching rain when he set his mind to it. But dysentery cannot just be endured and brushed aside by a mental effort.

Rest was at hand; Charles was now led by Donald

Cameron of Glenspean, sent out to Glenmoriston, where he joined the never-to-be-forgotten 'seven men'. Two Macdonalds, three Chisholms, a Macgregor and a Grant had formed themselves into a guerrilla group with their 'backs to the Mountain and their face to the Devil'. They had survived Culloden, knew that this campaign at least was lost for ever on that field, but were themselves determined never to admit defeat. They would take to the heights, shelter in caves and descend as Bruce had done before them to kill, harry and distress any Government forces or men they could get at.

When the Prince had scaled to their cavernous heights, one of them, John Macdonald, according to Ian Og of Borodale who had been one of the Prince's scouts and guides, turned as red as blood and addressed him:

> I am sorry to see you in such a poor stage, and I hope, if I live, to see you in a better condition, as I have seen you before the head of your army upon the Green at Glasgow (so the Prince did get some recruits from Glasgow): all I can do is to continue faithful to you while I live, and I am willing to leave my wife and children and follow you wherever you incline to go.*

Here the Prince really did rest and stayed with what he cheerfully called his 'Privy Council' for a little more than two weeks. He slept on a bed of sheltered heather and said that he 'was as comfortably lodged as if he had been in a Royal Palace'.

News that a strong force of the Government militia was encamped only four miles away induced the seven men to tell Charles that he must leave them. His person was too precious. They were quite prepared to stay and shoot it out with the militia if they had to but

* *The Lyon in Mourning*, Vol. III, p. 98.

feared that they might not be able to hold their Royal guest free from capture or death.

They sent a guide with Charles who now set out on one of his most tortuous tours of escape which puzzles even the meticulous Walter Biggar Blaikie, the author and compiler of *The Itinerary of Prince Charles Edward Stuart*. What we do know is that he reached much farther south to join Cluny Macpherson in his truly extraordinary 'Cage' constructed with skilful camouflage on the slopes of Ben Alder in the far south-east of Inverness-shire, near Badenoch. Here the Prince remained for a week, being joined eventually by Lochiel and his brother Dr Cameron.

Ben Alder in shape and appearance is unique among all the mountains of Scotland, indeed in all Great Britain. It lies, or rather abruptly stands up, as the last out-thrust of the Highland hills on the eastern side of the country. The three thousand seven hundred and fifty-seven feet of it look as if they were put up by immense man-made labour; for it is an almost perfect pyramid, apart from a few clefts or caves on its southern side. Its colour is a monochrome of yellowish grey; and anyone who is not deliberately dressed in bright startling colours disappears from view as soon as he begins to climb it.

In one of these clefts Cluny Macpherson had built out of long wattle rods a private house for use when on the run. He lived there like a gentleman and a chief. He had a number of his clansmen as servants, and, having in the old days taken some of his men to France, his cuisine had the advantage of being prepared by a French-trained chef. R. L. Stevenson, who took great pains to get historical details right, gives an accurate account of life in Cluny's Cage in his novel *Kidnapped*.

On 13 September, late at night, news reached Cluny's Cage that some French vessels had reached Loch-nan-Uamh, just where the Prince had landed on the mainland of Scotland fourteen months before. This had its immediate effect. The Prince and Lochiel as well as Dr Cameron prepared to make the perilous journey as speedily as possible so as to reach the ships, which had obviously been sent by the French Government to bear the Jacobites and the Prince back to safety. Cluny Macpherson remained behind to act as a Jacobite agent at home, though the Government might be highly suspicious of him.

The journey north to Morar and Arisaig took the party just under a week. The journey though successful was indeed perilous; for Government troops were on the look-out not only for the Prince but for fleeing Jacobites on nearly every square mile through which the fugitives passed.

That the Prince did get there and did eventually board the French vessels aroused the rumour current in both England and Scotland that George II's ministers were not anxious to capture Charles. The disposal of him would certainly have given the Government some headaches.

Would they have cared to try him and execute him? It would not have increased their popularity at home and abroad. By this time the Prince's exploits in success, defeat and in hunted flight had aroused great interest and even a kind of sympathy in Whig circles in Britain. In much of continental Europe, particularly in France whose ships had been sent to rescue him, and whose Court and Government were officially pro-Jacobite, the execution of the Prince would have given great offence. England did not want to quarrel with France on the Jacobite or any other question at that time. If they had killed the Prince in a fair fight on the battlefield or had him assassinated in a manner for which they could disclaim responsibility they would have been delighted. But the capture of the young man alive would have presented them with problems.

The rumours that the Government did not really want to capture him can be dispelled by a letter from the Commander-in-Chief, Lord Albemarle, to the Duke of Newcastle dated 15 October and now in the 1746 State Papers. The letter runs: 'Nothing is to me a more convincing proof of the dis-affection of that part of the country than that of the Prince lying so long concealed among those people, and that he should be able to elude our narrowest and most exact searches, and at last make his escape notwithstanding the great reward offered to apprehend him.'

Charles reached Loch-nan-Uamh on 19 September and boarded *L'Heureux*. The following day he left for France. From the time of his landing in Scotland, Charles had witnessed the devotion of his Highland followers, though it was only in the last few months that the intensity of their loyalty had been driven home. For the remainder of his life Charles Edward regarded them with a special affection. In the final years in Rome he often recalled the bracing winds and rain which had united hunted men, one of them a Prince, in the face of adversity. But he wondered especially at the suffering they were prepared to undergo on his behalf when information given to London could have secured them in comfort to the tune of £30,000. In sailing from the Western Highlands and Islands of Scotland for France the 'Bonnie Prince Charlie' of legend, song, poetry and fact sailed out of the history books, but not out of the memory of man.

Charles sailed on uninterruptedly and landed at Roscoff on 16 October 1746. Thence he moved to Morlaix. It seems at times as if events just moved for Charles, or against him – as if nature or destiny were actively interested in his movements. From Morlaix he wrote to his younger brother, Henry, Duke of York in Paris:

Dear Brother,
As I am certain of your great concern for me I cannot express the joy I have on your account of my safe arrival in this country. I send here inclosed two lines to my master (his father James) just to show him I am alive and safe and being fatigued not a little, as you may imagine. It is my opinion that you should write immediately to the French King, giving him notice of my safe arrival.... I leave to your prudence the writing of this letter and the wording of this letter, and would be glad no time should be lost in writing and despatching it.... It is absolute necessity I must see the French King as soon as possible, for to bring things to a right head. Warren, the bearer of this letter, will instruct you of the way I should wish to meet you in Paris. I embrace you with all my heart and remain

> Your most loving brother,
> Charles P.

Charles reached Paris on 17 October 'in perfect health and high spirits', and there met his brother who reported thus to their father James in Rome:

Charles did not know me at first sight, but I am sure I knew him very well, for he is not in the least altered since I saw him except grown somewhat broader and fatter (his fatness was probably the result of the large drams he had drunk in the Hebrides) which is incomprehensible after all the fatigues he has endured. I defy the whole world to show another brother so kind and loving as he is to me. For my part, I can safely say that all his endeavours tend to no other end but to deserving such goodness as he has for me.

Young Henry of York was then a very different character from the lofty, wealthy, yet truly religious Prince of the Church he was to become when he had received the Cardinal's hat. Naturally he was filled with admiration for his brother's famous exploits which had become the talk of France. For a brief period he hero-worshipped his elder brother and without a touch of jealousy, much though he would have liked to have been with him on his campaign. Nor was his view of Charles yet clouded with that disapproval which was to last till nearly the end of his brother's life.

But Charles wanted to see the King of France, not Henry. As he was uninvited, he would have to go on his own account to the French court. He rode to Fontainebleau, where Louis left his Council to greet the Stuart Prince and credit him with 'les Egalités des héros et des philosophes'. He arranged a reception at which Charles was to be received as the Prince Regent of Britain. All honour was to be given to the Prince, and Charles accepted the accolade in fine style. He arrived at the function accompanied by his retinue, and wearing the Stars of the Garter and St Andrew, but he mistakenly regarded the event as a French apology, and buttonholed Louis to ask for money and regular troops with which to effect another landing in Britain. Immediately the Frenchman became evasive, behaviour which heralded an era of disappointment for the young Prince.

In Paris Charles lived next door to his brother in a house rented from the Duc de Bouillon. The Princes dined together daily, but already their different temperaments had begun to widen the gulf between them. Henry was a retiring, devout man who paid scrupulous regard to French wishes. Charles was a human dynamo. His magnetism attracted widespread attention, and it was not long before his house became a centre for Jacobite society and intrigue. All the while, a wary French government kept watch and compiled reports upon Charles' various visitors, like the Lords Nairne and Lewis Gordon. At the same time they helped the Prince to maintain his estate with substantial subsidies. Lack of money remained a problem for Charles and through it France hoped to control his appetites. In 1747 the Comte d'Argenson calculated that Charles' venture in 1745 cost Louis 1,800,000 livres, besides the extra millions that were diverted from French coffers in order to bolster Stuart pensions and grants. What Charles failed to realize between 1746-8 was that France could no longer afford such a drain upon her resources. Economy was her aim, and among the measures which Louis necessarily undertook was the axeing of all future plans for an invasion of Britain.

Caught in a whirl of public acclaim, Charles was unable to separate the heady flattery of admirers like Madame Guéméne, whom d'Argenson accused of taking the Prince by force, from the more deceptive attentions of the French ministers themselves. He believed that Louis must now help him. Not once did he grasp the significant absence of direction from his father in Rome. James left all dealings between the Prince and Louis to his son. His caution was vindicated as relations between Charles and Louis deteriorated. The Jacobite King was horrified to discover that Charles had actually threatened the French court when a pension paid by d'Argenson to a Jacobite courtier was reduced.

The old King knew that his son did not have a foot upon which to base his aggression. At most Charles could retire huffily from Paris to Rome, but that was the last thing the Prince wished to do. In a moment of wisdom, Charles turned once more to Cardinal Tencin for intercession, only to explode when the statesman suggested that Charles should offer to cede Ireland to Louis in return for aid. Thenceforth his demands became more extreme and unrealistic. He wanted 'Either everything or nothing; *point de partage.*'

Faced with what he took to be the duplicity of Versailles, Charles turned desperately to Spain. The Spanish King, Ferdinand VI, was a peaceful man with no desire to involve himself with Charles Edward. But that did not deter the Prince. Uninvited, and in secrecy, 'so that this court should not hear from me till I let them know it', he travelled to Spain. There Ferdinand refused to grant him an audience, and only reluctantly agreed to a night visit during which the Spanish position was forcefully underlined. There could be no assistance.

But the failure in Spain was dwarfed by the reverse which greeted Charles Edward upon his return to Paris in early June. There he learned that his brother, Henry, Duke of York, had gone to Rome to become a cardinal of the Roman Catholic Church. Charles always regarded his brother's devoutness as a political drawback. He appreciated the crucial role which religion had played in keeping the Stuarts from the throne of England, and he himself took care never to offend either his Protestant or his Catholic followers. But Henry's conscience, or perhaps his more realistic appraisal of the Stuart future, led him to embrace the Roman Catholic faith in a fashion that was bound to have severe political repercussions. From St Ouen Charles wrote to his father in dire tones. 'I have received yrs of ye 13th & 20th June had I got a Dager throw my heart it would not have been more sensible to me than ar ye contents of yr first. My Love for my Brother and concern for yr Case being the occasion of it. I hope Your Majesty will forgive me not entering any further on so disagreeable a subject the shock of which I am scarce out of.'

In later years, the Prince accused James and Henry of conniving in a determined bid to keep him from a return to Britain. For twenty years Charles ignored his brother. As far as he could see, Henry's acceptance of a Cardinalate was as serious a setback as the bloody defeat on Culloden Moor in the previous year. Perhaps the Prince merely seized yet another excuse to explain his own failures, but others were also of his opinion. Even the Roman Catholic Father Myles McDonnell described Henry's action as 'a Mortal deadly stroke to the Cause'. The Comte d'Argenson believed that Cardinal Tencin and O'Brien were bribed by the English to persuade Henry to accept his cardinal's hat. The Duke of York too must have at least realized that the step would reduce his brother to extreme distress, for he took care to keep all the initial negotiations from Charles' ears, and afterwards wrote to the Prince in the most penitent of voices.

By becoming a priest, Henry had halved the possibilities of continuing the Stuart line. On Charles alone lay the responsibility of maintaining a challenge against the Hanoverian usurper. James would have liked his son to arrange a sensible marriage immediately on his return from Scotland. Then Charles had brushed aside every overture made by his father. Though by the summer of 1747 the need for Charles to beget heirs had grown more urgent, the Prince still regarded the prospect of marriage with singular disfavour. He countered his father's proposals with a candidate of his own, one far beyond his station, in a move calculated to ridicule the old King's concern.

Charles let it be known that he was going to sue for the hand of Elizabeth, the Tsarina of Russia and daughter of Peter the Great. The Tsarina was fourteen years older than Charles; her political inclinations were against the Stuarts and she was pursuing an alliance with the Hanoverian Government in London. Whatever might have been the true reason for these 'proposed proposals' for the Tsarina's hand, they shut up any further suggestions that he should hawk himself about in the marriage-market.

There is nothing to suggest that the Prince disliked women. In fact, he greatly enjoyed their attentions. He delighted in daily visits to the Opera, near which he lived, because he relished the flattery of female theatregoers. In Paris he had for a mistress a woman who was a cousin of the French King. The Princesse de Talmont was married to one of the House of La Tremoille, was the first cousin of John Sobieski and a cousin of Stanislas Leszczynski. She was also nineteen years older than Charles, but admired for her beauty, wit and vivacity by Voltaire, and even the acid Madame du Deffand. Charles flaunted this liaison openly. Association with the Princesse bore none of the responsibilities and burdens which legal marriage threatened. He could enjoy her company, damn her name, ignore her overtures as the mood took him with no recriminations whatsoever. What was more, he could concentrate all his attentions upon the really important work of gaining French government support for an invasion of England, a task in which Madame de Talmont's connections could prove useful.

Eventually the Princesse proved to be more of a nuisance than a help. French policy was guided not by the whispers which passed between cousins, but by the peace overtures being conducted at Aix-la-Chapelle during the summer of 1748 to end the War of the Austrian Succession. At first the Prince thought very little of these negotiations and believed that nothing would come of it.

In one of his rare letters to his father he wrote: 'I

really do not think a peace so esy at present to be compassed as people are willing to flatter themselves with.' But as the Conference seemed to prosper, the Prince at last took notice of it. It seemed to him that if all the powers signed and recognized the Hanoverians as the British monarchs, it would diminish the claims of his own House. He then drew up and published, for once with some dignity, a protest. King James in Rome had been carefully preparing another and more tactful protest, and was much put out when he learned that his impetuous son had forestalled him.

Charles' protest was very popular not only among the people of Paris but with the aristocracy. They felt their great country was humiliated by being forbidden to give shelter to exiles from whatever country and of whatever political flavour. This popularity only angered Louis and he implored King James to tell his son to leave French territory voluntarily. The French King even offered to give Charles two houses at Neufchâtel if the Prince would retire there peacefully. King James, as tactfully as he could, obliged. But Charles, relying on the evidence of the French people's liking for him in their midst, paid no attention. He wrote inconsequential notes to his father regarding the weather and his clothes. What he could not accept was the absolute necessity with which the French government regarded peace. The humiliation of a royal guest was not too large a price for Louis to pay.

The Prince did not help. He publicized his defiance, held himself aloof from Versailles and had a medal struck. On one side, Charles appeared in profile, with the words *Carolus Walliae Princeps* and on the other was engraved the words *Amor et Spes Britanniae*, a figure of Britannia and several ships. The message was plain. France needed peace because of the English Navy. Louis was furious at the insult, but when he heard that Charles was ordering large quantities of plate as if to furnish a new house, he offered to pay for the silverware. Only then did he discover that the silver was a gift to Madame de Talmont. His patience evaporated, and on 8 November the Duc des Gesvres carried a blunt message from the King to Charles Edward. Still the Prince was not perturbed. He ignored Gesvres and went to the theatre for the evening. There he made loud inquiries regarding the date of the next Opera ball so that all would know with what little esteem he held the French King's ultimatum.

By 22 October, many believed that Charles Edward had indeed defied Louis successfully. Madame de Talmont dined daily with Charles in direct contradiction of her husband's strictest warnings. The Prince even tried to rent a new house. But Louis was not finished. He would have peace with the English and if Charles Edward continued to remain so obstinately set against the prosperity of France, then he must bear the consequences of his ingratitude. On 25 October the French minister Maurepas himself visited the Prince to ask him not to inconvenience France further by remaining in Paris. That same day a letter from James reached the Prince via Versailles in which the same plea was made. On receipt of this communication, the Prince's servants departed from Paris, but Charles himself remained, apparently delighted at the embarrassment which he was causing the French King.

Then Louis struck. On 10 December Charles made his way as usual to the theatre, but in the Rue St Honoré a voice called out to him, 'Prince, retournez, on va vous arrêter. Le Palais Royal est investi.' Charles ignored the warning and continued on his way. At 5.15 he was arrested in the cul-de-sac outside the Opera. The whole arrest was carried out with military precision that bordered on farce. It was conducted by the Duc de Biron and effected by Major de Vaudreuil, who seized the Prince in the name of the King of France. In the street, a detachment of French Guards saw to it that the hero of the Forty-Five did not fight his way out of his confinement, while a further two companies of Grenadiers waited in the wings in case assistance was needed by the Guards. Besides a detachment of Mousquetaires, Biron also provided himself with axes and ladders in case the Prince locked himself in one of the houses near the Opera. Also there were a physician and three surgeons lest Charles' violence led to injury to any party. As it was, the Prince was taken without a struggle. He remained aloof, even while his captors bound him with silken cords. Only once during his uncomfortable journey to the Fortress at Vincennes did he speak to his captors, and then it was to ask wryly of an embarrassed Vaudreuil, 'Where are you taking me to – to Hanover?'

At Vincennes, Charles discovered that his gaoler was an old friend, the Marquis de Chatlet. Despite orders, Chatlet refused to bind his prisoner, but he did have the Prince searched thoroughly for any implement with which he might commit suicide. Confined in a room with only a wicker chair and a truckle bed, Charles once again found the strength which had sustained him through the months of hiding in the Highlands of Scotland. It was he, the prisoner, who had to comfort a deeply distressed de Chatlet. He learned with pleasure of the hostile reception which had greeted the news of his arrest in Paris. Even the Dauphin was reputedly angry with the King. For two days Charles remained at Vincennes. Then on 13 December came news that the Prince had at last consented to leave France voluntarily.

Happily, Louis abandoned plans to transport the Prince all the way to Rome. Instead he secured a promise from Charles that he would be out of France within eight days and that he would go neither to Avignon nor Lorraine. Furthermore he would neither come to Paris, nor stop at any major French town or city on his way. On 15 December Charles Edward left Vincennes in a post chaise, accompanied by Strafford

His arrest and expulsion from France formed a milestone in Charles Edward's life. He had been confronted with the weakness of his position in relation to that of a true head of state. It was actual power that mattered and not royal blood. Political pressure and the might of navies and armies had combined to throw him out of France. He was really no opponent for a King of France, nor an Ambassador from England for that matter. In many ways it was a confrontation similar to the one which the Prince had faced at Culloden. There the brutal facts of war and military strength had been rammed home against his most cherished dreams. Charles reacted to both crises by virtually refusing to accept the reality of the evidence with which he had been faced. Rather than abandon notions of an invasion of Britain, with or without French assistance, on both occasions the Prince behaved as though a return to Britain was imminent after a temporary setback. Perhaps he genuinely believed this in 1746, but three years later such optimism was unfounded. All through the years of mysterious flitting about Europe following his escape to Avignon, Charles conveyed the impression, at least to his father, that his elaborate secrecy and concealment was essential preparation to some fantastic excursion against the Hanoverians. The only explanation for such behaviour must be that the Prince deluded himself rather than face the truth, or perhaps he was unwilling to admit failure before his father and the Roman society he had quit many years before.

Despite the fury of Whitehall and Versailles, Charles lived in style at Avignon. On 10 January he was specially invited to a masked ball held in honour of the visiting Infanta of Spain. All was plain sailing with Rome. But then Charles became embroiled in an argument with the Archbishop of the Province. The cause of dissension was prize-fighting, a sport which Charles dearly loved and encouraged, and which the bishop, armed with a Papal Bull, was trying to discourage. Fortunately the squabble blew over and Charles continued with his life of trifles. He maintained a cordial but brief correspondence with Rome, much of which cannot be taken too seriously. One week he wrote to his father's secretary to tell him that he contemplated marriage with the Princess of Hesse-Darmstadt. By return of post he was informed that the Princess was at that time in Rome with her husband. Yet on 24 February he wrote to the Polish King at Luneville saying that he and the Princess had arrived in Polish territory, despite the fact that he was still at Avignon while the Princess was hundreds of miles farther east! He even referred to the Princess as 'la Princesse ma Femme'.

James was thoroughly perplexed by his son's behaviour. He complained that Charles had neglected matters of courtesy. He had not saluted the Pope upon his entry into Papal territory. He had angered the French King. Charles was more concerned with tantalizing the English government. On 26 February 1749, he left Avignon. On 11 April English agents reported that he had been seen in disguise in Paris. They feared he was about to marry Princess Radziwill. Simultaneous reports of Charles' appearance came from as far afield as Venice and Poland. In June Lord Kynford wrote from Moscow to say that Charles was definitely at Potsdam. Horace Mann discovered him, without money, in Venice, courting the second daughter of the Duke. In 1750 Lord Albemarle circulated a forged letter in the English press which claimed that the Prince had died of pneumonia on 24 August.

If Charles Edward's design was to confuse the British Government prior to an attack upon their territory, then he was eminently successful. No one in Europe really knew where he was at any given time. But the sad fact was that the preparation could be followed only by further preparation. There was no concrete action at hand, no cunning blow about to fall on the Hanoverians, however much Charles Edward may have relished the thought. During the years before 1765, the Prince's life consisted chiefly of visits to Paris, one to London in 1750 and mostly long sojourns in quiet towns like Basle and Bouillon. He lived under a variety of false names, for example, Baron Douglas, Bidolphe, Wm Bidle and the 'Wildman'. He sometimes referred to the French as Mr Orry and his father as 'Old Mr Douglas'. He was always short of money, and survived chiefly because of the generosity of staunch friends like the bankers, John and George Waters. He relied upon Jacobite supporters for funds and information and he used them to further conceal his whereabouts.

Though the Prince's behaviour shocked older Jacobites like Earl Marischal, his father firmly refused to condemn his son. James fervently believed that Charles had some grand design afoot. In the summer of 1750, the Prince asked that his Commission of Regency be renewed, and James readily complied, convinced that valuable action would soon occur. Instead of going to England, Charles spent the autumn of 1750 in the Convent of St Joseph in Paris. There, two of his most faithful servants, Madame de Vasse and her sister, Mlle Ferrand, looked after Charles intermittently for three years. They hid the Prince in a 'garde robe' during the day, and at night he would stroll along the corridor to another room where Madame de Talmont also happened to stay on occasion. In all Charles Edward appeared more determined to keep away from Rome than attempt another descent upon London.

In September 1750 the Prince did in fact go to London. He went at the invitation of English Jacobites and stayed at Essex Street, along the Strand, at the house of the notorious Lady Primrose. With typical audacity, he walked about London, taking in the sights. He looked at the Tower and ruminated upon methods for its capture. He met partisans along Pall Mall, whom he told that with 4,000 men he would again come to London to dislodge the present occupant of St James's.

He took one step which might have been important on this visit. He visited the church of St Mary's le Grand hard by what is now Trafalgar Square, abjured the Catholic faith and was received into the Church of England. When he got back he endeavoured to get this conversion publicized throughout Britain. His agents either failed to do so, or, equally probable, no one except a small group of non-juring clergymen of the Church of England took any notice. The whole gesture, courageous, futile, silly, and, by the standards of honour in his family, deplorable, fell flat.

By the second week of September, Charles was back in Paris. From there he journeyed to the Low Countries to which his former nurse, Clementina Walkinshaw, also happened to be headed. The legend says Clementina was summoned by the Prince, but her ostensible reason for travelling to the Low Countries was to take up a post as Canoness of a Noble Chapter at Douai. When Charles heard of her arrival on the continent he travelled to meet her and then brought her back to Ghent as his wife. From there, the couple travelled to Germany, and later to Liège, where they lived as Le Comte et Comtesse de Johnson. It was at Liège that Clementina gave birth to a daughter. The child was named Charlotte and quickly became her father's pride and joy. Wherever the Prince went, his daughter followed.

But not even the attachments of family could make Charles Edward abandon his charade. In 1753, following the arrest of Dr Cameron in Britain, Charles became fearful for his life. That was the reason for his flight into Germany. He was sufficiently calmed by his daughter's birth to settle for a time in Basle at the end of 1754, and the following year his major concern, as revealed in his correspondence, appears to have been a watch which he had ordered from Lucien le Roy in Paris. In March of 1754 he confessed to his father's secretary that there was very little news to cheer James. Two years later, he took his mistress and daughter to Flanders again, but at the end of the year was in Paris once more. In order to raise money, he hinted about a possible return to Italy, yet when money arrived from Rome he changed his mind and remained in Paris. In 1758 Charles found his last home till the end of his period of incognito at the Château de Carlsbourg at Bouillon. There he formed a friendship with the President of the Sovereign Court of Bouillon, a M. Thibault, which lasted through his most painful personal tragedy.

Throughout 1758 and 1759, Charles was greatly encouraged by the possible outcome of the Seven Years War. The French Minister, Choiseul, sought an audience early in February 1759, and a few days later Charles had a satisfactory interview with the French King himself. There had been overtures from Lords Blantyre and Clancarty in Scotland for an invasion of Scotland which the French seemed eager to assist. But Charles was wiser now. He was content to be sought by the French. He was willing to confer with them. He also knew that nothing solid would emerge from these discussions and he would no longer make a fool of himself merely to gratify the French. Nevertheless he dealt efficiently with a mission hastily despatched by James from Rome, and returned to his daughter only at the end of 1759 when the news of the fall of Quebec put paid to French schemes for an invasion of England.

On 9 January 1760, Charles Edward remembered

that he now had not seen his father for sixteen years and promptly despatched a letter to Rome to obtain funds to finance a visit. He eventually received 12,000 L., but then changed his mind and remained at Bouillon. He knew that his father and the Jacobite court disapproved of his liaison with Clementina and would do anything to break the relationship. They felt that the woman was a Hanoverian agent who would turn Charles against his own destiny. Rarely could there have been a woman less able to accomplish so difficult a feat. Her life with the Prince was far from happy. He treated her as his property, paid scant regard to her feelings, beat her when he was drunk, and did not let her go only because he was loath to part with any vestige of his belongings. He would not go to Rome because he knew that the Jacobite Court would also try to separate him from his beloved Charlotte. Thus when James fell ill in May 1760, the Prince continued to wait at Bouillon, despite the need for his presence in Rome should the King die.

James recovered from his illness in June, and with his return to health, the Prince's vitality also increased. But his high spirits were short-lived. On 22 July Clementina took her child and left for Paris. The loss of his daughter reduced Charles to months of helplessness. Desperately, he had the Paris convents scoured in order to find his daughter. Eventually one of his scouts, the Abbé Gordon, dealt Charles yet another blow. He informed the Prince that Charlotte was under the protection of the King at Rome. The Prince was enraged. There was nothing he could do to have his daughter returned. To the Abbé Gordon he wrote, 'I take this affaire so much to heart that I was not able to write what is here above, shall be in ye greatest affliction until I guet back ye childe, which was my only Comfort in my Misfortunes.' All Charles' anger turned upon his father. Once before James had conspired against him when Henry became a Cardinal.

Now he had taken away the one light in an otherwise miserable life. In defence, James pointed out that it was Clementina who had sought his assistance. 'It was many months before I had undoubted Information of her desire to leave you, to satisfy her own conscience in the first place, and to stop the mouths of those to whom she knew she was obnoxious and suspected, and lastly to be able to give her daughter in a convent a Christian and good Education.' There was really nothing Charles could do. Those who had once heaped calumny upon Clementina's head now referred to 'that poor woman'. James had endorsed her desertion and the kidnap of Charles' daughter. The Prince vowed rebellion. He would neither write nor speak to anyone till his daughter be returned. He would not shave. He would drink himself silly.

During his retreat Charles stayed chiefly at Luneville. He drank heavily, composing rhymes while in his cups: 'To Speke to Ete/To Think to Drink'. 'To ete to think/To Speke to Drink'. He even posted off his more profound thoughts to amazed servants. In sober moments, the Prince interested himself in science and was the proud possessor of an 'astromical telescope'. The greater part of his reading must have been in lighter vein, for among his library there abound such titles as: *Venus in a Cloister, or the Nun in a Chemise, The Brothel* and *The Art of Love in Six Cantos*. Although he was inundated with 'information' regarding the 'true state of England' Charles paid most of it scant attention. His horizon had narrowed. He was no longer interested in futile scheming.

Charles remained true to his vow. Despite occasional letters from Clementina informing him of Charlotte's progress, he could not be stirred. James made repeated efforts to have emissaries received by the Prince, but Charles turned them all back. He was not excited by the death of George II nor the prospect of restoration before George III settled in to the throne. Only when

James III by right of heritage King of Great Britain, Ireland and the Dominions was regarded in his permanent exile in Rome as the most respectable and least troublesome of throneless monarchs. He was recognized as King by the Pope and by the French and most Catholic Kings and Princes as a legitimate King to whom royal honours should be paid. The most practical and useful honour which came his way was a regular and by no means negligible pension from the Pope.

The reason for this respect and this pension was quite simple. James had tried to regain his royal birthright in 1715 and failed. After failure and various wanderings in which he scrupulously obeyed the monarch and government of any country in which he found himself, he settled down in Rome. Settled is the operative word; he had quite made up his mind to stay there, and never again to attempt to take his throne by force. It is obvious, too, that he disapproved of and discouraged any attempts by other people by force of arms to put him on the throne where he belonged. He was in every sense of the word a safe exile to give shelter to in such a place as Rome.

He must have been delighted when accounts reached him of his dearest Carluccio's triumphant successes at the beginning of the Forty-Five, and have been painfully fearful for him in the flight among the heather after Culloden; and consequently he had heard with the greatest fatherly relief of Charles' successful escape back to France. But why, oh why, did Carluccio linger on in France or anywhere else when he might come back to safety, comfort, affection and possibly even a pension in Rome?

Again the answer is simple. Charles upon his return,

as we have mentioned, immediately set upon trying another Forty-Five and with elusive French or Spanish help. This was not only incomprehensible to James, but also abhorrent. Failure was failure; and if it was the duty of a King to accept that elementary fact, how much more so was it the obedient duty of a Prince?

Charles would not recognize that fact. He knew that if he came back to Rome it would be a tacit admission that he had accepted failure. The Prince also had his other reasons; he was disgusted by what he could remember of the squabbling, ineffectual and worthless intrigues of Jacobite hangers-on at the Palazzo Muti. He knew that they were just beating about in the air with their vain dreams and taking in their own dirty washing of intrigue. Indeed they intrigued and quarrelled so noisily that the whole place was surrounded and sometimes penetrated by the spies and agents sent out or locally hired by the London Government. They must have had an easy job, for apart from reporting idle gossip there was nothing to say.

But there certainly would have been something to say and to report on if the hero of the Forty-Five had returned even for a short time to his father's palace. Charles had had quite enough evidence of the activities of such agents and even assassins where he was. He had no desire to go to the Jacobite Court in Rome which was, for all purposes, the continental headquarters of such individuals.

But King James, good, simple man that he was, knew nothing of such things, nor if he had would he have understood them. This simplicity made him even more amenable to the subtle Roman and Italian authorities.

They were, perhaps, really sad when the old man died; at any rate they genuinely mourned him. The Pope, after having his body laid out in state at the church of SS Apostoli just opposite the Palazzo Muti, gave him a royal state funeral culminating in his interment in St Peter's itself. The now elderly and exhausted Jacobite intriguers had no central figure to buzz around; they drifted away and dissolved. Even the shadow of an incarnate Cause had disappeared from the Palazzo, which was the official property of the Stuart family in Italy.

Henry, as was his right as a Cardinal, had an audience with the Pope. He implored His Holiness to continue to recognize the Stuart legitimist claims by acknowledging Charles as *de jure* King. He had the support of the French Ambassador to the Vatican, thereby giving the Pope the impression that he was acting under instructions from the French Court at Versailles. The Pope therefore did not wish to give a purely personal yes or no to the request, and fell back upon summoning a Congregation of Cardinals to advise.

In the meantime there were rumours in London that the Pope would continue his recognition as he had given it to James III on condition that France and Spain supported him. The British Ambassador in France spoke to a highly placed French Minister who reassured him that 'the only King of England France acknowledged was George III'. France would certainly not consider Charles as even a potential rival in exile. The French Ambassador to the Vatican was a close friend of the Cardinal of York, who had impulsively acted on his own and solicited in favour of Charles being recognized. The Ambassador got a sharp rebuke from Versailles for meddling in the matter. King Louis of France had decided to take no part in it. This decided the question put to the Congregation of Cardinals. They said (as their advice had been sought) that the Pope could not *per ora* grant the Cardinal of York's request on behalf of Charles his brother.

There was only one thing, then, for Charles to do. Despite Henry's advice he would come to Rome and chance his luck. On 21 January Charles wrote to

York: 'Have nothing more to add but to express the impatience I have to Embrace a Brother that is so dear to me, so remain your loving Brother, Charles R.' He reached Rome on 23 January and was evidently disappointed at his reception. His brother met him and drove him to the Palazzo Muti. Here Henry told Charles that the Pope would not acknowledge him even as a *de jure* King. After an outburst of rage, Charles decided to stay in Rome and see what his presence could do.

He was gratified by two things, one trivial. When they drove out together the Cardinal placed him on his right-hand side, a compliment a Cardinal would pay only to a King. His brother's generosity was not trivial, but gratifying. On King James' death the Pope had granted to Henry of York a pension of £1,200. Henry made this pension over to his brother, and from his private purse supplemented it by an annual sum of £1,800. But what pleased Charles most was the behaviour of the Scots, English and Irish Colleges who celebrated *Te Deums* in his honour as King, despite Papal orders against such celebrations.

That old gossip, Sir Horace Mann, the English Minister in Florence, wrote to the Secretary of State in London thus:

I have this morning received from Rome by an extraordinary conveyance that the indiscretion of the Pretender fomented by that of his adherents, had given occasion to fresh disturbances there, to the Pope, as in open defiance of his decision and of the notification that was sent by his order to all the Cardinals and to the chief of the Principle orders not to acknowledge his pretended titles, the Rectors and Students of the English, Scotch and Irish Colleges there, as well as the Superiors of two other Irish convents, dared to receive him with all the state that they were capable of, and to acknowledge the titles he assumes, in the most solemn manner that could depend upon them. Everything being privately settled for that purpose, the first visit the Pretender made was to the English Convent of St. Thomas, at the entrance of which he was received by the Rector, and by all the students in their habits of ceremony, who conducted him to a Chair of State, when a *Te Deum* was sung for his return by the title of Charles III, their Sovereign, after which he was conducted to the great hall of their College where they all kissed his hand. The same ceremony was practised for three days following in the Irish Churches which I have before mentioned. For which public contempt of the Pope's orders and Rectors of the English and Scotch Colleges as well as the Superiors of the two Irish Convents, were by order of the Secretary of State banished from Rome. An order was likewise sent to the Abbé Grant, who is agent there for the Scotch Roman Catholics and who has been very busy on this occasion not to dare to approach any of the Pope's Palaces, or to frequent his Ministers; at the same time the pension which he received from that Government has been taken from him.

Sir Horace had got some things wrong. The Pope was annoyed, but took no action save to remind the nuncios that he had not and would not acknowledge Charles Edward Stuart as King. Still, it must have been highly gratifying to Charles to have had the Rectors and students of the Colleges of the three Kingdoms acknowledging him in this public way.

Despite the Pope's annoyance, Henry was able to obtain an audience for his brother. As Cardinal, Henry of York was at once admitted to the audience chamber. Then after a while he took in his brother, who went down on his knees and kissed the Holy Father's hand. The Pope bade him rise; he stood and conversed amiably yet respectfully with the Pope for a quarter of an hour. 'God be praised,' the Cardinal wrote to a friend whose name we do not know; for though the letter is in the Cardinal's hand, the address is missing:

God be praised. Last Saturday after a good deal of battleying upon very trifling circumstances, I carried my brother to the Pope's privately, as a private nobleman, by which means he was certainly derogated nothing of his first pretensions, and has at the same time fulfilled with an indespensable duty owing to the Head of the Church. The visit went much better than I expected, the Pope was extremely well satisfied, and my brother well enough content, though I asked him very few questions, and so I hope to draw from it a great deal of good, provided my brother does not obstruct all by his indocility, and most singular way of thinking and arguing.

Andrew Lang supports Ewald in saying that it was on this visit to Rome that the Prince 'was privately reconciled to the Pope by his brother's intervention'. On the same page he also cites Ewald with approval for a report from Sir William Hamilton who had come to Rome from Naples in 1767. Hamilton reports that Charles 'appeared to me to be absorbed in melancholy thought, a good deal of distraction in his conversation and frequent brown study ... He told me time lay heavy on him.' It certainly did; and there is evidence that he sought the anodyne for boredom once again in drink.

The Cardinal of York wrote of him at this time: 'He has singular tenderness and regard for me ... and as singular an inflexibility and disregard for everything that regards his own good ... I am persuaded we should give some ground as to everything, were it not for the nasty bottle, that goes on but too much, and certainly must at last kill him.'

Maybe Charles saw more of Roman society; in 1767, however, he broke clean off and forever from the faithful Lumisden, his father's secretary, who, with some other companions refused to accompany him in his carriage 'when he was in no condition to go abroad'. According to Forbes, Charles now drank 'like one absent in mind when he was met with things that vex'd him, as too often was the case'. But the Prince's whole life was not one long hangover. He spent his summers at Pisa and winters at Rome and was according to one visitor, 'of middle height, bloated, heavy, with a sleepy face, but clear blue eyes, light brown hair, a portly, but noble presence and still extremely graceful'.

His faithful Scots adherents at home or abroad were now concerned with his marriage prospects. A legitimate heir was desirable. France, too, was of like mind. The French Court cared nothing for Jacobitism, but regarded the presence of a continuing *de jure* Stuart monarchy in Europe as a useful thorn in the English Hanoverian side. Charles, too, must have felt it politic now to think of marriage and of begetting heirs.

The French had been very steadily losing both face and ground to Hanoverian Britain. But the nation that was inflicting these losses on them was, in so far as its domestic policies were concerned, far from being contented. In 1777 Dr Samuel Johnson took Boswell's breath away – a pleasurable experience which 'Bozzy' frequently enjoyed in the Doctor's company – by stating: 'If England were fairly polled, the present King would be sent away tonight, and his adherents hanged tomorrow.'

French agents in Britain as well as ordinary perceptive visitors must have been aware that despite the United Kingdom's sensational victories overseas and the beginnings of the British Empire in the east in India, as well as in the west, the ordinary man at home found life disagreeable. Never before had there been so many corrupt politicians and venal men in high places. The people knew this, and though they were not taxed so iniquitously as we are today, they knew they were being milked by the men in power.

Though not caring a scrap for the Cause, the French Ministers felt it strongly desirable that a *de jure* succession of legitimist monarchs should continue in Europe. Not only would these legitimist Kings be a thorn in Britain's side, but (vain thought) they might even get back again on the throne of the United Kingdom. If so, peace in Europe or, at best peace between France and Britain would ensue.

Therefore the French encouraged the Prince to marry before it was too late for him to sire an heir. They employed an Irishman, Colonel Ryan, an officer in the French service, to tour round Europe to discover a suitable royal bride.

His choice finally settled upon Louise, Princess of

Stolberg, a daughter of Prince Gustavus Adolphus of Stolberg, and of Lady Charlotte Bruce, herself the daughter of the distinguished Scottish house headed by the Earls of Elgin. The Elgins claim and with some justification to be descended from King Robert the Bruce, the victor at Bannockburn. The Stewarts were descended from a sister of the Bruce married to Walter the Steward – hence their name. Therefore to social eligibility was now added something highly appropriate – her inherited blood.

Louise's father had been killed in a battle fighting for Austria, leaving her mother almost penniless and with four daughters. She was anxious to get husbands for them as soon as possible; for the pension allowed her by the Empress, Maria Theresa, though adequate, did not go a long way. She was glad, therefore, when King Charles, stimulated by the Irishman's description of her, chose Louise the eldest. She was twenty.

Modern romantic writers have poured out their sympathy upon Louise at twenty being given in marriage to a man of fifty-two. What they forget in this age of protracted adolescence, is that a young woman of breeding and any pretensions to good looks in the eighteenth century was in danger of being left on the shelf at twenty, especially if she had three younger sisters of marriageable age.

Their sympathy is wasted upon Louise. She had been hardened in the marriage-market for four years already. When the marriage by proxy in Paris was unduly delayed, it was she who had hurried it up by grappling with the problems of ecclesiastical law and with other such details as the pension the French Government had promised Charles before his marriage. Later she was to write to the French Ministry to claim that the pension should really be paid to her. She was an egotist, a profuse letter writer in which the pronoun 'I' proliferates; she also had a little learning upon a wide number of subjects, and was accounted among her friends to be what we now call a blue-stocking. She was an adulteress as well, an unusual combination.

She had a fine natural complexion, beautiful teeth and eyes. Her luxuriant hair was blonde – an attractive feature for a woman in Italy where nearly all women have raven hair. She had a tart and occasionally witty tongue. Though not strictly speaking a beauty, she attracted men strongly; it is easy to see why.

After the considerable difficulties put forward by the Empress Maria Theresa which necessitated the marriage by proxy in Paris, Louise met Charles at Macerata in northern Italy. Not by design, but by the chance of her unexpectedly quick journey. They met on Good Friday. It had been stipulated by Louise's mother that the wedding should take place *and* be consummated on the day they met. Good Friday was about the least suitable day of the year for meeting one's bride for the first time, marrying her and consummating that marriage, all within a few hours; but Charles had to do it, and presumably managed it. We should have heard from the bride's never-ceasing tongue or pen if he had not.

On Easter Sunday they entered Rome. The Cardinal of York had sent state coaches to meet them with outriders in scarlet liveries and white cockades. They drove down thus to the Palazzo Muti in the Piazza SS Apostoli.

Louise was genuinely enchanted by the wealth and display of Jacobite hospitality that was showered upon her. Her brother-in-law the Cardinal called the next day and gave her many presents including a gold box with his portrait on it set in diamonds. Inside it he had put a draft for 40,000 crowns – that was at that time the equivalent of about £10,000. As the Prince had already added 3,000 livres a year to her personal allowance, she was not doing too badly.

To begin with the marriage went so well that it looked as if it was going to be a success – Charles remained perfectly sober for some time. When he was frustrated, wandering, on the run or under a grievance, just or unjust, he had recourse to the bottle as all his acquaintances and much of Europe knew. But now he was happy and sober. Forbes wrote that the Prince 'now enjoys more ease and quiet than formerly, and has never been seen concerned in the least with liquor since . . .' He took great pleasure in his wife's attractive appearance and natural vivacity. It would be too much to say that he fell in love with her or even loved her on sight; but he was attracted by her and much stimulated by her natural vivacity.

The Queen, as she was now known in her own circle, was a social success in Rome. A young Swiss man of fashion, Carl Victor Bonstetten, called her 'The Queen of Hearts'. Some have speculated that her career of adultery began with him. If so, it is difficult to see where and how they managed it. Charles, right from the beginning, was very watchful of her – so was Roman society. She did, however, write to Bonstetten saying that he was the kind of lover she wanted, because he knew how to make love only when she and he were alone. It has been maintained that this was only schoolgirl sentimentality. In view of Louise's future career of adultery this is at least debatable.

All Jacobites in Scotland, England, Ireland or elsewhere were eagerly waiting to hear the news of the birth of a Royal heir. Those who were not Jacobites also looked for news of it. Had it happened it would have been of general and widespread interest. None came. This need not have been Charles' fault. He was still sexually potent at the age of fifty-two – most men are; and even his enemies a year later were to accuse him of ravishing his wife when she did not feel like it.

It is more probable that Louise was barren. Her

career of adultery and, after Charles' death, of steady fornication produced no children, born still or quick. It is extremely unlikely that she or her lovers would have condescended to use those crude contraceptives of the eighteenth century described by Boswell. Maybe Louise was responsible for the rumours of false pregnancies which circulated about her; at any rate she talked enough about them to justify curiosity.

It does not, however, justify the behaviour of the English-Hanoverian spies. They bribed the laundry maids to let them see and examine the Queen's dirty linen before it went to the wash. By keeping this up for many months, and by regular examination at certain periods of the month, they hoped to find evidence that would be useful to them in establishing her possible pregnancy. They were disappointed.

Louise's chatter about her false pregnancies was responsible for that fantastic pair, 'the Sobieski Stuarts'. The story they put about and in which they believed themselves, was that a British warship under Captain Allan had called at Genoa. To him was delivered a mysterious bundle containing a male infant. It was explained to him that this was the son of Charles who wanted it to be taken away from Italy (where it would be in danger of being killed) and brought to Britain. This alleged son married and had two sons who were convinced they were of royal descent. They settled on an island in the River Beauly in romantic circumstances. One of them had a supposed resemblance to King James III; the other to Charles I and on this resemblance alone a number of established people in the Highlands believed in their claim. That this preposterous pair got away with their story is a tribute to the spirit of loyalty still existing in the Highlands then, but it was an outrage on common sense. They published a book on Scottish tartans, almost all of them invented by the authors. On the authority of this bogus book rest more than half the tartans displayed at Highlands gatherings.

At the end of August 1774 the Prince and his Princess moved to a villa between Asa and Parma. Charles had left Rome rather than face the slights which he was bound to suffer during the festivities surrounding the Pope's imminent Jubilee. The move was not welcomed by Louise. She found it dull there, and, as there was no opera in Florence she had to go to the Casino dei Nobili which she left at ten in order to resume her prolific and gossipy correspondence with her large acquaintanceship.

It was here that boredom aroused her tart tongue or rather pen in a letter to her husband: 'Puisque votre Majesté ne veut pas entendre raison quand on lui parle ...' She mocks at his age, the decline of his one-time good looks and above all at his infirmities. At this time he was seriously and painfully ill. He was enduring day and night asthma in this period of great heat; moreover his legs had never recovered from the hardships he had suffered after Culloden and were so painful that they had broken out in ulcers.

Louise does not let him off any of these infirmities on which she comments ironically. She concludes by saying she is sending to all her friends the memorial which she enclosed with this letter. Whether she did do this we do not know; for no copy of the 'memorial' survives. Perhaps she did not circulate it; perhaps she did not even compose it. It may have been no more than an idle if vicious threat of a woman suffering from boredom and concentrating all that sense of being bored upon her bed-ridden husband.

The really puzzling question is what it was that inclined Charles to keep this letter. Perhaps he was too ill to destroy it, but merely let it fall beside his bed. Louise may have picked it up and kept it – if not for posterity then at least for other people to see.

A week later Louise wrote to Bonstetten in Rome complaining of the intense heat. She told him: 'Almost, yes almost two days ago I saw when I was to become mistress of my own destiny. Death and disease danced above the head of my lord and master.' There is not much comment one can make on that death-wishing letter except to point out that Louise had signed it as Queen Louise R, whereas in public the couple used the title of the Count and Countess of Albany. At the same time Louise R was carrying on a fervid flirtation with two young Englishmen visiting Florence.

Horace Mann says that these flirtations were carried on with the approbation of the Count of Albany: * 'But with such vigilance, *he* says, as at all events, not to render the legitimacy of an Heir to the Crown dubious. This occasions much mirth here.' Louise's posthumous supporters put forward this letter of Mann's as a proof of her innocence. But is it? The sneer of '*he* says' does not sound like a proof of innocence. There can be little doubt that Charles was now beginning to have suspicions of his wife's behaviour.

Another letter from Mann says:

He (Charles) goes every evening to the Theatre, where he sits in a corner of his box in a drowsy posture, but is frequently obliged, by sickness at his stomach, to retire to the common corridor ... visitors, however, to his wife go thither as usual. He is jealous to such a degree that neither there or at home, she is ever out of his sight. All the avenues to her room, excepting through his own, are barricaded. The reason he gives for this is that the succession may never be dubious.

We owe something to Sir Horace Mann's incurable love of gossiping on paper to his friends, but there is

* These and most details in this chapter derive from Mann's official correspondence with the Secretary of State in London and his unofficial letters to his friend Horace Walpole.

much in it that is distasteful. He describes Charles' illnesses in unsavoury detail. But this is but one more example of the paradoxical quality of the eighteenth century. In it men could combine cruelty and what seems to us a strange relish in disgusting behaviour with a capacity for creating beauty in the arts, especially architecture.

In 1777 Charles bought the Palazzo Quadagui, which is still today as it was then. Above it there is a weather vane, and on it the initials C.R. (Carolus Rex). It was in this palace that Charles' humiliation was made complete. In the eighteenth century in Italy the *cavaliere servente* was a recognized and usually a respectable figure. He was an admitted admirer of a married woman of fashion who would accompany her to her box at the opera and to other public places when her husband did not feel inclined to go.

Louise's *cavaliere servente* was Count Alfieri, a poet and playwright of immense fertility and versatility who in his lifetime had won international fame. His work was largely inspired by the cause of a united Italy in place of the peninsula divided into separate states. Idealistic causes of this kind usually produce poets, playwrights or authors whose works give them much popularity at the time. Sometimes that popularity survives the triumph of the Cause, sometimes it does not. Alfieri is an example of the latter kind. His name is well remembered as a romantic figure of his time, but his poems are now largely unread, his plays unperformed.

Alfieri is far too often referred to as a genius. He had, if it is not stretching the use of the word too far, a genius for living by using his fantastic energy and undoubtedly handsome appearance. But a genius for living does not usually survive death; and the dust thickens upon the literary fruits of his remarkable personality when he was alive.

Charles received his wife's *cavaliere servente* Alfieri

for many months into his house at the Palazzo Quadagui; but it was probably not until some time in 1780 that he became aware that the carroty-haired, dashing Alfieri had become more intimate with Louise R. than the role of *cavaliere servente* permitted. We do not know what he saw or what was the incident that enlightened him, but the shock of it turned him back once again to his old anodyne of drink.

Drink is about the last thing anyone suffering from physical jealousy should take as an anodyne; it only inflames the most persistently torturing of all passions. That Charles was now drinking too much was evident to all then. Things were working their way to a crisis, and that crisis was described by Louise.

According to her, on the eve of St Andrew's Day 1780, when Charles had been giving and drinking a number of toasts to the Patron Saint of Scotland, he grew so inflamed that he forced his way into her bedroom and having accused her of infidelity, ravished her. She repeated this story all over Florence. Sir Horace Mann, of course, gloated, but we have no evidence other than Louise's story to support it. Biography after biography contain accounts of this scene as if it were an established fact.

Charles when heated with wine may well have told her that he knew about her relations with Alfieri, but there is no evidence other than that of Louise's to convict him of aggression. The probability is that it was invented to provide an excuse for her escape from Charles, which she soon managed. Young Dutens, of French Huguenot extraction, travelling through Italy, and from whom we have a full account of that escape, does not say a word about this St Andrew's Eve ravishment as an excuse for her escape.

Louise chose an Irishwoman living in Florence, the widow of the Florentine nobleman Orlandini, to assist her in this escape. The Irishwoman, the daughter of an officer in the Austrian service, had been living with an impoverished young adventurer named Geoghegan, also Irish. Madame Orlandini, who had been to breakfast at the Palazzo Quadagui, suggested that they should all go to inspect the needlework at the convent of the Little White Nuns. On arriving at the steps of the convent Geoghegan was there as if by chance. Louise and her confederates walked rapidly up the steps, followed slowly by Charles. Louise at once gained an entrance, but before Charles could follow, the door was closed. Geoghegan said that when the ladies had gone in the nuns had uncivilly closed the door. Charles knocked and banged, but in vain. The Mother Superior came, and speaking through the grille, explained that Louise had fled to the convent as a refuge; she would stay there under the protection of the Grand Duchess.

From the convent Louise began her campaign of letter-writing in defence of her flight; she addressed herself to the ecclesiastical authorities in Rome, principally to her brother-in-law the Cardinal of York. This had the desired effect – Pope Pius VI wrote to say that Louise should have his protection if she came to Rome. Louise promptly took action and set out for Rome, accompanied at first by Alfieri, who later got out of the coach so that her proclaimed innocence should not suffer; she arrived alone, and retired to another convent there.

Sir Horace Mann reported home thus:

> The mould for any more casts of the Royal Stuarts has been broken, or, what is equivalent to it, is now shut up in a convent of Nuns under double lock and key of the Pope and the Cardinal of York, out of reach of any dabbler who might foister in any spurious copy. Histories may now close the lives on that family, unless the Cardinal should become Pope, and that would only produce a short scene of ridicule. . . . At present she is

to have half the pension of twelve thousand Crowns which the Pope gave her husband. This will affect him more than the loss of his wife.

Having fled to a convent in Rome, her immediate concern was how to get out of it, to resume her affair with Alfieri. They corresponded with each other using the *noms d'amour* of Pipsio and Pipsia – onomatopaeic words to imitate the sound of kissing. This was not enough for them; Pipsio went south to Naples to sulk, but Pipsia once again proved her capacity for managing affairs in her favour.

In less than three months she got round the 'silly' Cardinal of York – the word 'silly' quoted from a letter of Mann's still meant, even as late as the eighteenth century, 'simple', ready to be easily influenced towards benevolence. The Cardinal allowed her to be installed in an apartment of his official *Cancelleria* – his residence in Rome when he came there from his see in Frascati. He also reduced Charles' pension by about a half, giving the remainder to Louise. The French Court, too, which had largely arranged Louise's marriage, was sufficiently impressed by her lying, or at least exaggerated letters, to grant her a pension of twenty thousand crowns for life. She was not doing too badly on money. The only bar to her contentment was that Pipsio was banished from Rome. Pipsia wanted more from him than passionate letters. Both Pipsio and Pipsia were egotists, but their egotism was complementary, and they needed to have physical expression in bed together.

She managed to grow thin and ill – determined egotists can produce these physical effects merely by willing them to happen. She succeeded in persuading her acquaintanceship in Rome that her symptoms were the after effects of Charles' brutality to her. She schemed to get Alfieri back to Rome on a visit and got him to make a present of a specially bound and produced copy of Virgil to the Cardinal of York to play upon his 'silliness'. It worked; Alfieri settled down in Rome, poured out a string of tragedies, while riding in the Campagna with Louise. The relationship between the pair would have been obvious to anyone except the 'silly' Cardinal of York and the benevolently inclined Pope Pius VI. Charles wrote asking for Alfieri's banishment from Rome on account of his association with his wife Louise. But he wrote in vain. Alfieri's fame and romantic appearance and manner had had their effect. The Pope merely said that he wished he had more gentlemen like Count Alfieri in Rome.

Sentimental women supporters of the scheming Louise, such as the Marchese Vitelleschi, claimed that Louise's attitude towards the handsome Alfieri was merely an intellectual one. This is foolish; proof of Alfieri's physical affair with Louise R. is to be found in a sonnet cut out from his collected works, but which unfortunately for the pair emerged in the appendix of *Studii Alfierani*. They were having a splendid time; the only thing that would have completed their happiness would have been the news of Charles' death – and that, according to reports, did not look so far off.

It apparently soon became very near when a courier was sent to Rome in March to announce that Charles was dying, and that if his brother the Cardinal of York wished to be in time he should post at once to Florence. For reasons which we do not know, the Cardinal could not go at once, but did manage a journey to see his brother in April who had by then, as a result of his unconquerable vitality, recovered – bad news for Louise R. Even worse news for Louise in 1783, if she heard it at the time, was that Charles upon his recovery legitimized his daughter Charlotte, creating her Duchess of Albany.

The results of his recovery produced other bad results for Louise and Alfieri. When the Cardinal did see his brother he was to receive from him a full account of Louise's adulteries and general misbehaviour. He may have been shown the infamous letter from Louise to her husband when he was ill – the letter quoted earlier in the chapter. At any rate, for the time it cooked Alfieri's goose. The following is an extract from one of Sir Horace Mann's letters back to England:

> I formerly gave you an account of the fracas in the Pretender's family, by the Elopement of his Wife, whom everyone pitied and applauded. The tables are now turned. The cat, at last, out of the bag. The Cardinal of York's visit to his brother gave the latter an opportunity to undeceive him, only proving to him that the complaints laid to his charge of ill-using her were invented to cover a Plot formed by Count Alfieri who ... had imposed upon the Grand Duke, the Pope and the Cardinal and all who took her part.... On his (the Cardinal's) return to Rome he exposed the whole to the Pope, and obtained an order from him for Count Alfieri to leave the Pope's State in fifteen days....

This was all very well, but how was the confusion of Charles' marriage with Louise to be resolved? Most fortunately, in November 1783 Gustavus III of Sweden was travelling through France and went out of his way to see Charles, with whom he struck up a friendship as a fellow King. At any rate Gustavus applied his practical as well as generous mind to Charles' problems. He put his financial affairs upon an orderly basis and made them more comfortable by being the agent for their increase.

But, above all, he arranged a formal and recognized separation from Louise which pleased everyone; though complicated arguments had to be used with the Cardinal of York before he would lend his important agreement. King Gustavus must also have seen Louise in Rome, for she displayed an unusual generosity. She surrendered her marriage pension and the Sobieski jewels which she had appropriated as her own property when she had left the Palazzo Quadagui.

When Alfieri heard of the official separation between Louise and her husband – her 'freedom' he would have called it – he decided to join her openly at once; his audacity, however, stopped short of suggesting that such a return should take place in Italy where they would have been under the eyes of the Church and particularly of Charles' brother, the Cardinal.

He therefore fixed the assignation for 'perpetual joy' at Colmar near the Rhine. And so in August 1784, at the Inn of the Two Keys, Pipsio and Pipsia met again. Pipsio was speechless with happiness. One of the most credulous of Louise's biographers, Miss Vernon Lee, says that they passed two months together at the inn enjoying platonic ecstasies.

It is characteristic of Louise's obsession for writing gossipy letters that she should now have bombarded the Cardinal of York with bitter letters about his brother Charles' behaviour. But for what purpose? There was no more money to be squeezed or sucked out of the Cardinal, she had no practical reason for keeping on good terms with him. It is just possible that she may have heard through one of those channels which are only open to professional gossipers that Charles was now at last beginning to enjoy the most contented period of his life since he had returned from Scotland and the Forty-Five.

His daughter Charlotte had come to stay and look after him, and, as we shall see, to lighten his declining years. Had Louise heard this, what one can only call her bitchiness would have further envenomed her poisonous pen.

Louise and Alfieri continued at intervals over two years to use the inn at Colmar as a place where they could in private practise their platonic ecstasies. And it was there that enters our story, if only briefly, a character who throws light on Alfieri. This was a young man engaged by Alfieri as a secretary, and his name was Gaetano Poldoni, the grandfather of Dante Gabriel Rossetti. He took a strong dislike to his employer and his mistress, and one ought to take his strictures on them with a pinch of salt. But his letters and scraps of writing spring to life and have an echo of the truth about them when he is on the subject of the Count Alfieri – his highly scented red hair, his blue cloak lined with scarlet and above all his longing to be admired especially by the people for whom he affected a contempt. One can see him, hear him and smell his over-scented ambience, as one reads. Unfortunately Poldoni left no account of Louise.

Louise and Alfieri had moved to France, a France upon the eve of the Revolution, and were living in Paris. Alfieri's old mother knew about her son's liaison with Louise; and it was to her that Louise wrote a characteristically self-pitying and abusive letter about Charles. She had not seen him for some time, but he obstinately insisted on remaining alive; her letter ends thus: 'He drags out a miserable life, abandoned by all the world, without relatives or friends, given over to his servants.'

She founded in the house in Paris which she shared with Alfieri a salon ruled over by herself as the Queen of Great Britain and Ireland.

All the trappings of royalty were on show – plates bearing the Royal Arms, servants in scarlet livery had to call her 'Your Majesty' and had to walk out backwards from her presence; she even had a throne decorated with the Royal Arms. Despite his Republican views, widely propagated by himself, Alfieri enjoyed the situation of having a Queen as his openly acknowledged mistress. He hated France, and even the outbreak of the Revolution did not lessen his sense of inferiority towards the French. He, the internationally celebrated poet and dramatist, never recovered from the mortification of being asked by a French man of fashion whether he wrote comedies or tragedies.

As the Revolution became more savage Paris became too uncomfortable for a dilettante Republican poet; and the pair sought refuge in England where Louise, who had lost her pension under the Revolutionary French Government, had hopes of extracting one from George III. The idea was not as absurd as it sounds. The first King George 'born a Britain' had, despite his ridiculous and pathological fits of obstinacy, a genuine tenderness towards Jacobite relics; it was one of his most generous qualities. But despite her presentation at Court Louise's hopes failed.

The war that broke out between Britain and France drove the pair back again across the Channel. France they found impossible, and went south to Florence. The prolific Alfieri was still making money by his work, and Louise had a pension of 6,000 crowns from an arrangement made after Charles' death, so they were not in want.

The preposterous poet now decided to teach himself Greek with the notion of translating or adapting Homer with the aid of a lexicon, and locked himself up in retreat on this task by day and night. This gave Louise opportunities for a flirtation, to put it at its mildest, with a young French painter François Xavier Fabre, a monarchist exile in Florence. She was repeating the habits she had acquired when married to Charles and when his elderly sleepiness allowed her to commit adultery with Alfieri in the same house as her husband – possibly in the same room in which he was snoring.

In 1803 Alfieri died and Louise, dumpier and more Germanic than ever, set up her Court in Florence in absurd style. It was a Court in which the French language was supposed to predominate. It is to be hoped that the Queen who faced her courtiers while seated upon a domestic throne had improved her knowledge of French since the days when she had written the celebrated letter to Charles during his illness.

Why devote even these few pages to such a degrading figure of fun? I do so because she was the last Stuart Queen and cannot be allowed to slip away unnoticed. She has, moreover, had her defenders, but they are mostly sentimental Englishwomen; they find themselves in acute difference from the French and Italian writers, some of whom knew her. I conclude by quoting Sir Compton Mackenzie who has delved deeply into eighteenth-century Jacobite history, generous and sympathetic where he can be so, but devastating where the subject calls for it:

> She was entirely without religion. She had no faith in humanity. She was mercenary. She was a liar. She was cold to the very core of her being. She was pretentious. She was self-complacent. Such humour as she had was of the privy. She began life as a chatter-box with good teeth and pretty complexion. She ended as a dowdy, interminable old bore in a red shawl.

It is a grateful task to turn from the disagreeable events of the last chapter to the story of how the last days of Charles were sweetened by his daughter Charlotte. 'Lady Charlotte Stuart' as she passed in society had been the only child whom Charles had begot from his liaison with Clementina Walkinshaw; after her legitimation she became, as we have already said, the Duchess of Albany.

But before touching on her last act of pure benevolence and kindness, I must turn to her past. In 1772 the Countess d'Albertstrof (Clementina Walkinshaw), her daughter 'Lady Charlotte' and Charles were all in Rome. Charles offered to see his daughter but insisted that she should come unaccompanied by her mother Clementina. Understandably and with some spirit, the girl refused – taking the ban upon her mother as an act of rudeness, or at least one of lack of charity; so nothing came of it.

There was also a rumour current in the early nineteenth century, recounted by Sir Walter Scott, that Charlotte had married and produced a son. This was the Count Roehenstart in whom Lady Bute in 1815 saw a strong resemblance to Madame d'Albertstrof (Clementina Walkinshaw). There is no evidence at all that Charlotte had married Roehenstart or anyone else.* However, there is a possibility that it was Clementina who had a child and that one of them was by Count Roehenstart. The resemblance that Lady Bute detected in Roehenstart was to Clementina, not Charlotte. The early nineteenth-century Roehenstart was probably the grandson of Clementina.

* There have been historians who claim that Charlotte had three children by Archbishop Ferdinand de Rohan by 1783, and these were looked after by Clementina.

What is more interesting, in the face of Charlotte's refusal to see her father alone and without her mother, was her complete obedience to him in other commands. This devotion seems to us to have encroached quite unnecessarily on her personal and private life. He forbade her to take the veil and enter a convent, or to marry. It would seem that what was passing through the Prince's mind in those earlier days was the possibility of legitimizing Charlotte so that she would be his heir as Queen of the Kingdom in the event of a Stuart restoration.

If she were to become a nun that would rule her out of the succession as effectively as his brother Henry had ruled himself out by taking Holy Orders and becoming a Cardinal. What would also rule her out of the succession in those remote eighteenth-century days would have been her marriage with someone not of royal blood. And Charles saw precious little chance of effecting a royal marriage with his bastard daughter even if he had made her legitimate, so it is unlikely that there is any truth in the early nineteenth-century story that Charlotte did marry.

As we have seen in the last chapter one of the most odious of the letters that poured from the pen of Charles' wife Louise was that one to her lover Alfieri's mother speaking with gusto of Charles' state, 'wretched and abandoned by all save his servants'. In fact, Charles was at that time entering the contentment of his last years. Charlotte had come to him, or was about to do so; if she had not already come Charles was enjoying a pleasing friendship with the musician Domenico Corri.

Charles was fond of music and even as a youth well before his twenties had learned to play the violoncello. Corri visited him most evenings and has left us an account of them. They sat together in a room hung with crimson damask lighted with candles. Sometimes they would play duets with Corri at the harpsichord, sometimes Charles would play unaccompanied old Scottish and Gaelic melodies on the violoncello, the French horn, the flageolet or the bagpipes; invariably the evenings would end with *Lochabar no More* and with the elderly Prince in tears.

These musical evenings with Domenico Corri, pleasant though they were, did not assuage Charles' loneliness. As soon as the separation from his wife had been achieved and formalized, he decided to have someone of his own blood near to him. Accordingly he sent his servant John Stuart to Paris to bring back with him his daughter Charlotte. She responded by coming at once. Charles' choice of a companion in his declining years could not have been bettered.

A tourist writing in the *Gentleman's Magazine* saw her in Rome later and said of her: 'She was a tall, robust woman of a very dark complexion and a coarse-grained skin, with more of a masculine boldness than feminine modesty or elegance, but easy and unassuming in her manners, amply possessed of that volubility of tongue and that spirit of coquetry which the women of the country where she was educated have at all times been particularly distinguished.'

She was certainly strong-minded and may have given the appearance of robustness – though we now know she bore in her a malady of the liver which was to kill her not long after her father's death – a malady which she may well have inherited from her grandmother, Clementina Sobieski. But what about the 'spirit of coquetry'? We see not a jot of it in her behaviour as long as she was living with and devoted to her father.

It has been implied that, in taking over the running of Charles' establishment, she bullied him. She did not; she introduced some efficiency into his household, helped to reduce his melancholy drinking, was instrumental in helping to make up the long-standing quarrel between him and his brother the Cardinal, thereby bringing Charles back into the practice of the Faith of his birth; and finally she lightened the last years of Charles' life by her affection expressed in the most practical way. Those who know the facts of Charles' physical decline can feel nothing but gratitude towards this tall, robust, efficient, but doomed young woman who, after years of neglect was so generous in spirit that she gave herself up to making the last three years of this prematurely aged man as happy as it was possible for her to do.

Difficult though it may be to believe, Louise, Charles' wife, has had her posthumous admirers. Charlotte has been accused of 'being too clever' for her stepmother; deliberately exacerbating the difference between Charles and his wife who had long ago left him; but this is nonsense.

What she did do was (in the process of making up the old bitter difference between Charles and his brother Henry) enlighten the Cardinal on the outrageous behaviour of Louise. This took some doing, but she managed it. In Major F. J. A. Skeet's *Charlotte, Duchess of Albany** there are gathered together letters from her to the Cardinal which at length produced their cumulative effect.

A characteristic letter from Charlotte who supposed that she had offended the Cardinal contains this:

> I deeply regret for having incurred your disgrace. Deign to read this an instant: one favourable word will reanimate my courage and fulfill my wishes. Deign, my Lord, to say this word. An indisposition caused by the intense grief which overcomes me, and the journey to Pisa, which must take place to-morrow prevents me from urging more.

The result was that in 1785 the Cardinal of York wrote to Charles:

* London. Eyre and Spottiswoode, 1932.

I conjure you to do what lies in you to prevent a *quidam* (in this instance meaning a person of uncertain origin) like Alfieri from gaining his ends by a union so offensive to our family.

Then the Cardinal goes on significantly to show that he has now no ill-will towards Charlotte:

I am greatly obliged to your daughter for interesting herself so much on my behalf. It proves the kindness of her heart, to which everyone bears witness.

So began the reconciliation of the long-standing difference and coldness between the two brothers – a difference which had its origin in 'the brave old days before the tonsure' when, as we have described in an earlier chapter, Henry Duke of York ignominiously and secretly fled from Paris after Charles' return from Scotland and became a Cardinal in Rome.

Now that inhospitable flight was far in the past, and the memory of it was being obliterated by Charlotte's sweet-natured diplomacy. Touched by his niece's letter the Cardinal replied addressing her as 'My Cousin' and going on to say:

I do not lose an instant in expressing my regret for having hurt you in my last letter.... Since you appear so anxious for my friendship and my confidence (which greatly pleases me) I can assure you sincerely that you have both, and that in the course of our correspondence I feel certain that we shall learn to esteem one another ... I beg you to let me know that you are perfectly at ease again in yourself.

It was not an easy task for Charlotte to look after her ageing father. Nor can she have found the running of his household a smooth affair. It was a richer and more elaborate establishment than that which she had been accustomed to during her years in France. Moreover she spoke only French and does not seem to have picked up more than a word or two of English from her mother. French was the *lingua franca* of established society in Europe then, but she must have found her lack of Italian difficult in the ordinary affairs of life in the Tuscan capital. She did her best to learn it, and speaks of her efforts to do so in one of her letters. Italian is not a difficult language for a French speaker to acquire; moreover Tuscan Italian was and still is the most perfect and clear Italian in the whole peninsula. Any difficulties she may have had were recompensed by the warm welcome she received from her father and the assiduous affection he poured on her in his efforts to give her entertainment and company.

Meanwhile the happier relationships between Charles' household and his brother the Cardinal, which had been entirely fostered by Charlotte's efforts, continued to prosper. Charles wrote happily in his own hand (not an easy feat for him these days) about the social success Charlotte had achieved by being presented to the Grand Duchess of Tuscany – for Charles to correspond with his brother on pleasing matters was a happy novelty.

These friendlier relationships between Charles and the Cardinal had an effect; they were concerned with Charles' practice of the Faith in which he had been born. Charlotte was deeply gratified to learn from her uncle the Cardinal that Pope Pius VI had written to him congratulating her on her religious influence on her father; for Charles had performed his Easter duties that year of 1785, 'with edification'. This must have meant that he had sloughed off his assumed Protestant Anglicism – the result of his visit to London in 1750 – and had done so without any formality or fuss.

Charles, unlike a number of his Stuart, Polish and

Italian forebears, was not much concerned with religion. Elcho says that 'his religion was to seek'; and Elcho's envenomed tongue is always suspect, but in this instance he was guilty of exaggeration only.

Charles, however, did not revert from the impulse that sent him to his Easter duties in 1785, and was to die later in Rome fortified by the Rites of the Church. Nevertheless his earlier casual attitude towards the Faith, which deeply distressed his father and brother, is worth examining.

His superficial apostasy into Protestant Anglicanism during his private visit to London in 1750 was not so much cynical as naïvely expedient. He was at that time, while he still had hopes of being recalled as Regent to the throne in London, quite prepared to respect the Church of England, of which he would officially have been head, and might quietly have practised Catholicism, if only to please his father James III in Rome. This, after all, would not have been so very different from what his grandfather James II had done when he was reigning. Charles, of course, would never have taken the bit between his teeth as his grandfather did and tried to press the Faith on the whole country with the fantastic notion of reconverting the whole country to Catholicism. Charles in 1750 was wise enough to know that England would never again tolerate a Catholic sovereign, though Scotland for dynastic reasons connected with the name of Stuart, and Ireland for different and domestic reasons, might well have done so. It is possible, even probable, that with childish simplicity, he went through the form of Anglicanization, but with mental reservations. On the other hand, one should remember his extraordinary boyhood, in which he was battled for by Catholic and Protestant tutors; and he might have, if called to the throne, pronounced himself an Anglican.

This would not have been a very dignified proceeding, but it had its precedents. Charles II willingly died a Catholic and warmly welcomed the Scottish priest Father Huddlestone to reconcile him at his ending. He was strongly attracted to Catholicism during his lifetime and when he was on his throne admitted it, concealing the sincerity of his feeling by jesting about it in his characteristic way. He put his spiritual bet upon the gamble of being in a position to be reconciled when he would be certain that he was dying, and was very lucky that his flutter came off.

Charles Edward mellowed in his daughter's company. He gave balls for her, took her often to the theatre where his private box was hung 'with crimson damask, the cushions, velvet with gold lace.... The Count is much blessed with it.' The writer of these words was Horace Mann who even admits that the effect was pleasing. He goes further and says some (for him) flattering things about Charlotte, Duchess of Albany. The old epicene was more of a woman than a man in his gossip, and therefore inclined to that unfortunate quality in some women's conversation – sniggering denigration. It says much for Charlotte's natural charm that Mann was clearly influenced by it. Incidentally, in the same letter he says that Charlotte much resembled her father in his youth. Hence her charm, a quality of which Charles was redolent in the days of ardour, hope and advancing success.

That charm achieved its most remarkable result when it brought about the long-wished-for meeting of her father, her Cardinal uncle and herself at Perugia. At this happy meeting Charles agreed that, accompanied by his daughter, he should go back to pass the winter in Rome.

Her charm seems to have crossed the seas. When Charles gave a large dinner-party in Charlotte's honour on St Andrew's Day 1784, he invested her family with the green ribbon of the Thistle. In the unlikely event of any of the Courts in Europe hearing of it, they would have regarded the investiture as the empty gesture of a *fainéant* exiled King with no power to invest anyone with anything. But Robert Burns, somehow, somewhere in Scotland heard of it, and the following verses are from '*They've wranged the Lass of Albany*':

> *My heart is wae, and unco wae,*
>    *To think upon the raging sea,*
> *That roars between the gardens green*
>    *An' the bonnie Lass of Albany.*
>
> *This lovely maid's of royal blood*
>    *That ruled Albion's Kingdoms three,*
> *But oh, alas! for her bonnie face,*
>    *They've wranged the Lass of Albany.*
>
> *Alas the day, and woe the day,*
>    *A false usurper wan the gree,*
> *Who now commands the towers and lands*
>    *The royal right of Albany.*
>
> *We'll daily pray, we'll nightly pray,*
>    *On bended knees most fervently,*
> *The time may come, with pipe and drum*
>    *We'll welcome home fair Albany.*

It is surprising that the audacious loyalty to the House of Stuart expressed especially in the last two verses did not get him into trouble. But then at that date Burns was but small fry in England; if, indeed, people had heard of him there at all it would only have been as an obscure North British versifier who wrote in the Scotch dialect. Proud as Charles was of his 'high Scotch blud', it is 'improbable', to quote Andrew Lang, 'that the exiled family ever heard of their greatest laureate'.

Charlotte's charm which brought the exiled Prince to Rome meant that the long untenanted but much haunted Palazzo Muti was reopened and came into some life again. The ghosts of long-dead Jacobites, intriguers and Hanoverian spies must have perceived this reoccupation with languid interest. Charles gave dinner-parties and musical soirées; and now that the long coldness between Charles and his brother had ended the Cardinal must surely have visited him and his niece in the old house where they had both been born.

Did Charles ever step across the road to the Church of SS Apostoli to show his daughter the memorial bust of Queen Clementina Sobieski, his mother and Charlotte's grandmother? Did he stop but a few yards further to visit the smallest church in Rome, Santa Rita, devoted to prayers for 'desperate causes'? Did the Palazzo Muti survive this reopening and partial quickening into life after Charles' death? One cannot say. The Palazzo after Charles' departure would become the official property of his brother the Cardinal, who could not as a Cardinal live there in Rome. He would have been unlikely to have sold or let this place of haunting memories. When the Revolution burst the bounds of France and swept over Italy and Rome, Napoleon may have farmed it out to some of his attendants; but it would hardly have been grand enough for them.

When in Florence, a visitor questioned the Prince about the campaign of the Forty-Five. That visitor must indeed have been ill-mannered to press this obviously broken and prematurely aged and ill man about the famous deeds of his youth. Charles, however, endeavoured to satisfy his curiosity, spoke of the raising of the standard at Glenfinnan, the march to Derby and the retreat, but when he came to Culloden and the atrocities committed by the English troops under the Duke of Cumberland and to the hideous scenes at Tyburn or at Carlisle when the executioners tore out of their bodies the still quivering hearts of his Highland followers, he broke down; he choked and fell in a fit upon the floor.

Charlotte, who had been in the next room and had heard the sounds of her father's distress of voice and of his fall, came quickly in. 'Oh, Sir, what is this? You have been speaking to him about Scotland and his Highlanders; no one dares to speak about such things in his presence.'

The older Charles grew, and the nearer he got to death, the more strongly did his 'high Scotch blud' overcome all the other strains in his mixed ancestry; his youth came back upon him – not only the youth of his ardour and endurance but the youth which had brought such cruel distress to humble Highlanders who shared and indeed had much more Scotch blood in their veins than he had – Scotch blood which they had shed for him.

In Rome, the son of the Comte de Vaudreuil asked as a distinguished foreigner to be presented to the Prince. This was the son of the man who long ago had arrested the Prince in Paris and expelled him from France – thus beginning the downward career of the fugitive Prince with all its degradations and humiliations, which he himself had exacerbated by his own (at times understandable) folly and wildness. At first Charles did not know the identity of his visitor; when he did it was too much for his now sensitive and ageing mind surrounded normally by such kindness and sympathy. Again unconsciousness was to come to his aid; again he fell upon the floor in a paroxysm.

Charlotte nursed her father at his ending and fell ill at the task. It was probably that mysterious malady of the liver which overcomes its victims at times of strong emotion which laid her low; she recovered in time when she learned that her father was *in extremis*, and was able to tend him. There is a tradition that he died in her arms on 30 January 1788 and that the date was changed to 31. The reason for this curious evasion of the 30th was that 30 January had seen the tragedy of

Charles I's public execution in Whitehall in 1649. The thirtieth had in consequence been a date of ill omen for all Stuarts.

The Cardinal of York came to his brother's spiritual aid when he heard that he was dying and, for some reason at which we cannot even guess, the pages covering that time in his diary have been torn out. So a certain mystery remains about the exact day of Charles' death; but I am sure tradition does not lie when it says that the old man died in his loving daughter's arms. There is no official doctor's death certificate surviving; perhaps there was none.

There is no question that Charles intended his now legitimized daughter to be his heir in all things, including what remnants there were to his rights of succession. He had prepared medals for her and the designs for them are explicit. On one of them Charlotte is pointing to the Stuart arms, and her eyes are fixed upon a vacant throne; in one of the other medals a ship is approaching the shores of the United Kingdom; and the motto on it is *Pendet Salus Spes Exigua et Extrema* – 'Salvation depends on one small last hope.'

Not much more is left to tell of Charlotte's brief life. Her uncle, the Cardinal, took much grateful pleasure in her company. He always referred to her as Her Royal Highness. If, as we have shown above, Charles had intended her for the succession, Charlotte had too much tact to speak of that intention in the presence of the Cardinal King Henry IX of England and I of Scotland.

What did it matter? 'The Lass of Albany' was ill and nearing her own end from the strange liver complaint which may be an inheritable and exclusively female malady as haemophilia is an exclusively masculine one. She had an operation in an attempt to cure it; it failed and she died on 17 November 1789. At her request she was buried without much ceremony in the Church of San Biagio.

Charles died of apoplexy on 30 January 1788 in Rome. His posthumous reputation in the popular mind is a refutation of Shakespeare's lines that he puts into the mouth of Cassius: 'The evil that men do lives after them; the good is oft interred with their bones.'

The long period of frustration, evanescent hope, drunkenness and continual fear of the assassin's knife that began with Charles' ignominious expulsion from Paris and France in 1746 and ended only with his last few years in peace with his daughter Charlotte has been entirely obliterated in the popular mind, which only recalls him as the Bonnie Prince Charlie of legend. One could attribute this to charity or, in Scotland, a partly subconscious sense of loyalty to the 'Auld Stewarts', our own 'Auld Stewarts' whom we lent to England to govern her. But that also would on our part be too charitable; the real reason for the obliteration of Charles' years of despair is that people do not know about them, or choose to ignore them.

The memory of Charles Stuart as 'Bonnie Prince Charlie' lives on; and, however confused the historical idea of him may be, it is a good thing that it should live on. It is a good thing that it should be expressed on topical occasions in the heartfelt lament for him by Lady Nairne – 'Will ye no' come back again.'

He was, when among us, admirable because he was ardent, arduous, magnanimous to his foes and charitable to them when they were wounded or dying. He would not at any time in his life tolerate the notion of assassination, or the removal by cunning force of those who stood in the way of his family's access to the thrones of their forefathers. For him, if the thrones were to be regained, they should come either by popular acclaim in peace, or by war according to the rules of warfare. And admirably he played that game according to those rules when he marched with his Highlanders from Moidart south through Scotland and her capital to England and Derby.

He not only led his men but mingled with them, for his step was so youthfully rapid and hopeful that he could go backwards and forwards on the route encouraging his men in English and in the Gaelic he was rapidly acquiring. It was the memory of the Young Prince among his followers – his triumphal progress through Scotland, his victory at Prestonpans, his successful and brilliantly manoeuvred march into England – that remained in the tenacious memory of the Celtic Highlanders.

While in later years Lady Nairne was to compose the famous lament for the Prince in the English language, there was another one in Gaelic, a contemporary one immediately after the failure of the Forty-Five. Of it Andrew Lang says:

> Such was the end of an auld sang, and practically the beginning of the new songs on Bonnie Prince Charles. The contemporary lament was left for an obscure Highland bard to chant in Gaelic verse, that unconsciously reproduces the Greek lament for Bion. The King [Lang was writing of the time when Charles had succeeded his father] would not have had it otherwise ... his heart was constant to his highlanders. Farewell unhappy Prince, heir to such charm and to such unmatched sorrows; farewell most ardently loved of all the Stuarts.

Nearly all writers on the last Jacobite attempt on these islands admit that if Charles had persuaded his officers and above all Lord George Murray to march on London from the halt at Derby he would have reached it. But, as some of them add, could he have held it even had George II fled down the Thames back to Hanover – as we now know he was preparing to do? How could a purely Highland force have held down the great city, the capital of England and of newly-made Britain since 1707? But we now know that a considerable proportion of purely English and London Jacobites were awaiting Charles. He would not have had to hold the city with his Highlanders alone.

There are, of course, detractors, Whig writers who express their animus against the House of Stuart by denying that Charles, if he had reached London, could have been an influence for good. In the rising, commercially prosperous country of Britain what role, they ask, could a king have had? Kingship, they say, as a force of any influence in Europe and particularly in Great Britain and Ireland was beginning to die. Charles' presence in London as king would have been negligible. Would it? Was the influence of royalty dying?

Charles himself was to die on the eve of the French Revolution which later under Napoleon was to topple so many kings from their thrones. Yet, when Napoleon went, kingship returned to Europe irrepressibly. The throne of Britain was imperilled but never conquered by Napoleon; and only a few years after he had gone, there was to ascend the throne in London and at the heart of Empire, Queen Victoria. Who is there to say that Victoria lacked power as a monarch? And have her successors been without influence? There is even today something more in our monarchy than pure 'mystique'.

If that is so today, how much more would it have been true two hundred years ago?

In death Charles was not abandoned. They erected six altars in the antechamber of the palace where more than thirty Masses were said in the thirty hours immediately after his death. The Office of the Dead was chanted by the Mendicant Orders in the antechamber.

The Irish Franciscans of St Isadore, who had administered the Last Rites of religion, alone were allowed to see his body. The Cardinal arranged funeral honours due to a dead monarch in the cathedral at Frascati. After a cast had been taken of the face, the body was embalmed and placed in a coffin of cypress wood. The coffin plate was inscribed 'Carolus III Magnae Britannae Rex'. The obsequies lasted three days, the first the funeral service, the second the entombment, the third the requiem. The coffin was placed in the crypt of St Peter's near his father and mother where those who are faithful to the memory of the last members of the direct line of the Royal House of Stuart can, and do still, place white roses on the tombs.

# Bibliography

## Primary Sources

Despite its notorious partiality, the general collection of correspondence made by Henrietta and Alistair Tayler from the archives at Windsor Castle (*The Stuart Papers at Windsor*, London, 1939) provides some of the most interesting background material concerning Charles Edward's life prior to 1745. The work must be treated with reserve, but it does capture the atmosphere of Jacobite life, with all its squabbles, intrigue and make-believe. For an appreciation of the significance of the rift which separated the Prince's parents, one need only glance at the correspondence which passed between King James III and his devoted, but critical servant in Scotland, George Lockhart. This, besides a wealth of information about Stuart affairs and hopes in Scotland, is contained in two volumes of *The Lockhart Papers*, with a commentary upon the affairs of Scotland by George Lockhart of Carnwath (London, 1817). The British Museum also possess a miscellany of Jacobite tracts (C.115,i.3), some of which afford an insight into the developing legend of Bonnie Prince Charlie. Of individual documents, perhaps the *Copy of a Letter ... from Gaeta* (Anon., London, 1734) reveals something of the young Prince, although it cannot be treated as an impartial description of his bravery in the trenches, for it was definitely circulated as Jacobite propaganda.

The majority of tracts issued at the time, even when purporting to be 'true and impartiall' narrative, contain undiluted propaganda. By far the richest collection of eye-witness accounts, letters, documents, proclamations and stories is that which was made by Robert Forbes during the years following the battle of Culloden (*The Lyon in Mourning*, by the Reverend

Robert Forbes, A.M., Bishop of Ross and Caithness, 1746–1775. Publications of the Scottish History Society, Vol. XX–XXIII. Edited by Henry Paton, and published at Edinburgh in October 1895.) *The Memorials of John Murray of Broughton, Sometime Secretary to Prince Charles Edward 1740–1747* (Publications of the Scottish History Society, Vol. XXVII, Edinburgh, 1898) indicate the flimsy series of chances upon which the venture rolled into history, and also the misinformation upon which its conception was based. Murray was savagely critical of Jacobite organization and suggests that wilful misrepresentation and concealment were factors which led to the destruction of Stuart hopes. It must be remembered that he wrote most of his account without recourse to documentary or verbal evidence, long after events had occurred, and only shortly after he himself had turned King's evidence against his former associates. Nevertheless, the 'Memorials' are more reliable than the vivid commentary by David, Lord Elcho (*The Affairs of Scotland*, Edinburgh, David Douglas, 1907). Elcho was jealous of Murray and suggests that he was a Hanoverian spy. But he also impugned Charles Edward with all manner of Italianate foppery, besides cowardice and desertion at Culloden. Elcho's distortions reveal the ease with which spite can warp history; Charles Edward had neglected to repay to Elcho a debt incurred during the early months of the expedition. Another highly personal, but entertaining account of the Forty-Five is that of the Chevalier de Johnstone (*A Memoir of the 'Forty-five'*. 1820). A sharp sense of the fear with which news of the Scottish approach was met in England enlivens a critical collection of correspondence made by Winifred Duke in 1952. (*The Rash Adventurer. Being Records of Prince Charles Edward's Expedition into England during the Last Months of the Year 1745*. Robert Hale, London, 1952). For the Whig reaction in Scotland there is no better source than *The Culloden Papers*

(London, 1815), which contain much of the correspondence between Duncan Forbes, the Lord President, and various government officials who were concerned with Scottish affairs. There is also an excellent
study of Argyllshire by Sir James Fergusson (*Argyll in
the Forty-five*, Faber and Faber, London, 1951) which
consists chiefly of correspondence between various
Campbell agents. Another modern collection of source
material which concentrates upon the reactions of both
Scots and English to the Forty-Five is that made by
Donald Nicholas (*Intercepted Post*, Bodley Head, London, 1956).

Special mention should be made of a contemporary
history of the invasion by a foreigner who was not personally involved in the expedition, but who was given
the details in later years by the Prince himself. The
*Commentary on the Expedition to Scotland made by
Charles Edward Stuart, Prince of Wales* written by
Padre Giulio Cesare Cordara, S.J. in 1751 (Miscellany
of the Scottish History Society, Third Series, vol. IV,
pp. 1–176) is perhaps the history Charles himself would
have written.

Very little material is readily available for the
period of Charles Edward's life after 1746. There are
numerous letters in State Papers respective to the years
in question which indicate the interest that the British
government took in the whereabouts and activities of
Charles Edward during his years of wanderings, and
after his return to Italy. The study of Charlotte Stuart
by Major F. J. A. Skeet (*Charlotte, Duchess of Albany*,
Eyre and Spottiswoode, 1932) is one of the very few on
Charles Edward's daughter. There is another by Henrietta Tayler mentioned later in this bibliography.

*Secondary Sources*

For an idea of the place which the Forty-Five, and the
career of Charles Edward, held in the overall develop-

ment of Stuart and Scottish fortunes, there is no better study than that by George Hilton Jones: *The Mainstream of Jacobitism* (Harvard University Press, 1954). With Jones' study as a critical comparison one may also gain some reward from the more partisan volume of Sir Charles Petrie's *The Jacobite Movement* (London, 1948–1950), particularly in connection with Scottish affairs and the characters of their leaders. Also invaluable for an understanding of Highland society, the behaviour of the clans and their leaders, and their peculiar predicament in 1745 is John Prebble's classic *Culloden* (Penguin Books, 1967).

There are innumerable biographies of Charles Edward. Most of them concentrate upon the period around 1745, and very few have anything to say about the Prince's childhood. Studies like that of the Baroness Nobili-Vitelleschi: *A Court in Exile* (Two vols. 1903) are cumbersome and unreliable. Charles has always been a popular subject and perhaps the best general biographies are those undertaken by popular authors like Compton Mackenzie (*Prince Charlie*, Nelson, 1938). Winifred Duke has also written a balanced biography of the Prince (*Prince Charles Edward*, 1938). Among the more recent biographies, the study by Peter de Polnay (*Death of a Legend. The True Story of Bonnie Prince Charlie*, Hamish Hamilton, London, 1952) merits special attention especially with regard to the period after 1746. De Polnay has used material lodged in the Ministry of Foreign Affairs at the Quai d'Orsay in Paris to reconstruct the years of Charles Edward's incognito. Also useful in connection with the Prince's later life is the work of E. Dubois, *Les Derniers Jours de l'Exile* (Paris, 1866). Of the older biographies, only two are of any use. The first is Andrew Lang's *Prince Charles Edward* (Longmans, 1903); the other is the compendious work of W. D. Norrie: *Life and Adventures of Prince Charles Edward Stuart* (Caxton Publishing, London, 1903/4, 4 vols.). Norrie's book contains some excellent illustrations and much documentary material, but it relates chiefly to the Prince's expedition to Scotland.

The military details of the Forty-Five are comprehensively covered in *Battles of the Forty-five* (Batsford, 1962) by Katherine Tomasson and Francis Buist. Prebble's book (Op. cit.) also deals with this aspect, while W. H. Thomson: *The Levy on Manchester* (1952) analyses the Prince's military organization while providing a breakdown of the type of support Charles received in Manchester. Two studies by Walter Biggar Blaikie are invaluable with regard to the Forty-Five. One is a collection of papers under his editorship *Origins of the Forty-five and other Papers* (Publications of the Scottish History Society, Second Series, vol. II, Edinburgh, 1916). The other is his *Itinerary of Prince Charles Edward* (Publications of the Scottish History Society, vol. XXIII). The latter contains a critical treatment of much of the source material relating to Charles Edward's wanderings in the Highlands and is the only reliable account of the Prince's travels at the time. Winifred Duke's *In the Steps of Bonnie Prince Charlie* (1953) is a general travelogue of Charles Edward's movements in Britain. As a classic work of popular history one should also mention Eric Linklater: *The Prince in the Heather* (Hodder and Stoughton, 1965).

Compton Mackenzie's *Prince Charlie and his Ladies* (Cassell, London, 1934) is a readable attempt to deal with a puzzling aspect of the Prince's character. One needs to return to the work of Henrietta Tayler to appreciate the Prince's relationship with his wife and particularly with his daughter (*Prince Charlie's Daughter*, 1950).

# Index